Baby Basics

A GUIDE FOR NEW PARENTS

Anne K. Blocker, RD

Baby Basics: A Guide for New Parents © 1997 by Anne K. Blocker, RD

Library of Congress Cataloging-in-Publication Data
Blocker, Anne K.
Baby basics / by Anne K. Blocker.
           p.   cm.
Includes index.

ISBN 1-56561-090-3; $12.95

Edited by Jeff Braun and Linda Lynch
Cover Design: Pear Graphics
Text Design & Production: David Enyeart
Art/Production Manager: Claire Lewis

Printed in the United States

Published by
Chronimed Publishing
P.O. Box 59032
Minneapolis, MN 55459-9686

10   9   8   7   6   5   4   3   2   1

This book is dedicated to all the special people who have helped me learn about, experience, and navigate the parenting journey. Each of you has a special place in my heart.

To Dave, my husband and best friend—you make parenting fun at every turn. Thank you for your editing advice and constant faith in this book. Our children are lucky to have you as their dad.

To Katie and Marty—you have brought immeasurable joy, love, and laughter into my life. I cannot imagine a day without you. You capture hearts with your smiles and make each day an adventure. Experiencing the world through your eyes, whether it's the first winter snow, the magic of Christmas, or a walk through the forest, gives special meaning to life.

To Paul David—your short time with us taught me incredible lessons about the value of family, the preciousness of the miracle we know as life, and the unconditional love of God. In times of trials, you bring Heaven a little closer to Earth.

To my parents and in-laws, Rosemary and Leo Kriener and Jeanne and Maurice Blocker—you top the ranks in the grand-parent department. Thank you for sharing your parenting wisdom, and money-management skills, and for providing parenting relief. You are truly wonderful.

To Wilma and Curt Lien and Sue and Dean Burroughs—I wish all parents could be as fortunate to have such super child care providers. You have given our children two extended, warm, and loving family environments to grow up in. I couldn't go to work without you.

To parents everywhere—I respect the incredibly valuable contributions you make to humankind.

Table of Contents

Foreword   vi

Acknowledgments   vii

Chapter 1: **Medical Care**   1
How to Contain the Costs

Chapter 2: **Top Six Things to Do**   17
Before Baby Arrives

Chapter 3: **Maternity Clothes**   33
Looking Great Without Spending a Bundle

Chapter 4: **Nursery Furniture**   43
and Other Baby Products

Chapter 5: **To Grandmother's House We Go**   75
and Other Safe Travel

Chapter 6: **Baby's Basic Wardrobe**   91
Clothing for the First Year

Chapter 7: **The Diaper Dilemma**   107

Chapter 8: **Toys on a Budget**   121

Chapter 9: **Feeding Made Simple**   139

Chapter 10: **The Medicine Chest**   173
Knowing When to Go to the Doctor

Chapter 11: **Babyproofing Your Home**   191

Chapter 12: **Finding the Best Child Care**   215

Chapter 13: **Take This Job**   237
and Keep It, Share It, Downsize It, or Leave It

Chapter 14: **Investing in the Future**   259
and Other Financial Matters

Chapter 15: **Baby Yourself**   269
Making Time For You

Sources   285

Index   291

Foreword

Bringing up baby well is a daunting task. This book will:
- ✿ give you well-tested, down to earth advice on saving time and money caring for your baby;
- ✿ show you how to provide your baby with a safe environment; and
- ✿ provide expert advice on feeding your baby.

I have had the pleasure of not only knowing the author professionally, in obtaining expert nutritional advice for my patients, but also caring for her, her husband, and their two small children as their family physician. While raising her small children she has done an extraordinary job of bringing together all the information you need to care for your baby while saving time and money.

Her "baby comes first" attitude shines through this book. *Baby Basics* should be one of your first purchases. It will help guide all the rest. Start reading; you can't begin too soon.

Kevin L. Sand, MD, Family Practice Physician, Decorah Clinic, Mayo Health System

Acknowledgments

A project touched by many hands is better because of everyone who contributed. *Baby Basics* is no exception. Special thanks to each of the following people who helped me take this book from its conception and infancy through its many stages of development. Thank you to:

Rosemary Behrens, Julie Metcalf Cull, Debi Edwards, Sandy Hagen, Valeria Herold, Anastasia Kriener, Rosemary Kriener, and MJ Smith for your editing, proofreading, candid comments, and support, as well as "real parenting advice." I value your parenting opinions and experiences.

Evie Milbrandt and Linda Jones for always being at the other end of the telephone line when I need parenting advice. I treasure your sisterly honesty and support as we share the challenges of motherhood in the '90s.

Laurie Kimber for incredible word processing skills. Your assistance in keeping this book on schedule is greatly appreciated. I enjoy your sense of humor, dedication, and excitement for new adventures.

Dan Anderson, Iowa State Patrol and past Safety Training Officer; Dan Hageman, Investment and Certified Fund Specialist; Dr. Kevin Sand, MD, Family Practice Physician; Rose Ann G. Soloway, RN, MSEd, ABAT, Clinical Toxicologist at the National Capital Poison Center; and Brenda Whetsone, RN, Certified Lactation Consultant. Thank you for reviewing material and sharing your professional expertise.

Jeff Braun, for editorial faith, wisdom, and just the right sense of humor to give lots of fun and enjoyment to the publishing process.

Ann Balk, Sharon Bahr, Lois Bohr, Marlene Blocker, Nell Chmielewski, Darin and Jenny Gruenhaupt, Fran Gruenhaupt, Dan and Chris Hageman, Don and Kathy Hageman, Diane Hedlund, Anne Herold, Carol Johnson, Nancy Kriener, Rene Kriener, Linda Klimesh, Wilma Lien, Joan Lubke, Kim Lubke, Janice Marzen, Marianne Marzen, Roger and Lisa Pralle, Jenny Schaack, Barb Smith, Tim, Wiltgen, and Paul and Margie Woodruff for sharing real parents' comments and questions. You represent the wonderful diversity of parenting that is individual to each family and generation, yet is bonded by the common thread of love for a child.

CHAPTER ONE

Medical Care—How to Contain the Costs

"The street's abloom with pregnant women.
They stand next to me in elevators. I see them in movie lines…
Were they here before I was pregnant?"
—Phyllis Chesler

It's common knowledge that babies cost a bundle. That's part of what this book is all about—keeping the bundle from becoming the national debt by simplifying baby care. According to recent estimates, you can expect to spend at least $145,000 to raise your child to age 18.[1] If you want to send your child to college, tack on another $100,000 to $275,000 to the price tag for four years of schooling.

Although there is little you can do about the projected cost of a college education—besides starting to save now—you can take steps to hold down some of the other costs associated with raising a child. Let's begin with the significant costs of simply bringing your baby into the world.

Necessity Checklist

✿ **Secure health insurance coverage** for yourself and your baby.

✿ **Precertify with your insurance company** for baby's delivery.

✿ **Set up a flexible spending account.**

✿ **Request a written copy of your maternity and baby benefits from your insurer.**

✿ **Contact your hospital or birthing center** and ask about items you can bring with you to decrease charges on your bill.

✿ **Maintain a medical expense record** of all prenatal, labor and delivery, and postnatal care.

It All Adds Up

Prenatal Health Care

Prenatal health care will be the first expense you incur on your journey to parenthood. Because your health and lifestyle at conception and during the early weeks of pregnancy affect your developing child, health care professionals recommend that you see your physician or nurse-midwife as soon as you suspect you are pregnant. Some providers even recommend pre-conception care for ideal preparation for pregnancy.

Based on your health needs, your physician or nurse-midwife will determine the timing and number of follow-up visits. (There are many options for prenatal care, including a family physician, midwife, obstetrician, gynecologist, or perinatalogist. For simplicity, the health practitioner will be referred to as your physician in this chapter.) Typically, you will be seen monthly for the first 7 months, every 2 weeks during your 8th month, then weekly until delivery.[2] If you have a chronic condition such as high blood pressure or diabetes, your physician or nurse-midwife may require more frequent visits. The cost of these visits will usually be included in your physician or nurse-midwife's global prenatal and delivery fee. A brief description of some of the most common prenatal tests follows:

Prenatal Tests

Your prenatal care will most likely include a variety of tests and exams to monitor your health and your baby's development. Some of these tests will be performed during your regular prenatal visits; others may require additional visits or the use of outpatient services. You should discuss with your physician or nurse-midwife which tests are needed and when.

Urinalysis

Urinalysis is routinely performed during your first prenatal visit. You will be asked to collect a small sample of urine, which is analyzed for the presence of protein (which may indicate possible infections or kidney disease), sugar (a possible sign of diabetes), bacteria (which may indicate infections), and a hormone called human chorionic gonadotropin hormone (which confirms your pregnancy).

Because urine is routinely checked for proteins and sugar during pregnancy, you will be asked to bring a urine sample to all subsequent prenatal visits.

Urinalysis typically costs $15 to $25. The test may be included in your prenatal care package.

Blood Tests

Routine blood tests are usually performed at your initial prenatal visit, too. A small amount of blood is drawn from your arm and analyzed for blood type, Rh factor, hepatitis B, rubella immunity, anemia, and syphilis. The sample may also be screened to determine whether you are a carrier for toxoplasmosis, Tay-Sachs disease, sickle cell anemia, or other disorders.

Blood tests cost between $70 and $250, and the results are usually available in one week. You may need a repeat test during your 28th week to recheck for anemia.

Blood Pressure Check

Your blood pressure will be checked at each prenatal visit. An inflatable cuff is placed on your arm and a stethoscope is used to determine your blood pressure during diastole, or relaxation of the heart, and systole, or contraction of the heart. You may be asked to lie on your side during this test. Women who have high blood pressure before becoming pregnant receive special prenatal care to prevent complications. Because the blood pressure check is part of the prenatal visit, there is no additional cost.

Some women develop pregnancy-induced high blood pressure in the second half of pregnancy. Elevated blood pressure can be a sign of preeclampsia, or toxemia, a condition that leads to poor fetal growth and premature birth. Because of the seriousness of this condition, let your physician know about any sudden weight gain (more than two pounds a week), swelling in your hands and face, headaches, vision problems, or upper abdominal pain.[3]

Cervical/Vaginal Swab

A cervical or vaginal swab is routinely done during your initial prenatal visit to gather cells for a Pap smear. These cells are then analyzed for signs of cancer. The area around your cervix or vagina may also be swabbed to test for gonorrhea or chlamydia.

Some physicians swab the cervix again at 26 to 28 weeks to test for the presence of Group B streptococcus (GBS), a common bacterial inhabitant of the vagina that causes two or three of every 1,000 newborns to become ill or die each year. Screening for and treating GBS infection prevents the bacteria from being passed to your baby during birth.

A Pap smear generally costs $20 to $25, a GBS test, $40.

Amniocentesis

Amniocentesis is most often recommended for older expectant mothers or women who have a family history of genetic disorders. It is performed at 14 to 20 weeks gestation by inserting a needle through the abdomen to withdraw amniotic fluid from the amniotic sac. The fluid, which contains cells sloughed from the fetus, is then screened for genetic abnormalities.

The test can also be used to determine the maturity of the fetus in situations where premature labor might be dangerous or to rule out GBS infections near term. It costs about $300. Though the procedure is considered safe, there is a slight risk of complications; discuss the benefits and risks of amniocentesis with your physician before having the test.

Maternal Serum Alpha-Fetoprotein

Alpha-fetoprotein (AFP) is a screening test used to detect abnormalities, such as neural tube defects (open spine, brain, or abdomen). It can also detect some cases of Down's syndrome. It is most accurate when performed at 16 to 18 weeks gestation with a blood test. Follow-up confirmation tests with ultrasound or amniocentesis are performed on abnormal blood tests. If the follow-up test(s) indicates a birth defect, you may need to deliver at a specialized center.

The AFP test costs about $90 to $100.

Glucose Tests

At approximately 26 weeks gestation, your physician may check for gestational diabetes by administering a glucose challenge test. You are given a very sweet sugar solution to drink. One hour later, blood is drawn from your arm, and your blood sugar level is tested. If the 1-hour test comes back high, you will be given a second sugar solution and your blood sugar rechecked. If your blood sugar is high after the second test, you may be diagnosed with gestational diabetes. If this condition is present, you will need to follow a special diet. Untreated gestational diabetes puts you at risk for having a larger than average baby, which can make delivery difficult.

Glucose tests cost between $10 and $50.

Ultrasound

Although ultrasound can be performed as early as 5 1/2 weeks and as late as 40 weeks, most often it is performed between 16 and 20 weeks. Ultrasound is used to determine gestational age, and to learn the number of fetuses, as well as to identify potential risks or abnormalities. Sometimes gender can be determined.

While you lie on a table, a gel is applied to your exposed abdomen. A wand-like transducer emitting sound waves is then rotated over it, allowing images of the uterus and fetus to appear on a monitor resembling a TV screen. Often, the resulting sonogram is the first "photograph" you'll receive of your baby.

Ultrasound costs between $100 and $300. If you have insurance, check to see if this test is covered. Some plans will not pay for ultrasounds performed only to determine gestational age.

Nonstress and Stress Tests

If you are overdue or have diabetes or high blood pressure, your physician may perform a nonstress or a stress test to monitor fetal health in the weeks before delivery. In both tests, a wide belt is placed around your abdomen and used to monitor your baby's heart rate. The nonstress test indicates fetal health by measuring your baby's heart rate after you feel him or her move.

If the nonstress test results are not satisfactory, your physician may recommend a stress test. The stress test indicates fetal health by measuring your baby's heart rate in response to mild induced contractions of the uterus. If the test is negative, you will most likely be allowed to continue the pregnancy with close monitoring for another week. If the results are positive, delivery may be indicated.

A nonstress test costs between $50 and $150, the stress test, $150.

Labor and Delivery Costs

When your baby is born, your medical expenses can increase dramatically. These expenses include your physician or nurse-midwife's fee to deliver your baby, the hospital or birthing center's fee for your room and care during labor and recovery, and the hospital or birthing center's nursery charge for your baby's care after birth.

Projections by the Health Insurance Association of America indicate that you can expect your prenatal and delivery costs to average $5,250 if you have an uncomplicated, vaginal delivery and $8,700 if you require a cesarean section.[4] These estimates may be higher or lower depending on where in the country you live.

Postnatal and Infant Health Care Costs

Of course, medical costs do not stop with the birth of your baby. You will need a 6-week postpartum checkup, which may or may not be included in the physician or nurse-midwife's global charge. Your infant will need a series of well-baby checkups and shots. These begin when your baby is about 2 weeks old. In addition to these expected costs, unexpected costs can include bilirubin tests if your baby becomes jaundiced, intensive care charges if your baby is premature, and treatment of common childhood illness such as ear infections and bronchitis.

Importance of Health Insurance

Because medical complications can occur, estimating your total pregnancy and delivery charges can be difficult. The majority of pregnancies have minimal or no complications or associated increased costs. However, a high-risk pregnancy, surgeon fees, intensive baby care, delivery complications, or a baby born with special needs all are unfortunate situations that can cost thousands of dollars.

Securing health insurance coverage is the single best way to contain your costs for medical care before, during, and after your baby's birth. Depending on the type of coverage you choose and the services you require, you can usually expect your insurer to pay between 70 percent and 100 percent of your health care bill.

Despite the obvious benefit to having health insurance, currently 13 percent of all Americans are not covered.[5] Some people cannot afford insurance, have employers who do not offer benefits, or have plans without maternity benefits. Others are denied coverage because of past medical problems. If any of these situations apply to you, you may need to explore budget options and programs to obtain health care.

Depending on your financial status, you may be eligible to apply for Medicaid. Call your local Department of Health and Human Services or similar agency to see if you meet the financial guidelines. Programs such as Maternal Child Health and Women, Infant, and Children (WIC) also provide important prenatal health and nutrition services. Check your local telephone book for agencies in your area.

Some people opt for less coverage, higher deductibles, or co-payments to keep their monthly premiums lower. If you consider one of these options, be sure to set up a monthly savings program so you're able to pay these costs. The copayment is the amount for which you are responsible before insurance payments are made.

If you decide against health insurance coverage altogether, set aside a minimum of $200 to $300 per month to ensure you can pay for basic physician and delivery charges. In nine months you'll have $1,800 to $2,700 to put toward your medical bills.

Having health insurance coverage does not mean all bills are automatically paid. Most plans require some type of premium to be paid by you or your employer on a monthly or annual basis to be eligible for coverage. In addition, most insuring groups have a deductible, or a set amount of out-of-pocket dollars that must be paid before the insurer pays on claims. Deductibles of $250 and $500 are standard.

Once you have met your deductible obligations you will typically pay a 10 to 20 percent copayment on all remaining bills. What this means is that the insurer determines a reasonable charge for a given service, then pays a percent, usually 70 to 90 percent, of that charge. You are then responsible for the remaining 10 to 30 percent. After a set amount of out-of-pocket expense, usually $1,000 to $3,500, many insurance plans will then pay 100 percent of reasonable charges.

Sometimes insurance companies determine a provider's fee to be above "customary and reasonable" for the service you received. This means the insurer will pay the standard 70 to 90 percent on the portion they determine to be reasonable. You are then responsible for the remainder of the charge.

In such cases, the provider—a physician, clinic, or hospital — is sometimes willing to accept payment for what the insurer has deemed a "reasonable" charge. It's always worth asking for such an adjustment and demonstrating your consumer awareness of the need for cost containment. If the provider does not agree to accept the amount paid by your insurance carrier, you are responsible for paying the balance.

The following is an example of a charge above reasonable and customary:

Blood Test Charge: $18.00

Insurer's Customary and Reasonable Charge Limit: $12.00

Insurance Payment at 80 percent: $ 9.60
($12 x .80 = $9.60)

Your responsibility: $ 8.40
($2.40 [20% of the Customary and Reasonable Charge]
+ $6.00 [the fee charged above the Customary and
Reasonable Limit])

Some providers will waive the $6 portion of the fee above "customary and reasonable" limits or split the difference with you if you ask.

Changes in Health Care

Shortened Hospital Stays

A typical hospital or birthing center stay for an uncomplicated delivery and normal recovery is 24 to 48 hours. There is currently legislation in some states to require a minimum 48 hour stay. This is a considerable decrease in length of stay since the 1950s when a new mom spent 12 to 14 days in the hospital. Even in the 1970s, the average stay was 5 days. These traditional stays make 1990s births look like drive-through operations. Improved technology, changes in recovery time philosophies, and home health services all make shorter hospital stays possible.

Because health care costs keep rising, insurance companies have become more stringent on paying claims. Insurance company case managers and review agents are routinely involved in determining the length of time you and your baby can stay in the hospital. Unless there are complications to the delivery (such as a cesarean section) or recovery (such as hemorrhaging), the standard stay allowed by your insurance plan will be all the hospital time covered. Carefully review your insurance policy or contact your company's benefit department to find out how long you can plan to stay before being discharged.

Your doctor may determine you need more time to recuperate in the hospital. If this is the case, he or she must document the medical need for your stay. In addition, notification and prior approval from the insurer may be necessary to ensure bills are properly paid.

Home health coverage is often beneficial for new mothers and babies with short recovery stays. A home health or county nursing agency can provide breastfeeding support or referral for nursing and physical therapy services after your discharge from the hospital. Again, check your insurance policy to see if this type of service is covered. Hospitals or birthing centers often help make arrangements for such services at patients' request.

> ## " Real Parents Say...
>
> When our children were young and needing the doctor often, we had a lower deductible. Now we have a higher deductible. It saves money at this point in our lives when we use health care services less.
>
> *— Rose and Art, parents of three* "

Policy coverage varies widely from plan to plan. Ideally, you should obtain insurance coverage before becoming pregnant. Because not all plans include maternity benefits, make sure to check for this before purchasing a health policy. Some plans will not cover you if you were already pregnant at the time the plan was purchased. They may treat your pregnancy as a noncovered preexisting condition. Check for clauses in the plan stating the length of time the policy must be in effect before you are eligible for benefits.

If you should happen to change insurance carriers during

your pregnancy because of a change in employer or employment status, most companies will continue your coverage. The pregnancy may not be considered a preexisting condition because you were covered by an insurance plan before the change. For example, if your health insurance is provided through your partner's employer and he changes jobs (and consequently insurance) during your pregnancy, the prenatal, labor, and delivery charges incurred after the change should be covered under the new policy. One word of caution, though, deductibles and copayments may start over at zero, regardless of payments already made.

Insurance for Baby

Insurance coverage for the newest family member is also important. Some policies automatically include the baby on the mother's plan unless notified otherwise. Babies, however, don't always arrive on schedule so make sure this is covered by month 5 or 6 of your pregnancy. If you and your spouse both carry health insurance, you need to let your insurer know which policy you would like the baby covered under.

As with adult health insurance plans, policies for dependents are not all the same. Before selecting a policy for your baby, you need to ask the following questions:

- ✿ What are the deductibles and copayments?
- ✿ Are there any caps on newborn care, especially if my infant should happen to need special services?
- ✿ Is my baby covered under my individual policy? If so, for how long or do I need to purchase a family plan?
- ✿ What is the monthly premium?
- ✿ If my baby needs special home care like oxygen or nursing monitoring, will the insurance pay? How much and for how long?
- ✿ Are hospital nursery charges covered? How many days is my baby allowed to stay in the nursery?

✿ If I (mom) need to be hospitalized for an extended period of time, will insurance pay for my baby to stay also?

✿ If I have a boy and choose to have him circumcised, is this charge covered?

✿ Is well-baby care, including shots, covered?

✿ If a consultation is needed by an outside physician or pediatrician, is this service covered?

✿ Under what conditions can my baby's policy be terminated?

As with an adult policy, request that the insurer send you the specifics in writing.

Budget Helpers

In addition to being a savvy user of the health care system, you can help cut your health care costs in a number of ways.

Eat a nutritionally balanced selection of foods and exercise regularly. Eating well and staying fit increases your chances of having a healthy pregnancy and baby. By giving your body the nutrients it needs, you are also giving your baby a great start. Exercise helps you maintain an appropriate weight gain, build your endurance for labor, and enable you to recover more quickly. Check with your physician, though, for guidelines on exercising safely during pregnancy. Staying healthy can mean fewer trips to the doctor for specialized care. This, in turn, means lower bills.

Decrease your risk of complications by avoiding alcohol, drugs, and cigarettes. Use of any of these substances can lead to high risk pregnancies and complications for your baby. Babies born with complications require high-tech medical care at many times the cost of a delivery for a baby born without complications.

Babies born with complications related to maternal alcohol, drug, and cigarette use typically have more medical problems throughout their lives. So, for at least 9 months, don't drink alcohol, smoke, or take drugs. Give your baby a chance at a healthy future.

Check with your hospital or birthing center for a list of items you are allowed to take with you to keep your medical costs down. Many insurance companies will not pay for diapers, alcohol, sanitary pads, etc. By taking your own you can reduce your charges. For infection control purposes, make sure any items you take to the hospital have not been opened. Some items you may consider taking along include: disposable diapers, alcohol for baby care, Tylenol, and sanitary pads.

When the Bills Roll In

Paying the bills doesn't have to be the most painful part of having a baby. It is important to keep track of all services you receive, as well as receipts for any payments made. This information is important if you ever need to follow up on a bill, insurance claim, or payment.

File all claims to your insurance carrier promptly. The longer you delay, the longer payment of the bill is left unattended. Some carriers will not pay claims after a set date, often 6 to 12 months. Keep a log of what claims you filed and when.

Make sure you follow the rules established by your insurer. Sometimes precertification of services, second opinions, or preferred health providers are stipulated by insurers. If you do not follow the insurer's guidelines, you may not receive full insurance benefits.

Keep track of all the services you receive during your delivery and hospital stay. Ask for an itemized copy of your bill at discharge. Compare your records to the hospital or birthing center's bill. You may also receive a separate bill from your physician or nurse mid-wife. Compare these charges, too. If you notice an error, notify the hospital, birthing center, physician's office, or nurse mid-wife's office immediately and ask to review the charges. Some common billing errors include being charged for a private room when you did not request one, an incorrect number of days actually in the hospital, and items you did not use. Keeping a log of all services received and supplies used can make sorting through the bills easier.

Other Ways to Trim Health Care Costs

Ask for generic drugs if you need a prescription for pain medicine. Generic drugs can cost up to 50 percent less than brand name counterparts.

Use a telephone card to call friends and family. Hospitals bill high rates for long distance calls charged to your bill.

Take advantage of flexible health care spending accounts if your employer offers them. This type of account allows you to place an amount of your salary (determined by you) into a health care spending account. The money is exempt from social security and income tax. You may draw money out of your account to pay for out-of-pocket medical expenses, deductibles and copayments. (Flexible spending accounts can also be set up for childcare expenses.)

The tax savings can add up fast. A married couple with an annual income of $55,000 who put $2,000 into a flexible account can save up to $600 on taxes. Health care expenses paid through a flexible spending account cannot, however, be claimed as a deduction on your income tax return. You must use all the money in your account within the year. You can not get a refund on unused money.

Real Parents Say...

Although health insurance is a must, some health care can be provided for a lower cost through public health agencies. Shots, for example, are very inexpensive this way.

—*Deb, mother of one*

Securing Your Child's Future: A Financial and Legal Planner for Parents by Winifred Conkling, Ballantine Books, New York

Getting the Most for Your Medical Dollar by Charles B. Inlander and Karla Morales, Random House, Westminster, MD

The Savvy Patient by David Stutz, Consumer Report Books, Fairfield, OH; 800-272-0722

For additional information about state health departments and medical societies that provide free or low-cost health care or information, contact: Information USA at PO Box E, Kensington, MD 20895; 800-955-7693 or 301-942-6303. Ask for "Healthy Hotlines: Tips on How You Can Save a Bundle by Phone!"

For free information on maternal and child health issues, contact: National Maternal and Child Health Clearinghouse, 8201 Greensboro Drive, Suite 600, McLean, VA 22102-3810; 703-821-8955

If you need prenatal or child health care assistance, contact your County Relief Administration office. You may also want to check with major insurers in your state like Blue Cross-Blue Shield to see if they sponsor health programs for children in low-income families.

Books

Eating Expectantly: A Practical and Tasty Guide to Prenatal Nutrition by Bridget Swinney, Meadow Brook Press, Minneapolis, MN

Managing Your Gestational Diabetes: A Guide for You and Your Baby's Good Health by Lois Jovanovic-Peterson, Chronimed Publishing, Minneapolis, MN

No More Morning Sickness: A Survival Guide for Pregnant Women and **Take Two Crackers and Call Me in the Morning: A Real Life Guide for Surviving Morning Sickness** by Miriam Erick, Grinnen-Barrett Publishing, PO Box 779, 36 Winchester St. #8, Brookline, MA 02146

CHAPTER TWO

Top Six Things to Do Before Baby Arrives

"Love is an ocean of emotion entirely surrounded by expenses."
—Lord DeWar

As this chapter title suggests, there are a number of things that ideally you should do before your baby is born. You might be surprised, however, to find that picking out the best baby names, packing for your hospital stay, selecting nursery furniture, and child-proofing the house are not among this "Top Six" list.

Although other chapters focus on more immediate, short-term preparations, this one outlines some less visible, often forgotten preparations that can have important, long-term effects on your child's life. Most of these preparations require little or no money—just time and planning. So, before your baby's arrival propels you into the fast-paced world of parenting, you might want to take this opportunity to ensure the brightest possible future for him or her by writing a will, selecting a

Necessity Checklist

✿ **Make a will.**

✿ **Select a guardian.**

✿ **Get your finances in order**—set up an emergency fund and working budget.

✿ **Evaluate your insurance (life, disability) needs and purchase adequate coverage.**

✿ **Make maternity and family leave arrangements.**

✿ **Set up a legal and financial record keeping system** for all your important documents.

guardian, getting your finances in order, and making sure you have adequate insurance should anything happen to you. In addition, now is a good time to finalize your maternity or family leave arrangements and to set up a filing system for your medical and financial records.

#1—Write a Will

No doubt the last thing on your mind as you eagerly anticipate the birth of your child and the time you will spend together is the possibility that death could separate you. Yet accidents and illnesses resulting in death are too common. You need only to glance at the headlines or evening newscasts to readily confirm this.

Too many parents who work long hours both at home and away to provide for their child's daily needs fail to make arrangements for that child in the event they would die. In fact, two-thirds to three-fourths of adults under the age of 45 do not have wills.[1,2] If you do not have a will, you risk having a court decide your child's fate. In addition to selecting your child's legal guardian, the court and state may get a large chunk of the assets your child needs for clothing, food, shelter, and an education. Having a written will is the best way to prevent such a catastrophe should something tragic happen to you.

Basically, a will is your written instructions for how you want your earthly possessions divided. It designates who is to handle your personal and financial obligations, and who is to care for your dependent(s). You owe it to your baby to make sure his or her emotional and financial needs are taken care of. You can write a will on your own or have your attorney draft one. A plethora of books and computer software programs are available to take the confusion out of setting up a will.

Before you can give your possessions and money away, you need to know your financial net worth. Simply put, net worth is your current assets minus your liabilities.

Now is a good time to set aside a couple of hours to list all your assets, including cash, checking and saving accounts, investments, retirement funds, property, and personal valuables. From this total you will subtract your current liabilities, which could include a home mortgage, car loans, credit card debt, bills, and other loans. Many people are surprised to discover the value of their savings and other assets. Update your net worth annually.

Once you have determined your financial net worth, you need to decide:

Who will execute your will. This person(s) will inventory your property, pay your debts, distribute your property, and settle your affairs.

Whom you will name guardian of your child(ren).

To whom you will leave gifts. If you want to leave special possessions to certain people, make sure you state this in writing. Gift planning prevents family feuds from developing. Sometimes adults are worse than children when it comes to fighting over "toys" and other worldly possessions.

What guidelines to leave for paying taxes and any other debts. This way your executor will know that he or she is to sell your shares in Microsoft and IBM to pay the estate taxes and pass your great-grandmother's diamond brooch on to your daughter.

How to divide property, cash, and other assets left after gifts have been designated.

On a contingency plan in case someone can't fulfill a designated duty such as executor or guardian or if someone does not accept a gift.

With all this in order, you are ready to meet with an attorney or write your own draft will. If you write your own will, it is a good idea to check with an attorney about making it legal. See the Resource section of this chapter for will-writing references.

#2—Select the Best Guardian

Nobody can replace you as a parent, but in the event of your death, you owe it to your child to make sure he or she is cared for by a capable, loving substitute. You also need to designate a conservator, or guardian for the property, money, and other assets that your child(ren) will inherit should you die. The conservator controls the "purse strings" until your child is age 18 or 21, depending on state laws.

Selecting a guardian requires much consideration about who is best to raise your child. Before rushing to sign up grandparents, consider their age, the fact that they are possibly reaching their retirement years, and that they have already lived through having a teenager in the house at least once. Look for a guardian who:

- ❀ Likes children and is someone your child enjoys being with.
- ❀ Lives in an environment/home that provides a positive atmosphere for raising children, and would be a good role model.
- ❀ Would love your child and treat him or her as a birth child.
- ❀ Would be willing and able to carry out your wishes.
- ❀ Has similar parenting values, beliefs, and practices as you do.
- ❀ Is responsible.
- ❀ Is capable of managing the significant amount of money that would be passed on to your child.
- ❀ Shares similar moral and religious beliefs.
- ❀ Has regular contact with your family so your child is able to grow up knowing his or her grandparents, aunts, uncles, and other relatives.
- ❀ Lives in a community you would like your child raised in.
- ❀ Is loving, caring, considerate, and happy.
- ❀ Is in good health.

✿ Has the time and energy to devote to raising your child.

✿ Shares your educational values.

✿ Is willing to serve as your child(ren)'s guardian.

✿ It is also a good idea to name one or two alternate guardians in the event your designee is unable to fulfill the request.

Some parents set up a trust in the event of their death. A trust is a legal arrangement under which a person or institution, like a bank, controls property that you would leave to your child. There are a variety of different types of trusts. Talk with your attorney if you are considering this option.

#3—Get Your Finances in Order

Another necessary step to planning for your child's future is to get your current finances in order. This involves two things: establishing an emergency fund and setting up a working budget.

Emergency Funds

An emergency fund is money you put aside to cover day-to-day household and living expenses in the event of a crisis. Financial planners suggest an easy-to-liquidate fund equivalent to 3 to 6 month's salary.

If you don't already have such a fund, there is no time like the present to start one. Although building it may take some financial juggling, limited spending, and creative penny pinching, the security of knowing it is in place will be worth it. A word of caution, though. Remember what your emergency fund is for—a financial emergency.

Once you start setting money aside, it is easy to be tempted to spend "just a little" on a new baby swing or a weekend getaway. As harmless as this may seem, it is a practice you want to avoid. Spending money from this fund can leave you in a bind if your company suddenly decides to downsize or your job becomes unstable. Try to maintain spending habits as if that fund did not exist. Hopefully, you will never need the emergency cash and you can treat yourself to a reward later in life.

Reassess your emergency fund annually to make sure your savings keep up with your salary increases, inflation factors, living expenses, and future needs.

Working With a Budget

The best way to meet the projected costs of raising your child to age 18 is to start watching your spending and saving now. Before you can alter your spending and increase your saving, though, you need to know where your money goes.

Where Does All the Money Go? Some days it may seem as if money is short no matter how hard you work. With the additional expenses of caring for a baby, finances may only seem to get tighter. Many people are surprised at how quickly their paychecks disappear to cover weekly expenses. Some cannot imagine being able to save the 5 to 10 percent figure of their take-home pay that financial planners typically recommend. Others see no path to financial stability, let alone planning for a rainy day, college costs, or retirement dreams. Yet, these are important financial goals.

The first step to achieving these goals is to track both your monthly and yearly income and expenses to determine where your hard-earned money is going. You can track your income and expenses in a variety of ways. Computer programs like Quicken or Microsoft Money allow you to set up budgets, make future cash flow projections, and track your spending—all at the touch of the key pad. The traditional ledger pad, pencil, and calculator method works well, too.

Are You Spending Wisely? Now that you know where you are spending your money, you can begin to look at how wisely you are spending. This analysis requires you and your partner to share your financial goals, discuss future needs, and identify ways you may want to alter your spending habits.

For example, if you estimate your baby's delivery is going to cost you $1,000 in out-of-pocket expenses, do you have a plan for payment? Do you need to pay for roof repairs or is a baby stroller more important? Will you need child care after your baby's birth? Where will the extra money come from?

Listed below are questions you should ask yourself as you evaluate your current spending. If you are completing the analysis with your partner, it is helpful for each of you to answer the questions independently and then share your ideas. This may help you to come up with a plan you both find workable.

1. Do you have discretionary income at the end of each month?   Yes   No

> If no, your first task is to identify ways to decrease your expenses and/or increase your income to obtain a positive cash flow.

2. Where does your leftover, discretionary income go? Were there unexpected expenses?

3. What percentage of your income is currently invested in savings?

4. What are your future needs and wants?

5. Prioritize your list of needs and wants in order of importance, with "1" being the most important goal.

6. Identify three to five areas in which you could decrease your spending.

   1. _____   4. _____
   2. _____   5. _____
   3. _____

Setting Up a Budget Now that you know your current cash flow status and you have identified your future needs, you can begin the process of setting up a budget. A budget is simply a calculated forecast of future spending. Budgets can help you make buying decisions. Budgets, however, should not be carved in stone. If your needs, wants, income, or expenses change, your budget should change, too.

Budget success is most likely if all "spending" members of your household set up the plan together. This allows all affected family members (except baby, who needs you to make decisions in his or her best interests) to be involved in financial decision-making. This participation usually results in wiser spending by everyone.

The best way to save money for future wants and needs is to include these goals in your monthly budget. Treat savings and investment deposits like a regular bill to be paid. In essence, you are practicing the habit of "paying yourself first," as advocated by financial planners.

Making Your Budget Work Simply having a budget does not guarantee financial success. To make the budget work, you must compare it to your monthly expenditures. As you do this, you can adjust your spending and savings to meet your goals.

#4—Evaluate Your Insurance Needs and Purchase Adequate Coverage

Now that you have a clearer picture of your financial status, you can use that information to help you determine how much disability insurance and life insurance you can afford to buy to protect your income and secure your family's financial future in the event of a tragedy. Just as you buy auto insurance and homeowners insurance to protect your property, you need to protect your income in case you lose your earning ability through death or disability.

Tips for Buying Disability Insurance

Make sure your policy protects you against your inability to work in your present position. Some policies only protect you if you can not work at all.

Make sure your policy makes cost-of-living adjustments. This allows your policy to keep up with inflation.

Purchase a non-cancelable contract. As long as you make your payments, the policy can not be canceled or the premiums increased.

Make sure the policy does not distinguish between illness and injury. In either instance, you can not work and need an income, especially with a new family member.

Buy a policy that offers you residual benefits and salary while you are recuperating or can only work part time.

Shop for a policy that offers a waiver of premium during the period you are disabled. This keeps your contract in effect without your paying premiums during the time you are ill or disabled.

Check if the policy covers preexisting conditions.

Check if the policy covers pregnancy. Be sure to ask about the waiting period before benefits kick in.

Check the benefit period. Some policies only pay benefits for a certain number of months (like 15 to 60 months); others pay benefits until age 65.

Life Insurance

Experts disagree on how much life insurance is enough. A simple rule is that you need enough money to cover your dependents' immediate cash needs and living expenses. Lifestyle, the number of dependents you have, and other sources of available income will also determine the amount of coverage you need. Buying adequate life insurance is one of the most important things you can do for your child.

If one parent stays home to care for your child, consider life insurance coverage for this parent also. Though he or she may not receive a weekly paycheck, it would take a significant amount of money to hire someone to fulfill his or her work and child care responsibilities.

Tips for Buying Life Insurance

Assess your insurance needs before looking at policies.

Be sure you can afford the premiums, now and in the future, especially when considering cash-value policies.

Don't buy cash-value life insurance if you don't intend to stick with it. Cash-value types can be very expensive if you drop them in the early years.

Read your policy very carefully. Ask questions you are uncertain about. You typically have a 30 day grace period from purchase date to change your mind.

Review your insurance coverage every few years to make sure your needs and increasing income are covered.

Compare similar policies from different companies.

#5—Maternity and/or Family Leave Request

If you want to take time off when your baby arrives and return to your same job, it is important to discuss your leave plans with your employer early so both of you can make appropriate arrangements.

The Family Leave and Medical Act of 1993 represents the United States' first legislative steps toward making it easier for both women and men to balance their need to work with their family responsibilities.

How the Family Leave Policy Works

You may take up to 12 weeks of unpaid leave per year for birth, adoption, or foster care of a child, personal illness, or the illness of an immediate family member.

To be eligible, you must work for a company with more than 50 employees. You must have been on the job for the past 12 months and have worked at least 1,250 hours over the past year (slightly more than half time). If you and your spouse work at the same company, you are eligible for 12 weeks total between the two of you.[3]

You are entitled to your position or equivalent position (including pay, benefits, and working conditions) upon your return. You will receive company health and medical benefits during your leave. You may be asked to repay these costs if you do not return to work after the leave.

You may take the 12 weeks off intermittently or consecutively.

Your employer has the right to decide if two leave periods can be taken consecutively. For example, if one leave ended in December, you may or may not be allowed to take a second leave starting in January.

You may be required to give 30 days notice of leave whenever possible to receive substitute pay such as vacation and sick time or other paid benefits.

Employers may exempt employees who are the highest paid 10 percent; employers with fewer than 50 workers in a 75 mile radius are also exempt.

In addition, the Pregnancy Discrimination Act of 1978 states that an employer with 15 or more employees on the payroll must treat pregnancy, childbirth, and related conditions like any other medical disability. This means you are entitled to the same sick benefits and job security as any other employee with an illness.

#6—Set Up a Legal and Financial Record Keeping System

Now that your financial and legal matters are in order, it is a good idea to set up a record keeping system for past, present, and future important records. Otherwise, you may find yourself living the saying, "I finally got it all together but can't remember where I put it." Select a simple method that works well for you.

Items such as your will, power of attorney, duplicate safety deposit key(s) and special instructions to be carried out in the event of your death, you may want to leave with your attorney or a trusted relative or friend. Important papers such as birth, death, and marriage certificates, passports, financial papers, insurance policies, and other significant documents should be stored in a safety deposit box or personal safe.

In addition to safely tucking away important papers, it is important to have a complete list of what you have and where it is located. This list should be updated every time you change, add, or eliminate a record or important paper. The list should be readily accessible to enable you to keep it current. Once a year set aside 3 to 6 hours to review and update everything.

Keeping things organized and current makes it easier for you to find things quickly. It also makes it possible for someone else to locate papers in case of an emergency or death.

Some people prefer to keep this information on a home computer. If you choose this option, make sure you leave information about where the records are located and directions for accessing the computer software program. For added convenience, print a copy of your records and keep it with your will. Computer software programs and books designed to help you keep your records orderly are listed in the Resource section at the end of this chapter.

Smart Parents Do

Check out your insurance company before making your investment.
Call your local library for a listing of insurance rating companies.

Keep all insurance policies, important documents, and certificates of investment in a safe or safety deposit box.

Independent insurance agents can usually do more price shopping for you than those who represent just one company. Most agents are pretty reasonable. **However, don't let an agent pressure you into signing something you are not sure of.**

Take care of yourself. The best insurance policy is one that never gets used.

Budget Helpers

Avoid return-of-premium disability policies. These policies offer you a portion of your money back if you don't file a claim. However, they can cost up to 50 percent more than other disability policies. Opt for a less expensive policy and invest the difference in a savings plan of your choice.

If you've recently kicked the smoking habit, let your insurance companies know. Your premiums (life and health) may be reduced by as much as 40 to 50 percent.

You can save up to 40 to 60 percent on your disability premium by having a 90 versus 30 day waiting period for benefits to be available. Put the premium savings into your three to six month emergency fund. You will earn interest and save on premiums at the same time.

Pay all insurance premiums annually instead of biannually, quarterly, or monthly. The total premium is usually less because the insurance company has fewer administrative costs.

Consider taking advantage of employer insurance plans. They usually offer unbeatable group discounts.

Avoid buying life insurance for your baby. Most babies do not contribute to the family income. Statistically, your baby is not apt to die. The money may be better spent having more coverage on the family's breadwinner(s). If you like the idea of carrying life insurance on your child, consider buying a cash-value policy as a savings investment. This can be a good idea if you have a difficult time setting up savings plans. Remember, some money in life insurance investments is OK, but there are other investments that offer higher rates of return.

Check into buying the majority of your insurance coverage (home, auto, life, etc.) all from one company. You can often reduce your total cost by as much as 15 percent by taking advantage of multi-policy plans.

Books

A Parent's Guide to Wills and Trusts by Don Silver, Adams-Hall Publishing, Los Angeles

The Complete Will Kit by Jens C. Appel III and F. Bruce Gentey, John Wiley and Sons, Somerset, NJ

Securing Your Child's Future—A Financial and Legal Planner for Parents by Winifred Conkling, Fawcett/Columbine Books, New York

Wills: A Do-It-Yourself Guide by HALT, Halt Membership Services Department, 1319 F Street NW, Suite 300, Washington, D.C. 20004; 202-347-9600

Current Family Health Journal, Code #15497-8, Current, Inc., The Current Building, Colorado Springs, CO 80941; 800-521-7170 or 800-855-2880 (for the hearing impaired)

Brochure

To learn more about giving money to your children, contact the **Internal Revenue Service** (IRS) at 800-829-3676. Ask to receive a free copy of "Federal Estate and Gift Taxes" (Publication 448).

Computer Programs

For easy financial planning and record keeping, check out local computer stores, electronic stores, and some discount stores for programs.

Money, Microsoft Corporation, One Microsoft Way, Redmond, WA 98052-6399

Nolo's Personal Record Keeper, Nolo Press, 950 Parker Street, Berkeley, CA 94710; 800-992-6656

Quicken, Intuit, PO Box 3014, Menlo Park, CA 94026-9959; 415-322-0573

Quicken Family Lawyer, Parsons Technology, One Parsons Drive, Hiawatha, IA 52233; 800-223-6925

Parents' Guide to Money, Intuit, PO Box 7850, Mountain View, CA 94039-7850; 415-944-6000

R
e
s
o
u
r
c
e
s

R
e
s
o
u
r
c
e
s

Computer Programs (continued)

WillMaker, Nolo Press/Legisoft, 950 Parker St., Berkeley, CA 94710; 800-992-6656 (Note:

Wills are valid in all states except Louisiana)

Family Leave Information

Pregnancy Discrimination Act
For more information call the Equal Employment Opportunity Commission at 800-669-3362

National Association of Working Women, 614 Superior Avenue, Cleveland, OH 44113-9990; 216-566-9308

Other Information

To request your survivor's social security benefits call 800-937-2000 and request the "Personal Earnings and Benefits Estimate Statement"

To request a free estimate of your disability benefits call 800-772-1213

For information on vital records write: Consumer Information Center, PO Box 100, Pueblo, CO 81002 (ask for the U.S. Department of Health and Human Services' "Where to Write for Vital Records," Cost $1.75)

CHAPTER THREE

Maternity Clothes—Looking Great Without Spending a Bundle

"Ah, to be skinny herself! To sleep on her flat stomach, walk lightly again on the balls of her feet."
—*Doris Betts*

Now that you have taken care of some important but less obvious preparations related to your child's impending birth, it's time to focus on more immediate needs and how you can save money while meeting them. Depending on how far along your pregnancy is, that may well mean paying attention to a maternity wardrobe.

Contrary to popular belief, you don't have to spend a fortune to be comfortably and fashionably dressed during your pregnancy. The availability, selection, and pricing of maternity clothes have improved in recent years. In addition, today's fashion trends and fabrics make it easier to postpone or avoid buying maternity clothes altogether.

Necessity Checklist

- ✿ **2 supportive bras**—plan to purchase a larger size every two to four months

- ✿ **2 or 3 nursing bras** if you plan to breastfeed (purchase 1 or 2 during weeks 28 to 36)

- ✿ **2+ pair of comfortable fitting, low-heeled shoes**

- ✿ **5 to 7 pairs of comfortable underwear,** depending on how often you do laundry

- ✿ **Maternity pantyhose** (purchase between months 3 and 6, number needed will vary)

- ✿ **Maternity slip**—if you wear dresses or skirts to work

continued on next page

Necessity Checklist (continued)

✿ **Casual wear** (purchase 100% cotton); 3 outfits minimum—may double as career wear

✿ **Career wear** (purchase mix and match separates); 3 or 4 pairs of pants, 2 or 3 skirts, 1 dress, and 4 or 5 blouses

✿ **Dressy blouse and pants or skirt** for dress or social outings

✿ **Accessories**

✿ **Some type of clothing for exercising**

"Nice-to-Have" List

✿ **1 or 2 sleep bras** if extra support is needed at night

✿ **1 or 2 formal or evening outfits**

Let's Get Comfortable

You can continue to wear your regular clothing as long it feels comfortable. Even when your abdomen starts to swell and jeans and trousers feel tight, you may find you can get by for months by pairing a loose blouse or one of today's oversized tops with several styles of elastic-waist bottoms, including regular knit pants, leggings, sweatpants, or casual stretch pants. While this strategy may see some women through their entire pregnancy, you may find that somewhere between your fourth and seventh months you need to do some shopping (or sewing if you are handy with the scissors, sewing machine, needle, and thread).

The amount of maternity clothing you will need depends on several factors. If you must maintain a professional appearance on the job, you'll probably need to buy more articles than someone who can dress more casually the entire nine months. Where you live and when you're due will determine whether you'll need to buy clothes specific to any given season, such as a heavy, cold-weather coat or a swimming suit. Your interests will dictate whether you need aerobic wear or evening wear.

Generally the sizing in maternity clothing is comparable to that in other women's wear. So, if you wore a size 12 before you became pregnant, you will most likely wear a size 12 in maternity clothes.

For maximum comfort, 100 percent cotton is probably your best fabric choice. Because body temperature tends to rise during pregnancy, polyester and other "blend" fabrics may be uncomfortably warm. Consider the care instructions of an item before you buy it. Pregnancy itself can be exhausting. You may want to avoid clothing that needs lots of special attention, such as handwashing and ironing.

When you begin adding maternity pieces to your wardrobe, look for separates that can mix and match and work with your present wardrobe. Stick to the basics and try not to overbuy. This is one wardrobe you probably won't want to leave hanging in your closet.

What and How Much Should I Buy?

To create a basic maternity wardrobe, consider your need for the following articles.

- ✿ **Casual Clothing**
- ✿ **Work or Career Wear**
- ✿ **Bras:** Maternity, Sleep, Nursing
- ✿ **Underwear:** Underpants, Slips, Pantyhose, Support hose
- ✿ **Formal Wear**
- ✿ **Exercise Clothes**

Casual Clothing

Again, stick to knit pants or leggings, shorts, and tops. Knit dresses can be comfortable for lounging around, too. With a few accessories, these clothes work for a casual night on the town or a day at work. Women of average height can often find clothes at regular or discount stores with great, non-maternity prices.

Work or Career Wear

Basics and coordinating separates are the keys to dressing successfully for work. Pants and skirts in basic colors go nicely with almost any top. Your goal is to create six to eight different outfits without spending a fortune.

Changing the color of your stockings and accessories increases your wardrobe depth. Adding a scarf and pin can give an outfit an entirely different look at minimal cost.

Bras

Maternity Bras Bras specifically designed for pregnant women can be purchased at department stores and specialty shops; however, the only thing that seems to distinguish them from ordinary bras is the not-so-ordinary price. Many pregnant women find regular bras work fine, and they can skip an unnecessary expense. Bust size can change monthly during pregnancy, though. So even if you choose to stick with regular bras, plan to purchase new ones every two to three months to accommodate your blossoming bosom. Buy two in any given size; one to wear, one to wash.

When you buy a bra—regular or maternity—make sure that it provides adequate support, is comfortable, and allows a little room for growth. Women who favor underwire styles may find them uncomfortable in the evenings and during the final months of pregnancy when the baby's feet often seem to be up against the diaphragm.

> ### Real Parents Say...
>
> My breasts seemed to be the only thing expanding for the first six months of my pregnancy. I found regular bras from the Hanes and Bali outlet stores provided great support at super prices—a real plus when I was purchasing bras every other month.
>
> —*Emily, mother of three*

Sleep Bras Because of their increasing bust size, some expectant moms find sleeping with a bra on offers added support and comfort at night. Special sleep bras are available in some stores; in others, similarly made bras are marketed as "soft" or "minimum support" bras. If you choose a sleep bra, make sure it provides light to moderate support, is comfortable (cotton is best), does not cut or bind, and can be used as a nursing bra during night feedings if you plan to breastfeed. One may be plenty; wear it at night, wash it during the day.

Nursing Bras Bras specifically designed for nursing are not a "must" if you plan to breastfeed. Whether you use them is a matter of personal preference. Although they are designed to facilitate breastfeeding by making the breast more readily accessible, many women find regular bras or no bras at all meet this need just as well.

If you decide to purchase a nursing bra, look for one that you can open and close easily, ideally with one hand, and that has room in the cups for breast shields or nursing pads. Shop for it between your 28th and 36th weeks of pregnancy. After 36 weeks, your rib cage expands and it's hard to size a bra to fit properly after delivery. Since your breasts may become engorged when your milk initially comes in after delivery, make sure the bra fits comfortably in the middle hook position. This will allow you some additional room for those first few weeks of breastfeeding—before your rib cage begins to return to normal size and your breasts are less engorged. Again, two bras are plenty to start with. Keep all sale slips and receipts until you are sure the size and fit are comfortable for you.

Finding Your Correct Size To find your correct bra size, take two easy measurements; one to determine body size, one to determine cup size. Measuring yourself correctly may be difficult at this time; ask your spouse or a friend for assistance.

Body Size

1. Wearing a bra, stand erect and measure under your bust, around the band of your bra.
2. Add 5 inches to this underbust measurement.
3. The total equals your body size. If the total is uneven, round to the next even number.

Cup Size

1. Measure around the fullest part of your bust.
2. Subtract your body size from this bust measurement.
3. The difference determines your cup size. A 1-inch difference correlates to an A cup, a 2-inch difference to a B cup, a three-inch difference to a C cup, a 4-inch difference to a D cup, and a 5-inch difference to a DD cup.

Underwear

Most women are amazed to find maternity underwear so comfortable even though they lack sex appeal. They fit easily over an ever-expanding abdomen without creeping up the backside. Stick to 100 percent cotton. Buy at discount stores for super savings. Five to seven pair are necessary some time after your third to fifth month. It's a one time buy—most women find it hard to outgrow these. Some women also find that regular bikini-style underwear in a larger size works well.

Slips If you plan to wear skirts and dresses regularly, you may need a maternity slip. Many women find that purchasing an inexpensive to moderately priced half-slip in a size larger than normal works great, too.

Hosiery Once again, if your wardrobe calls for skirts and dresses, you will probably need a few pairs of maternity hosiery. Many women find regular pantyhose binding and uncomfortable around the waist. The panel section of maternity hosiery gives you support without restricting circulation. Purchasing a larger sized pair of pantyhose, though less expensive than maternity hose, can still restrict circulation and contribute to fluid retention in your legs. Hanes/Leggs outlets carry a nice selection of maternity nylons and stockings at reasonable prices. Avoid buying these at maternity shops where they can cost as much as $15 per pair.

Support Hose Although maternity support hose could win an "ugly duckling" award, you may need a couple pairs if you have a history of varicose veins or if your feet, ankles, or legs tend to swell. Many women find maternity pantyhose combined with a little leg exercise during the day work almost as well as support hose. If you wear knee- or thigh-highs, make sure they are not too tight around your calves or thighs, where they could restrict circulation. If you sit a lot during the day, take a stretch break every 30 to 60 minutes and put your feet up. (Tip: Sit forward in your chair whenever possible to avoid compressing the back of your legs above the knees. This helps prevent fluid retention in your legs and ankles.) For women who are on their feet a lot, try to not remain stationary for long periods.

Formal or Evening Clothes

Unless your social calendar is full, investing in formal evening clothes is probably not necessary. In large metropolitan areas, it may be possible to rent formal evening garments. Another option may be to pair a fancy blouse or dressy accessories with your work clothes to add a softer touch for evenings out.

Exercise Wear

Most women find knit shorts, sweats, and T-shirts work fine for exercising. If you are headed to the gym, health club, or beach and need something more, catalogs and stores specializing in exercise gear are included in the Resource section at the end of this chapter.

Nursing Clothes

Nursing tops are not a must for nursing. Many moms find they do just fine with loose-fitting tops that button down the front or lift up easily. You may want to forget about wearing a dress that zips down the back

> **Real Parents Say...**
>
> I found a pair of denim maternity jeans and shorts a great investment. They go with everything!
> —*Linda, mother of two*

for now. When your baby's hungry, the last thing you need is a zipper struggle.

Nursing nightgowns make evening feeding easy if you can find one that fits properly. Some have openings that reveal all of you to the world and others seem impossibly undersized. An oversized T-shirt works just as well for lounging and sleeping. You can probably own three for the price of one nursing gown. These tops or nighties are in the wash all the time because leaking can be a regular occurrence during those first months.

Smart Mom Tips

Be careful about buying too many clothes too far in advance. It's often hard to tell what your size will be in the months ahead.

Make sure you wear comfortable shoes. The extra weight you are carrying and the relaxation of ligaments can cause feet to swell, expand, and change in size. Your balance may be slightly off, too, due to the extra weight and relaxing ligaments. Wearing a moderate to low heeled shoe (1/2 to 1 inch) is both practical and safe.

Accessorize, accessorize, accessorize. Coordinating scarves, eye-catching jewelry, and pretty hair ties can draw the eye away from your ever-expanding middle and add style to your fashions.

Buy or make coordinating separates. Mix-and-match separates can extend your wardrobe as your lifestyle dictates.

Keep your face and hair looking fabulous. This is an easy, inexpensive way to energize you and bolster your self-esteem.

Save all receipts—especially when you are buying for the future. Buy at stores that have an accommodating return policy.

Budget Helpers

Become a borrower. Borrow clothes from someone who has recently had a baby. Even borrowing two or three items can give your wardrobe—and your spirits—a boost. Most women who have just had babies don't ever want to see their maternity clothes again. Return the favor should they become pregnant again.

Shop consignment stores or garage sales. Maternity clothes can usually be found in great shape at low prices. Shopping consignment stores or yard sales in affluent areas of your community can sometimes lead you to the best deals.

Resurrect the sewing machine. Even if your sewing skills are rusty, you can save lots of money by making skirts, knit pants, shorts,

T-shirts, and jumpers such as those from McCalls, Simplicity, Butterick, and Kwik Sew. Stick to quick, easy patterns with simple lines and elastic waistbands.

Shop and swap with another person. If you have a friend that is expecting about the same time you are, consider shopping together and swapping dresses and nonbasic items periodically. This is a great way to mutually increase your clothing selection.

Shop discount stores—especially for underwear and casual clothes. Cotton underwear can be found at discount stores for about half the price of a maternity shop. Knit pants and tops can also be found in these stores. If you need tall sizes, however, you will probably need to shop the stores or catalogs listed in the Resource section, visit a maternity shop, or sew your own.

> ### Real Parents Say...
>
> I borrowed maternity clothes along with purchases of my own. I frequently wore my husband's shirts around home. At work, I basically had five dresses, adding regular jackets for cooler weather and variety.
>
> — *Cheryl, mother of one*

Buy regular clothes in a larger size or shop "one size up" stores. Oversized clothes and larger sizes often work well for the first two trimesters. These clothes are often more stylish and less expensive and can be worn when you bring baby home. Often regular bras in a larger size and bikini style underwear fits fine for the first three to seven months.

Raid your spouse's closet. Boxy shirts paired with a sleek skirt or leggings can be stylish at a minimal cost.

Shop at maternity outlet stores or through catalogs. A number of quality stores and catalogs are listed in the Resource section of this chapter.

Set a budget for maternity wear. How much do you normally spend on clothes during a year? Use this amount as a guide.

Maternity Wear Catalogs and Outlet Stores

Mother's Place, 6836 Engle Road, PO Box 94512, Cleveland, OH 44101-4512; 800-829-0080

J.C. Penney Company, Inc. (request the Baby and You Maternity catalog), Catalog Division, Atlanta, GA 30390-0370; 800-222-6161

Dan Howard's Maternity Factory Outlet, Catalog Customer Service, 4245 North Knox Avenue, Chicago, IL 60641-1904; 800-9 MONTHS for a catalog or 800-263-6700 for an outlet store near you. Fax: 312-777-0057

MothersWork, 1309 Noble St., 6th Floor, Dept. P6, Philadelphia, PA 19123; 800-825-2286 or 215-625-9259

A Pea in a Pod, 2800 W. Storey Road, Irving, TX 75038; 800-733-7373

Hanes/L'eggs/Playtex/Bali Outlet, One Hanes Place, PO Box 748, Rural Hall, NC 27098; 800-300-2600. Fax: 800-545-5613

Mothercare; 312-263-6700 for a store near you

Motherhood; 800-929-4428 for a store near you

Fitness Wear for Expecting Exercisers 4R MOMS 2B; 800-666-2127 for a store near you

Title Nine Sports Mail Order, 1054 Heinz Street, Berkeley, CA 94710; 510-549-2592

CHAPTER FOUR

Nursery Furniture & Other Baby Products

*"You know that having a baby has drastically
changed your life when you and your husband go on a date
to Wal-Mart on double coupon day."*
—Linda Fiterman

Welcome to the world of baby furniture and accessories. As you shop around, you are sure to notice just about everything imaginable from baby-sized tables and chairs to miniature recliners, not to mention thousands of other "baby-only" products. These baby-only, use-for-less-than-two-years items include high chairs, swings, jumpers, monitors, and on and on.

Your challenge as a new, cost-conscious parent is to meet baby's needs at a bargain price. The fact is, infants need or want very little besides food, shelter, warmth, and love. In addition to baby's needs, your purchasing decisions will also be affected by your family situation, lifestyle, child care needs, and budget. Basic baby gear will typically include a crib, car seat, high chair, and stroller.

Safety should be your number one concern when selecting any baby product. Each year more than 86,000 children under the age of five are treated in U.S. hospital emergency rooms for injuries attributed to nursery furnishings.[1] Look for products that have the Juvenile Products

---

Necessity Checklist

✿ **Crib**

✿ **High chair** (purchase by months 4 to 6)

✿ **Stroller**

✿ **Car Seat** (See Chapter Five)

Manufacturers Association (JPMA) certified seal, which indicates products have been tested in an independent lab and meet safety criteria set by both the JPMA and the Consumer Product Safety Commission. JPMA certification is a voluntary process.

Product manufacturing is only a piece of the safety puzzle. Remember, the crib, high chair, and other baby gear can only meet safety claims when used as intended. As your child's guardian you will want to ensure the best use of your baby's equipment.

So you are ready to furnish baby's room. All you need to do now is buzz over to your favorite baby shops and away you go. Just a quick little shopping trip, pick out the colors, and set up a delivery date. Or if you are a handy do-it-yourselfer, you can skip the set up fee and delivery date arrangements; by sunset, the baby's room should be ready to go.

Slow down, oh new parental one. There are a few things you need to know before you head blindly into baby mania. Before leaving the comfort of your living room, make a list of your most needed items. The items listed earlier (a crib complete with mattress, car seat, high chair, and stroller) do not all need to be purchased now. Actually, baby will do just fine for the first 4 months with only a crib and car seat. (For car seat specifics, see Chapter Five.) All other baby furnishings are highlighted in this chapter. Use the guidelines included in this chapter when comparing product safety features.

In the coming months and years you will find many products for your baby — some of which you will recommend to every new parent and some of which you will consider a waste of money. Start with the basics and add more if you wish. Just make sure to place safety concerns at the top of every decision checklist.

Both used and new products can be either safe or unsafe. Most baby products are a convenience, and yes, helpful from time to time. Your baby, however, will probably prefer to dance in your arms than swing back and forth, smile at your face than gaze at a mobile, and play with you on the floor than jump in a jumper. No product in the world can take your place.

Cribs

Besides your arms, the crib is the place baby will spend a majority of his first few months of life. More than 10,500 accidents involving cribs were reported in 1995, making them the fourth most dangerous nursery product.[2] Selecting this piece of furniture must be done carefully.

Contrary to crib advertisements, price and quality are not necessarily proportional. A new crib can cost from $100 to $750 or more for a designer one. However, before you faint from sticker shock, realize you can get a well-made, baby-safe crib for $150 to $300. If you are considering a beautiful imported model, remember your child will use his crib two years or less. At $750 for a top-of-the-line imported model, you are paying $1.03 a night for baby's bed—that's not including a mattress, bedding, blankets, and sleepwear. And, to top if off, Junior will never know if he rested his weary head in a designer crib or not.

Take the following crib safety guidelines with you on your crib hunt. Whether you are shopping at a specialty shop, a baby megastore like Baby Superstore, a discount or department store, through the mail, or borrowing from friends, keep crib safety your top priority.

Crib Safety Guidelines

- ✿ **Slats are spaced no more than 2 3/8 inches (60 mm) apart.** A larger space could allow baby's head or body to become lodged between the slats, resulting in injury or even strangulation.
- ✿ **Check that no slats are missing or cracked.**
- ✿ **Mattress fits snugly in the crib.** There is less than two fingers width between the edge of the mattress and the sides of the crib.
- ✿ **Mattress support is securely attached to both the head- and footboards.**
- ✿ **Corner posts are no higher than 1/16 of an inch (1.5 mm)** to prevent entanglement of clothing or other objects

worn by your child. Remove corner post extensions or decorative knobs.

✿ **No cutouts in the head- and footboards that could allow head entrapment.**

✿ **Drop-side latch cannot be easily reached by your baby or young child.**

✿ **Make sure the crib is sturdy.** If it wobbles when you shake it, it may be unsafe when your baby begins bouncing and climbing.

✿ **Look for a crib that meets federal safety standards** and the JPMA (Juvenile Products Manufacturers Association) seal of approval.

Assembly and Maintenance Guidelines

✿ Tightly secure all screws or bolts.

✿ Re-tighten all nuts, bolts, and screws periodically.

✿ Whenever a crib is moved, be sure all mattress support hangers are secure.

✿ Check mattress support hooks regularly to be sure none are broken or bent. An open or broken hook may allow the mattress to fall.

✿ Never use a crib with broken or missing parts.

✿ If a crib has been dismantled, put it back together with screws one size larger than the originals to ensure everything fits together tightly.

✿ Plastic teething rails should be securely attached. Remove or replace cracked or loose rails. They can cut or pinch an exploring tongue or finger.

For Added Safety

Do not put baby on a water bed. Babies can easily roll to the edges and get wedged between the mattress and the bed. Infants caught in this position have been known to suffocate.

Remove all crib toys which are strung across the crib or playpen when baby begins to push up on his hands and knees or is five months of age, whichever is sooner.

Remove bumper pads as soon as baby can pull to standing. Some ambitious youngsters have used the pads to assist their climbing efforts out of the crib.

Avoid using the crib as a playpen.

Once your child is 35 inches tall or has tried to climb out of the crib, transfer him to a regular bed.

Never use dry cleaning plastic or trash bags as mattress covers. The plastic may cling to your child's face and cause suffocation.

Adjust the mattress to the lowest position as soon as your child can stand up.

Always lock the side rail in its raised position whenever you place your child in the crib.

If the crib is placed near a window, make sure there are no window blinds or shade cords within baby's reach.

Never put a string or ribbon around your child's neck to hold a pacifier.

Never hang a laundry bag or any stringed object like a toy on the crib post. Baby could get caught in the item and strangle.

Check out other cribs baby may be sleeping in—including those at day care and grandparents' houses. Share these crib safety guidelines with them.

What About a Used Crib?

A used or borrowed crib can be a great way to save on baby expenses. However, you must be careful to apply the preceding safety guidelines to any crib you consider using. No amount of money can replace your baby if the crib is unsafe.

All cribs manufactured in the United States since February of 1974 have been required to meet Consumer Product Safety Commission (CPSC) safety standards. However, this is only one step in ensuring crib safety. Many cribs are imported or have become unsafe with years of wear and tear.

If you opt to use the crib stored away in grandma's attic or one on loan from a friend, you can do so safely by following these additional safety precautions recommended by the CPSC:

Look for cribs without designs and openings in the head- and footboards. Any opening between the crib post and robe rail (the horizontal piece along the top of the crib) could lead to strangulation.

Corner posts should be unscrewed or sawed and sanded off flush with the head- and footboards.

Make sure the crib has no missing slats. All slats must be securely fastened in place and no more than 2 3/8 inches apart.

Use a mattress that fits snugly. You should not be able to get more than two fingers between the crib and the mattress. If the mattress is too small, there is a chance that baby could get his head caught between the mattress and the crib.

If you refinish or paint the crib, check the product label closely to make sure it is safe for use on baby items. Do not use a paint that contains lead. After refinishing the crib, allow it to dry completely so there are no residual fumes for baby to inhale.

Remove or replace all used or cracked teething rails.

Smart Parents Do

Rotate the crib mattress every two months for longer wear.

Shop for your crib by your sixth or seventh month of pregnancy.
Many stores do not keep cribs in stock and to special order can
take anywhere from four to sixteen weeks.

Look for a crib with good mattress support. A crib with a set of
springs provides more comfort for baby than those with a cardboard or plywood bottom.

Try out the side release. Look for a crib with a release that is easy
to operate with one hand because baby will most likely be in
your other arm. A quiet release is also a must when trying to lay
a sleeping baby down for a nap.

Make sure you can adjust the mattress height. This saves your back
from excess strain and is a necessary feature as baby grows.

Check the directions for ease of assembly.

Budget Helpers

Buy a crib with a single-drop side instead of double-drop sides. You
will save about $50 to $100. Unless you have a very large baby's
room, one side of the crib is usually against the wall.

Avoid designer brand cribs and baby specialty shops. The mark-up
is high on cribs and accessories.

Avoid the combination crib/youth beds. Most children make the
transition from crib to twin bed easily. These beds require special
sized bedding and won't save you from having to buy a full sized
bed later. If you worry about baby falling out of bed, place your
used crib mattress on the floor, close to the bed. If Junior accidentally rolls out, he'll land on the mattress and cushion his fall.

Be cautious if purchasing a metal crib. They can be poorly made
and have safety problems. Check welded areas between parts

carefully. Look for sharp edges on which fingers can get cut and clothing caught.

Consider buying from mail order catalogs. JC Penney (800-222-6161), for example, has well-made cribs at reasonable prices. Although mail order prices are not a lot less than retail prices, you may find the convenience worthwhile.

Linens

Baby's room is a place where you can spend anywhere from a little money on basics to a small fortune on a room with coordinated walls, linens, and other special touches. Your personal style and overall baby budget will determine how much you decide to invest in decorating. Coordinated rooms are beautiful, no doubt, but decor hardly matters to a baby who usually spends the time in his room sleeping. To save money, it may be more practical to wait to decorate when your child is older and he can help choose a design that reflects his own personality.

Listed below are suggested baby linens to help you get started. You can always add more later.

- ✿ **1 or 2 Mattress Pads.** The fitted style stays put the best.
- ✿ **2 Fitted Crib Sheets.** It's important to have a spare for speedy changes when you don't have time to wash. Flannel sheets are nice if you live in a cold climate. Look for sheets with a high thread count (ideally, 200 or more threads per inch).
- ✿ **1 Set of Bumper Pads.** Look for pads that are washable, thick, and soft. Avoid filling that feels gritty. Dacron-brand filling is one good choice. Look for 6- to 7-inch ties at the tops and bottom. A neutral, plain colored or white bumper pad coordinates with most sheet patterns and allows you decorating versatility.

✿ **5 Receiving Blankets.** Receiving blankets come in a variety of sizes. The larger ones last the longest. Infants quickly outgrow the smaller sizes. It seems you will find uses for these blankets for years. For example, keep one in your car to cover your car seat when it is a hot day; keep one in the diaper bag for an emergency changing.

✿ **1 Good Blanket or Quilt.** Choose a weight appropriate for the climate in your area.

Avoid pillows, lambskin, and fluffy bedding. Babies have been known to suffocate on these while they sleep.

Never use an electric blanket. Babies can easily overheat. Moisture, like drool or urine, can potentially increase the risk of electrical shock.

Avoid items sewn with nylon. Nylon on sheets and other bedding can melt and break in the dryer and become a choking hazard.

High Chairs

Many parents find a high chair indispensable when their baby begins sitting up and eating solid food — usually 4 to 6 months of age. After that you will use the chair at meals and snack time every day. A sturdy chair is a must since baby may be in it until he is two or three.

Surprisingly, this essential piece of baby furniture is involved in over 7,300 injuries each year, according to the U.S. Consumer Product Safety Commission.[3] Most accidents occur to children under the age of 1. The majority of injuries result from falls from the chair. An unrestrained baby can easily slip or climb out of a chair in less time than it takes to run to the

> ### Real Parents Say...
>
> I liked the high chair with a swing tray that wraps around for ease getting baby in and out. The larger tray also had ample room for baby's food and its size made it harder for baby to grab things from the table.
>
> —*Anne H., mother of five*

refrigerator to refill the sippy cup with juice.

As with the crib, check the chair over thoroughly for safety features before purchasing or using one. If you are tempted by a wooden chair with old fashioned charm, evaluate it for safety. Expect to pay $50 to $120 for a new chair.

Safety Tips

- ✿ Never leave a child unattended or unrestrained in a high chair.
- ✿ Select a chair with a wide base for stability.
- ✿ The crotch and waist straps should be independent of the tray.
- ✿ Make sure the tray locks securely.
- ✿ If the chair is a folding model, make sure it has a device to lock it in place and keep it from collapsing.
- ✿ Caps or plugs on the legs or other tubing should be securely attached. Look for any loose pieces your child could pull off and choke on.
- ✿ Pull on the straps and belts to check for sturdiness. Make sure the restraint system is easy for you to use. If it is hard to fasten, you may not consistently secure it when sitting a wriggling infant down for lunch.
- ✿ Never allow your child to stand in the chair.
- ✿ Keep the chair far enough away from the table, counter, wall, or other objects that baby could use to grab things from or push off of.
- ✿ Do not let other children hang on or play around the chair. They can easily tip it over with baby in it.

Smart Parents Do

- ✿ **Look for a chair that is easy to clean** because you will be doing this at least three to six times a day.

- ✿ **Wrap-around trays are great for keeping more of baby's food on the tray instead of on the floor.** Smaller trays, on the other hand, are ideal for washing in the dishwasher.

- ✿ **Padded seats may be more comfy for baby than wooden styles.**

Budget Helpers

- ✿ **For money-saving ideas** on any baby product, see the Budget Helpers section at the end of this chapter.

- ✿ **Search through grandma's attic or borrow from friends.** Check the chair for safety.

Strollers

A stroller makes almost any outing with your baby more convenient. Three types of strollers are available. The umbrella stroller, the conventional stroller, and the jogging stroller. Next to walkers, strollers are the second most potentially dangerous piece of baby equipment. According to the Consumer Product Safety Commission, they are involved in more than 14,400 injuries each year.[4] Choose one with safety in mind.

Umbrella Stroller A lightweight, inexpensive stroller that can be carried on your wrist like an umbrella when it is folded. Great for short trips or outings on very smooth surfaces—like shopping center floors. They usually come with no special features. Cost is $20 to $30.

Conventional or Lightweight Stroller A beefed-up version of the umbrella stroller, the conventional stroller often has features such as reclining seats, storage pouches, brake systems, and more. Price ranges from $150 to $300.

Jogging Stroller A large three-wheel stroller designed for taking baby walking or running with you. The large tires and aluminum frame make the stroller easy to push at speeds up to 15 miles per hour. Great for walks in the country or on bumpy streets where other stroller wheels do not function well. Cost is $150 to $300.

If you opt to take baby jogging with you, remember to always have him wear an approved helmet and buckle him securely in the stroller. This may mean baby has to wait to go on his first jogging outing until a helmet fits properly and he has adequate neck strength.

Always try the stroller before you buy it. Besides looking at the price tag and comparing special accessories, look for safety features, too.

Safety Tips

- ✿ Look for a stroller with a wide base that will resist tipping when baby shifts from side to side.
- ✿ Make sure the brake is convenient and firmly locks the wheels. Brakes on both wheels are best.
- ✿ Never leave your child unattended in a stroller.
- ✿ Always secure the seat belt.
- ✿ Do not hang purses, cameras, or shopping bags over the stroller handles as this could cause it to tip over. Use strollers for their intended purpose — transporting baby.
- ✿ When using a convertible buggy-stroller in the carriage position, the leg openings must be closed to prevent baby from slipping out and possibly being strangled.
- ✿ Follow the weight limits set by the manufacturer. Too much weight in a stroller could be dangerous, causing parts to break.

Smart Parents Do

✿ **Check to make sure the vinyl or fabric is easy to clean.**

✿ **If you are trying to limit expenses, avoid buying a stroller carriage.** Your baby is only in it three to six months and the limited use may not justify the spendy price.

✿ **If you plan to have more than one child, consider a double stroller right from the start.** The extra space can easily be used to hold diapers and blankets. And you will have room for two if a second child is in your future plans.

✿ **Look for a stroller with an adjustable handle** so both you and your partner can be comfortable pushing it. Adjustable handles allow you to push the stroller without straining your back.

✿ **A canopy is nice for keeping the sun off baby on hot days.**

✿ **Make sure you can comfortably push the stroller** without kicking your toes into the wheels.

✿ **Check that you can push the stroller with one hand** in case you are carrying packages in your other hand. This is especially important with an umbrella stroller that you may be using when shopping.

✿ **Try turning corners** to see if the stroller steers easily.

✿ **Make sure you can work all the stroller parts easily.** For maximum satisfaction and minimum frustration, you should be able to take it up or down in seconds.

✿ **Select the type of stroller that best meets your needs.**

Real Parents Say...

We prefer the great outdoors so we opted for a jogging stroller and search out the mall rental models whenever we go shopping.
—Anne and Dave, parents of two

Strollers that have big wheels in both the front and back make it easier to steer than the styles that have the smaller wheels in the front.
—Kathy and Don, parents of one

We invested in an umbrella stroller for quick trips and convenience. This works especially well in shopping malls.
—Dan and Chris, parents of one

Budget Helpers

✿ **Check out the new strollers that double as car seats.** The
car seat portion latches into the stroller frame. Various models are available through the Perfectly Safe
catalog. See Resource section.

Other Baby Products

The following are descriptions, safety tips, and parent comments
on other baby accessories. Only you can best decide which items
you and your baby need. Remember to buy with safety in mind.
This list is not inclusive; new products appear on the market
daily.

Remember, all the following items are conveniences. Your
baby (and you) will survive and continue to develop appropriately with or without the following items. The most common crit-
icisms of baby products are their safety and their potential use as
a substitute for parental attention. Chosen and used carefully,
these products can be safe. None of the items listed can replace
your loving care, constant supervision, and steadfast attention.

Bath Ring or Bath Seat

A seat or ring for baby to sit in while in the bathtub. The three-
or four-legged device is designed to give 6- to 12-month-olds
added support while in the bathtub. Cost: $15 to $25.

Safe Use: Never leave baby alone or with a sibling while in the
bathtub. A baby can drown in only a few inches of water. Only
fill the tub with enough water to cover baby's legs. Make sure all
the suction cups are securely attached to the bath ring. Suction
cups must be attached to a smooth surface to hold properly.
Nonskid or textured bathtub surfaces do not allow for adequate
suction and holding power.

Things to Consider: The suction cups can accidentally release,
allowing the bath ring and baby to tip over. Baby can slip

between the legs of the seat and become trapped under water. Once baby can climb, about 7 to 9 months, he may try to climb out of the seat. Where will you store it?

Smart Parents Do: If you choose to buy a bath ring or seat, select one made of sturdy plastic, with good suction cups on the base.

Baby Bathtub

A miniature bathtub for babies up to 6 to 8 months old. Many manufacturers claim this can also be used for toddlers. However, it is sometimes difficult to contain a toddler in a full-sized tub, so it seems unlikely that the infant tub will slow him down. Cost: $15 to $30.

Safe Use: Never leave baby unattended. Make sure the tub is not near the edge of a table, counter, or changing table. Be careful not to bathe baby in the kitchen sink. Faucet edges can be sharp; garbage disposals can be dangerous if accidentally turned on.

Things to Consider: Where will you store it?

Smart Parents Do: Save the money and give baby a bath in the bathtub. Lay a thick towel in the bottom of your bathtub. Fill the tub with a small amount of water and rest baby on the towel while bathing. Some parents opt to take a bath with baby. If you like this option, have your partner nearby so you can hand baby to him or her before you get out of the tub.

If you like the idea of an infant-sized bathtub, you can buy a soft foam bath cushion for about $5. Baby lays on the cushion in the full-sized tub. Wring the pad out and let dry when done using. Easy to store and inexpensive, too!

Real Parents Say...

My sister lent me a baby bathtub and we never used it. For the first sponge baths, we used a basin from the hospital and later we used the big tub. I had a large bath sponge to lay him on in the tub. It worked great!
—*Sandy, mother of three*

Budget Helpers: Shop garage sales or consignment shops for baby bathtubs. They can often be found in almost-new shape for little cost.

A 16 x 24 inch shallow plastic storage container with a thick towel or foam bath cushion in the bottom can be used as a baby bathtub. When baby outgrows it, you have a useable storage container.

Baby Carrier

A baby seat with a cloth cushion that usually adjusts to three or four positions. The carrier is used around the house to sit or recline baby in. A carrier is used for a baby's first 6 to 8 months or until he starts to crawl. Some carriers even have a rocking base and/or toy attachment bar for an added price. Cost: $25 to $50.

Safe Use: Absolutely not to be used as a car seat. Always buckle and strap baby in securely. Look for a carrier with both a waist and crotch safety strap. Look for a carrier with a wide base and nonskid feet for stability and slip resistance.

Things to Consider: How long will you use the carrier?

Real Parents Say...

I liked a baby carrier of some type. Keeping baby close by when he was awake makes getting things done easier.

—Linda, mother of three

Smart Parents Do: If you like the idea of a baby carrier, buy an infant car seat that can double as a carrier. You'll save about half the cost and have one less item to store or sell. If you plan to use a used car seat, check out the safety precautions in Chapter Five.

Budget Helpers: Shop garage sales or consignment shops for carriers. They get limited use and can often be found used in almost-new shape at a not-so-new price.

A baby carrier is a great item to borrow from a friend because baby uses it for such a short time.

Front or Back Baby Carrier, Sling, Snugli, or Backpack

Back or front carriers are designed for keeping infants up to 40 pounds close to you while allowing you to have your hands free. Slings, a different version with the same purpose, also allow you to keep baby close. Cost: $25 to $95.

Safe Use: Make sure the carrier has a restraining strap to secure the child. Check so leg openings are small enough to prevent baby from slipping out, but large enough to prevent chafing. Check that framed models have no places where baby could get pinched. Back carriers should have a padded covering over the frame to protect baby's face. When using a carrier, bend at the knees when stooping over, not at the waist, to prevent back strain. Don't wear baby in a carrier while cooking, drinking hot liquids, or handling chemicals. An accidental spill could burn baby.

Things to Consider: Can you get baby in and out of the carrier without any assistance? You will often need to do this in a hurry. Look for a carrier you can get a sleeping baby out of without waking him. Look for a carrier with good head support for baby. It defeats the purpose of a carrier if you constantly have to support baby's head and neck with your hands. Look for a carrier with well-padded shoulder straps that adjust easily and a broad waistband for back support. Try the carrier on for a proper fit. If you are not comfortable, baby won't be either.

Smart Parents Do: Getting baby in and out can be an adventure in baby gymnastics, so try out different models with baby before you buy.

Look for a carrier that can be

> ### Real Parents Say...
>
> I had a Snugli but my sons were 9 lbs. 9 oz., and 10 lbs. 7 3/4 oz. and they were hard on my back. Consider the season of the year before making your purchase. If you have a November baby in a cold climate, you may not be walking outdoors with an infant until April. By then he can ride in the stroller and he may be too heavy to carry in the Snugli.
> —*Lois, mother of three*

washed easily and has a snap-out bib to protect both carrier and parent from spit up.

Borrow from a friend before you buy. Trying the carrier out for more than a few minutes in the store is also helpful.

Keep all sales receipts until you know baby likes to go everywhere you go.

Budget Helpers: Shop for outdoor-type carriers in late fall or early winter for best sales and end-of-season deals. The off season for camping and backpacking gear can be a chance for great savings.

Watch for April baby sales, times when stores offer special discounts and clearance sales when cloth designs come out. Stores often put last year's design on clearance to make room for new merchandise.

Changing Table

A table with a covered pad and safety straps on which you can change baby's clothes and diapers. The changing table, used for infants until age 1 or 2, depending on baby's mobility skills, can either be freestanding or part of a child's dresser. Cost: $60 to $150 ($200 to $500 if part of a dresser).

Safe Use: Never leave baby unattended; you never know when your infant will master the skill of rolling over, and a fall from a changing table is a long drop. Make sure the table has safety straps. Always use the safety straps. Select a table with easily accessible drawers and shelves that you can reach without taking your eyes off baby. Look for a table that is sturdy and does not rock when baby moves.

Things to Consider: Look for a table that is waist high for maximum back comfort when changing baby.

Smart Parents Do: Consider a dresser with a convertible top as a changing table. This eliminates storage problems when baby outgrows the changing table, and you won't need to buy a new dresser for baby's clothes. However, shop around; some models are expensive. Look for a cover that's easy to clean.

Budget Helpers: Shop garage sales or borrow from a friend.

Cradle or Bassinet

Designed as a smaller space for the first 3 months of life. Provides baby with a cozy transition from womb to crib. Cost: $50 to $150 without mattress, bedding, and skirting.

Safe Use: Look for a bassinet with a sturdy bottom and wide base to prevent baby from falling out. Follow the manufacturer's instructions for appropriate size and weight of babies who can safely use the cradle or bassinet. Check the screws and bolts periodically to make sure they are tightly secured. Make sure the legs lock in place when the bassinet is in the upright position. Mattress and padding should fit snugly and be smooth; never use pillows, they are a suffocation hazard. Trim off decorative bows and ribbons to prevent accidental choking or strangulation. Make sure cradle slats or spindles are placed no more than 2 3/8 inches apart. There should be no missing or broken slats.

Things to Consider: Look for a bassinet that folds down easily and can be taken on trips or overnight stays with grandparents. If you have an older child, be careful that they don't tip baby out of cradle or bassinet. A crib or bassinet is nice if you want baby in your room for those first months of midnight feedings.

Real Parents Say...

We have changed both our children in the crib, on a bed, and on the floor. A towel or lap pad underneath keeps things from getting soiled. It is a great way to cut costs and you do not have to worry about falls when they are already on the floor.

—Linda & Joseph,
parents of two

An antique "dry sink" with a towel bar makes a neat changing table. Much more versatile later on. You can't put an old changing table in your living room when you are done with it!

—Rose and Art, parents of three

Smart Parents Do: Skip all the fancy bassinet coverings. Baby will never remember it and it is a hassle to launder.

Budget Helpers: Borrow, buy used, or shop discount stores for great prices on both bassinets and mattresses.

Exersaucer™ Walker Alternative

A baby entertainment system designed like a walker with a bottom, for babies 6 months old until they walk. Baby can rock, spin, or bounce, while forward movement is limited. Cost: $30 to $60.

Safe Use: Never leave baby unattended. Make sure all toys are securely attached. Keep baby out of the kitchen area and away from cords or things he could pull over on himself. Watch baby so bouncing and rocking doesn't cause the Exersaucer to tip over.

> ### Real Parents Say...
>
> If possible, borrow a swing, walker, baby jumper, or other items and see if baby and you like them before buying. Our son hated his $30 jumper so we never really used it.
>
> *—Dan, father of one*

Things to Consider: As with walkers, Exersaucers may impede walking.[5] Because forward movement is limited, they may be safer than walkers.

Smart Parents Do: Keep a constant eye on baby.

Budget Helpers: Borrow or buy used. Buy at Toys-R-Us or at a discount store. Save receipt in case you need to return it.

Hook-on Chair

Used as a substitute for a high chair, starting with babies 4 to 6 months old until age 1. Hook-on chairs attach to the end of your table. Care needs to be taken so the chair does not detach from the table resulting in a fall for baby.

Safe Use: Never leave your child unattended. Look for a chair with a clamp to lock it on to the table for additional safety. The restraints should be easy to use. Always fasten baby in the seat; never allow him to stand in the seat. Do not place the chair where your child's feet can reach the table supports and he can use it to push the chair away from the table. Do not place a regular chair under a hook-on chair. Do not clamp the chair onto a card table. Do not use with a glass, marble, loose-top, or single pedestal table; do not use with a tablecloth or hook onto a leaf of a table—all of these items can be unstable and could result in a fall for baby. Frequently examine the chair for any loose parts or screws.

Things to Consider: Will we have to buy a high chair as baby gets older, anyway? Handy for traveling and dining in restaurants.

Smart Parents Do: Keep the receipt until you are sure the chair works with your table.

Budget Helpers: Borrow or buy at a discount store where you can return it if it does not work well with your table.

Jumper

Basically a cloth baby seat with two long straps secured to the center of a door frame. The springy device allows a 6- to 9-month-old, who is suspended a few inches off the ground, to "jump" up and down.

Safe Use: Never leave baby unattended; baby walkers and jumpers were associated with 22,500 product-related injuries and deaths in 1995.[6] Be aware of the weight limit as specified by the manufacturer. Be very careful if there are other children around who may give baby an extra push or bounce. Check the overhead clamp regularly to make sure it is secure.

Tie or move jumper out of baby's reach when not in use so he doesn't become tangled, caught, or strangled in it.

Things to Consider: As with walkers, these types of devices may hinder creeping, crawling, and walking practice; overuse may also cause dizziness or head injuries.[7] Check that your door frame is strong enough to hold baby's weight and movement (kitchen remodeling could make the jumper's overall cost expensive).

Smart Parents Do: Try one out if possible before buying—let baby be the judge if he wants to practice high-jump training before his first birthday.

Budget Helpers: Borrow if possible.

Mobile

Black and white or colorful designs that hang above cribs, used until baby can stand in crib and reach the mobile. Whether mobiles stimulate learning is debatable. Some babies love them while others couldn't care less. Cost: $20 to $60.

Real Parents Say...

If you're going to spend the money, we liked the musical type. Alison seemed to love her musical moving mobile the best.
— *Debi and Nick, parents of two*

Safe Use: Take mobiles down as soon as baby is 5 months old or can pull to standing; he could pull down the mobile and become tangled in the strings.

Smart Parents Do: Lie flat on your back and look at the mobile from baby's point of view; it's amazing how many two dimensional designs are sold—baby sees little or nothing of the design. Look for a three dimensional model if you want a mobile.

Budget Helpers: A great "wish list" item.

Consignment shops often carry these at great prices.

If you are crafty, make your own out of fabric, bright colored objects, or other interesting shapes.

Monitor

A portable, two-piece device that allows you to listen to baby from another room. It is generally used until your child quits taking a nap. A monitor allows you to work away from baby, either in another room or in the yard or garden, and still monitor if baby is sleeping. Cost: $25 to $60.

Things to Consider: Look for a monitor that can be used both with an electrical outlet or batteries. A baby monitor is like a radio transmitter, so don't be surprised if you pick up conversations from somebody else's monitor or cordless phone. A word of caution: avoid carrying on a private conversation close to the base unit of the monitor—your neighbors or other cordless phone users may pick up your conversation. Try switching phone channels or consider purchasing a 900 Mhz cordless phone (about $150) to prevent interference problems between monitors and cordless phones.

Smart Parents Do: Save your receipt in case you need to exchange or replace the monitor.

Budget Helpers: Buy at a discount store.

Borrow from friends.

If buying used, make sure you try it out to see if it works; monitors often wear out after a few years of use, so a used model with no warranty may not be a good deal.

> ## Real Parents Say...
>
> We wouldn't live without one. Great for a two-story house and being outdoors.
> —*Sandy and Rick, parents of three*
>
> I never used my monitor with my September baby because we have a small house and weren't outside much. By the time he was 6 months old, I could hear him cry even when I was outside
> —*Lois, mother of three*

Night Light

A soft light for baby's room at night. Usually uses an electrical outlet. Cost: $5 to $35.

Safe Use: Keep the electrical cord and/or plug-in away from baby and baby's crib.

Things to Consider: May be useful when checking on baby late at night. Soft light is less apt to wake baby.

Smart Parents Do: Avoid leaving on all night unless you want baby to get used to sleeping with a light on.

Budget Helpers: If you do not mind a dimly lit room, use a 40 watt bulb in the main light fixture and skip the night light; the lower wattage light is soft for checking on baby at night. Sunlight usually provides ample lighting during the day. Buy at a discount store. A nice idea for your baby shower "wish list."

Pacifier

Looks like a nipple with a hard shield attached. Babies up to 8 months old have a need to suck; whether it is on their thumb or a pacifier is a matter of parental preference. Cost: $1 to $4.

Safe Use: Make sure the pacifier shield is large enough and firm enough not to fit into baby's mouth. Make sure the guard or shield has holes in it so baby can breathe if it accidentally gets stuck in his mouth. Check so the pacifier nipple is free of tears or holes. Do not attach rings, cords, or strings to the pacifier. Never fasten a pacifier around baby's neck. Pacifiers deteriorate with age and use, and with exposure to sunlight and food. Make sure to inspect them frequently. Never substitute a bottle nipple for a pacifier. They do not have a mouth guard to prevent choking.

The safest models are made of one single, molded piece.

Things to Consider: What is your personal philosophy on the use of pacifiers? Because they tend to fall on the floor and are handled a lot, they are a potential germ collector for baby.

Smart Parents Do: If you decide to use a pacifier, have three or four in stock so you can clean them frequently and rotate them when they fall on the floor.

Budget Helpers: Buy at a discount store. Packages of two or three are usually less costly than single packs.

Playpen

A contained environment for infants to 2-year-olds to play in. Cost: $60 to $120.

Safe Use: If you buy a mesh playpen, look for netting with very small weaving, smaller than the buttons on baby's clothing. If the playpen is wooden, check so the slats are no more than 2 3/8 inches apart. Check the top of the rails; replace, recover, or remove worn teething rails or torn vinyl. Never leave an infant unattended in a mesh playpen with a drop-side down; he could roll between the mesh and the mattress and suffocate. Do not string items across the top of the playpen. Never use a playpen with holes in the mesh sides.

Things to Consider: How long will your baby use a playpen? Where will you store it? Some parents find the playpen often becomes a giant toy and storage box.

Smart Parents Do: The portable travel playpens are nice for traveling and visiting family and friends; they fold up for easy storage. Look for a style that is easy to assemble and take apart. Look for a floor pad that is easy to clean.

Budget Helpers: Borrow from friends and family or buy used.

Shop from discount or wholesale catalogs or at discount stores.

Watch for baby sales — especially in April.

Safety Gate

Used at the top or bottom of stairs or in open doorways to keep baby out of potentially unsafe area. Used from crawling to toddling — 4 to 6 months to about 3 years of age.

Safe Use: Do not use accordion-style gates with expandable enclosures and V-shaped or diamond-shaped openings; a young child could easily get his head caught in the gate. If the gate has vertical slats they should be no more than 2 3/8 inches apart.

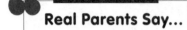

Real Parents Say...

We loved our metal Century Gateway child security gate. It was the best one we found. Priced at under $40, it fit nicely into our budget. It was expandable to fit a variety of areas and heavy-duty to withstand our child.
—*Sharon and John, parents of two*

Choose a gate with a straight top edge and a rigid mesh screen; if you choose a gate with V-shaped or diamond-shaped openings, the V-shaped openings should be no wider than 1 1/2 inches to prevent head entrapment. Be sure the gate is securely anchored to the doorway or stairway it is blocking; a determined child could push a poorly secured gate over and fall. If the gate is held in place with a pressure bar, install the gate with the bar away from the child; an adventurous climber could use the pressure bar as a toehold and use it to scale over the top of the gate.

Things to Consider: Where will you use the gate(s)? Measure the doorway or opening and take the dimensions with you when you shop. Make sure the gate fits the doorway properly.

Smart Parents Do: Take the gate down when your child starts climbing over it; dangerous falls could result. Look for a sturdy latch system—you may be opening and closing the gate 20 times per day; a latch that does not work well can be an unneeded aggravation.

Budget Helpers: Buy a sturdy gate. A flimsy gate that does not hold up well will cost you double your investment if you have to replace it.

Shop for gates in pet stores or through pet catalogs. You can sometimes find the exact gate for $5 to $10 less than in the baby department. Watch for baby sales—especially in April.

Baby Swing

Comes in two styles: a wind-up manual version or a quieter, battery operated model. Some even play music. Of course, the fancier the features, the more you pay. It seems babies either love or hate swings—there is little in between. If your child enjoys the swinging motion expect to pay $40 to $120 for the luxury. Most swings are designed for babies up to 25 pounds, but 3 to 8 months of age is prime time for maximum use.

Safe Use: Never leave your baby unattended. Always fasten the safety waist and crotch belt so baby can not slide out. Always observe the manufacturer's weight limit for baby. Look for a model with a stable, wide base. If other children are around, make sure they don't give baby an extra little push. Avoid the cradle swings; babies have been known to suffocate when getting wedged in the bottom of the swinging cradle.

> ### Real Parents Say...
>
> We never used ours much.
> —*Lois, mother of three*
>
> Only used for a short time—not really a necessity.
> —*Marsha, mother of two*
>
> We purchased our swing used for $20. Both of our children used it for about three months each. We have loaned it to friends, also. Because it gets minimum use, it was a great "used-buy" investment.
> —*Marie & Michael, parents of two*

Things to Consider: Look for a model that is easy to get baby in and out of; some models make it near impossible not to clunk baby on the head when you lift him out. A swing is not a substitute for hugging and cuddling.

Smart Parents Do: Try before you buy; save your receipt until you are sure baby appreciates this newest gadget.

Budget Helpers: Borrow or buy used. Once again, swings are only used for short periods. Manual, wind-up swings cost less. They are slightly noisier than their battery-operated counterparts, but because they do not run continuously, they are less apt to be overused as a "babysitter."

Baby Toiletries

Shampoos, lotions, oils, creams, and other products are all available in "baby-formulated designs" intended for infants until they are 1 or 2 years old. Soap and lotion are the basics. A mild soap can be used for washing both baby's body and hair. You may need baby oil if your little angel develops cradle cap.

Safe Use: Do not use baby powder; it can form a powder cloud over baby and cause respiratory problems if inhaled. Look for products that are dye- and perfume-free.

Things to Consider: If you receive samples of products during your hospital stay, try them to see if you like them before buying large quantities. You usually get more samples during your pregnancy than you will use in the first 6 months. Castile soap works great for a head to toe baby wash; a bar lasts a long time and it is gentle and non-drying to baby's skin.

Smart Parents Do: See Chapter Seven for diaper products and ointments.

Budget Helpers: Use coupons and shop at discount stores. Avoid buying baby toiletries in grocery stores, where prices can be double.

Try purchasing store or generic brands. They are often less expensive and of equal quality.

Walker

A seat suspended on a frame with four to six wheels. This creation, which is intended for 6-months-old until walking, allows baby to zoom through your house at an amazing speed, months before he can even walk. Walkers, though they give baby a newfound freedom, are also the number one cause of nursery product-related injuries. The U.S. Consumer Product Safety Commission reports 22,500 walker-related injuries for children 15 months or younger in 1995.[8] Cost: $35 to $60.

Safe Use: Never leave baby unattended; do not use walkers as babysitters. Look for models with a wide wheelbase for stability. The side coil springs should be covered to prevent finger pinching. Make sure the seat is securely attached to the frame. Avoid exposed joints; some models can pinch or amputate little fingers. Keep all stairway doors closed and place gates at the tops of all stairs to prevent falls. Keep a baby in a walker away from all cords, hot stoves, and tablecloths. Use only on smooth surfaces; rugs and thresholds can cause tripping and tipping.

Things to Consider: Walkers do not help infants learn to walk faster; the American Academy of Pediatrics recommends not using walkers because they may interfere with the natural development of walking.[9] An infant in a walker can move 3 to 5 feet per second.[10]

> ## Real Parents Say...
>
> Walkers are OK but can also be dangerous, especially with steps. Our daughter flipped hers one night and landed on her head. Even with only two steps she had a huge bump.
>
> —*Patty, mother of two*

Smart Parents Do: Be cautious about purchasing this product unless you can give baby 100 percent of your attention while he is buzzing all around the house. The risk for accidents is great.

Budget Helpers: Buy at discount stores.

Borrow—baby uses it for such a short time.

Avoid models that are more than a few years old. Old-style, X-framed walkers are no longer being made because these designs are responsible for many injuries, including finger amputations. Be careful not to buy these models at garage sales.

Instead of buying a walker, consider making a special play area on the floor where baby can roll, crawl, or scoot freely.

Baby Wipe Warmer

An electrical warmer that wraps around a variety of sizes of baby wipe containers. Makes wipes warm for diaper changes. Cost: $20.

Safe Use: Keep electrical cord out of baby's reach.

Things to Consider: Warmers can cause wipes to dry out faster.

Smart Parents Do: If a warm baby wipe is desired, use a warm washcloth for wiping baby's bottom. Save the $20 and put it toward a savings bond for baby.

Budget Helpers: Check out consignment and secondhand shops.

Note: Safety tips in this chapter were adapted from the U.S. Consumer Product Safety Commission Guidelines for safe nursery furniture. Though this product list is not inclusive, it does cover the most common baby products on the market today. Each major juvenile product company has their own line of high chairs, cribs, strollers, and more. You may find it helpful to write companies for product catalogs. For additional safety information, contact the U.S. Consumer Product Safety Commission, Washington, D.C. 20207; telephone: 800-638-2772 or 800-638-8270 for the hearing impaired. Further product research and safety guidelines may also be obtained by referring to Consumer Report publications.

General Budget Helpers

Borrow from friends. Carefully check products over before using them. Babies only use most products for a short period of time. Many parents sell or share furnishings in great shape. Before buying or borrowing any equipment, check if the used product model is on a recall list. Call the Consumer Product Safety Commission at 800-638-2772 for recall information or contact the manufacturer.

Post want ads on a bulletin board or in a newsletter at work. Know the features you are looking for and be prepared to make an offer. Request any product operating manuals also.

Watch local papers and work bulletins, and listen to "swap shop" radio programs for good deals on used baby furnishings. Ask other parents at day care or in parenting groups if they have used items to borrow or sell.

If you have a nearby friend or family member who is expecting 2 to 6 months before or after you, consider buying some products together and sharing them. Swings, jumpers, carriers, and other product "conveniences" are easily shared.

Shop discount stores for high chairs, baby carriers, swings, and toiletries, and save about 25 percent off the specialty store prices.

Use coupons for all baby toiletries like soap, shampoo, and lotions.

Check out discounters. Baby on a Budget, a Texas-based mail order discounter offers great pricing. Call 800-575-2224 for information.

Consider baby megastores like Baby Superstore (803-675-0299) or Lil' Things (817-649- 6100). Both specialize in carrying brand name products at hard-to-beat prices.

Watch for sales. April is traditionally baby sale month.

Check out Baby Catalog of America. They have great prices on strollers and other baby gear. (See Resource section.)

Shop consignment shops and garage sales. Much baby equipment is hardly used and can be found for 50 to 75 percent off the retail price at these sales. Take along the safety tips from this chapter.

If possible, try all items before you buy and save your receipts in case you need to make a return.

If you have problems with a product (new or used), write the manu-facturer.

R
e
s
o
u
r
c
e
s

Books

Guide to Baby Products by Sandy Jones and Werner Freitag, 4th Edition, Consumer Reports Books, Yonkers, NY

Baby Bargains by Denise and Alan Fields, Windsor Peak Press, 1223 Peakview Circle, Boulder, CO 80302, 800-888-0385

Catalogs

Baby Catalog of America, 719-721 Campbell Avenue, West Haven, CT 06516; 800-752-9736 or 203-931-7760

JCPenney Company, Inc., (request the "For Baby" catalog) PO Box 10001, Dallas, TX 75301-3114; 800-222-6161

One Step Ahead, 950 North Shore Drive, Lake Bluff, IL 60044; 800-274-8440 or 800-950-5120

Perfectly Safe, 7245 Whipple Avenue NW, North Canton, OH 44720; 800-837-KIDS or 800-837-5437. Fax: 216-494-0265

The Right Start Catalog, Right Start Plaza, 5334 Sterling Center Drive, Westlake Village, CA 91361-4627; 800-548-8531. Fax: 800-762-5501

For information on baby slings call: NoJo, 800-854-8760; Parenting Concepts, 800-727-3683

Other Information

To write for product safety information or to report a product hazard or product-related injury or recall information, contact: U.S. Consumer Product Safety Commission, Washington, D.C. 20207; 800-638-2772 or 800-638-8270 (hearing impaired)

For information on baby product safety, write for the booklet, "Safe and Sound Baby." Send a SASE and your request to: JPMA Safety Brochure, 2 Greentree Centre, PO Box 955, Marlton, NJ 08053; 609-985-2878

CHAPTER FIVE

To Grandmother's House We Go and Other Safe Travel

"Whenever we travel, whether it's to the sitters or on a vacation, it's not just a trip, it's an adventure."
—*Anonymous*

As you wrestle to secure your wriggling baby into her car seat, you wish for an extra pair of hands. You hear the latch click and check your watch. Thirty seconds—not bad! Your Olympic-level buckling-up skills are getting better every day.

You may have been tempted more than once to just let baby ride in someone's lap. And, as relatives are quick to remind you, *"You* never rode in a car seat." But, each time you consider not buckling up baby, you recall a car seat could save your child's life.

Knowing the fatal dangers of allowing your child to ride unrestrained, you opt to spend those extra 30 seconds making sure every ride is safe.

According to the National Highway Traffic Safety Administration, a child riding unrestrained in a vehicle is twice as likely to be killed in a crash than a child who is properly secured in a safety device.[1] A car seat could save your child's life. This may be the most important item you will buy for your child. It's a law in all 50 states

---

Necessity Checklist
✿ **Convertible car seat**

"Nice-To-Have" List
✿ **Infant car seat**
✿ **Booster seat** (needed when child outgrows the convertible car seat)
✿ **Children's cassette tapes**
✿ **Infant rearview mirror**
✿ **Window shades/sun protectors**
✿ **Car toys**

that infants and children, usually up to 3 or 4 years of age or 40 pounds be restrained in a child safety seat. Even then, it's best to use a car seat until your child is large enough to correctly fit in your vehicle's safety belt—usually 5 to 7 years of age or 50 to 60 pounds.[2]

Motor vehicle accidents are a leading cause of death among children under the age of 5, with more than 800 children killed in 1994 and more than 50,000 injured.[3] Buckle up every time you travel, even when it is close to home. Most fatal accidents occur at a speed less than 40 miles per hour. Using a child care seat correctly can reduce the risk of fatal injuries from a crash by 69 percent for infants and 47 percent for toddlers.[4]

In an accident, a car seat prevents a child from:

- ✿ **Becoming a missile.** An unrestrained baby in a 35 mile per hour crash is thrown forward with a force of more than 300 pounds. This is like a head first dive from a three story building. At this speed an adult would not be able to hold onto the child.

- ✿ **Crashing into the interior of the car.** A child who hits the dashboard at even five miles per hour can suffer fatal head injuries.

- ✿ **Being thrown from the car.** Seventy-five percent of people thrown from vehicles are killed.[5]

In addition to traveling safely, parents often find children riding in car seats are: better behaved; less likely to distract the driver; and more likely to fall asleep while traveling.

Types of Car Seats

There are basically three types of car seats: infant, convertible, and boosters.

Infant Car Seat

The seat reclines slightly and can be carried from vehicle to house with ease; most come with a three-point harness that secures above baby's shoulders and at crotch. Use from birth to 20 pounds.

Features to Look For: Are the belts easy to adjust for a proper fit in the vehicle? Does the car seat secure and remove easily from the car? Does the seat have an easily removable, washable cloth liner for comfort and easy cleanup? Does the seat have molded handle grips for easier carrying? Is there a provision for snapping the seat into the handle of a shopping cart? Is the carrying handle adjustable?

Potential Advantages: A baby carrier and car seat all in one. The smaller size allows for a better fit for infants. It doubles as a portable shopping cart seat.

Potential Disadvantages: An infant car seat is used for only about 4 to 8 months or until baby reaches 20 pounds. At this point you must purchase a convertible car seat. Cost: $35 to $50, plus the cost of a convertible seat when baby reaches 20 pounds.

Safe Use: Seat must be positioned rear facing. Use for infants only up to 20 pounds. Do not use in the front passenger seat if your auto has airbags. Do not use in the front seat if your vehicle has automatic seat belts, unless your owner's manual provides specific instructions on how to do so correctly. Make sure the seat fits properly in your vehicle.

Real Parents Say...

We never allow the children to ride in the car without being in their seats. They don't fuss because they have never known it to be any different.

—*Lisa and Roger, parents of two*

Convertible Car Seat

These seats can be used for infants and children up to 40 pounds. The seats come with three- and five-point harness systems, T-shields, and/or arm rests. Safety is dependent on correct use.

Features to Look For: Does the seat remove easily from the car? Does the seat recline easily? Are the reclining positions easily adjustable? Can the vehicle seat belt remain buckled or do you need to buckle and unbuckle it every time? Does the harness easily adjust as baby grows? Is it easy to get baby buckled into and out of the car seat? Does the seat have an easily removable and washable cover for baby's comfort and easy cleanup?

Potential Advantages: You only need to buy one seat. The seat remains in your vehicle at all times.

Potential Disadvantages: May be too large for small infants. If you have two vehicles consider buying a car seat for each vehicle to avoid constantly transferring the seats.

> " **Real Parents Say...**
>
> A car seat saved our daughter's life. She was buckled in her car seat in the back of a Ford Explorer. The driver of the vehicle lost control on a patch of ice at 55 miles per hour; the vehicle landed on its top, and was totaled. All passengers were buckled and escaped without a scratch.
>
> —*Anne and Dave, parents of two* "

Safe Use: Seat must be positioned rear facing until infant weighs 20 pounds. Seat faces forward in an upright position thereafter. Remove T-shields and arm rests (on those styles) when using with infants up to 20 pounds. Do not use rear facing in the front seat if your vehicle has passenger airbags. Many manufacturers currently recommend not placing any child safety seat in the front seat if the vehicle has passenger airbags, due to the force with which the airbags can inflate in a crash. Make sure your car seat and vehicle are compatible (check your vehicle's owner's manual). Make sure the seat fits properly in your vehicle. Use a metal locking clip, supplemental belt, or other device to keep the seat secure if it tends to rock or tip to the side. Do not place the seat in deeply contoured or bucket seats; they prevent most seats from resting properly. Avoid using the car seat with any type of motorized shoulder harness system. Do not use in the front seat if your vehicle has automatic seat belts, unless the owner's manual provides specific instructions on how to do so correctly.

Booster Car Seat

These seats are designed for children from 40 to 60 pounds depending on the child's height and weight. The seat should be used until your child is large enough to see out the vehicle window and comfortably use a standard adult belt.

Features to Look For: Does the seat have a removable shield designed for use with shoulder/lap belt? (This feature is designed so your child can be properly restrained as she continues to grow.) Is the restraint easy to fasten? Is the seat easy for your child to get in and out of? When your child sits in the seat, is her neck comfortably supported by the booster or vehicle seat?

Potential Advantages: The seat allows the older child to be properly restrained until she is large enough to comfortably and safely use a standard adult seat belt. The seat allows child to see out the window. Booster seats are typically easy to move from car to car.

Potential Disadvantages: Some styles of booster seats may not offer neck support for your child when riding in the back seat. Hard plastic type seats may not be comfortable, especially for moderate to long trips.

Safe Use: Typically designed for children heavier than 40 pounds. Read the car manual carefully for weight restrictions. All other safety criteria for convertible seats apply to booster seats, also. Make sure the seat fits properly in your vehicle. Make sure the lap bet fits snugly across your child's hips.

General Safety Tips

Car safety is extremely important. Car seats must be used properly every time in order to keep your precious passenger safe.

Read the directions of both your car and car seat owner's manuals carefully. Between twenty-five and fifty percent of all car seats are used incorrectly, according to the National Highway Traffic Safety Administration.

Use your car seat. It's more dangerous to leave your child in a car seat unrestrained than to put him unrestrained in the back seat.

The safest spot to place your child's car seat is in the center of the back seat; if that position is not available, the back seat is still safer than the front.[6]

Always buckle the car seat restraints.

Always place infants who weigh 20 pounds or less rear facing because the infant's back is the strongest part of the body.

Never put a rear facing infant seat in the front seat of a car that has a passenger airbag system. In an accident, an inflating airbag could push the infant into the seat.

Built-in child safety seats in vehicles are designed for children heavier than 20 pounds.

If your car has door-mounted safety belts you may need to have your dealer install a special adapter belt.

Never use a child safety seat in the front seat of a vehicle with automatic safety belts, unless your owner's manual provides you with specific instructions on how to do so correctly.

Do not use a plastic infant feeding seat as a car seat. These seats are not strong enough or designed for car usage.

Never use a household booster seat, telephone books, or pillows to boost a child or as a substitute car seat.

When putting baby in the car seat, make sure you place her bottom and back flat against the seat. If you leave a gap, you may not be able to properly adjust the straps for a secure fit.

Make sure the car seat is at the appropriate reclining or upright position. A rear facing seat needs to recline at a 45 degree angle. A forward facing seat should be in an upright position and not reclined. Check you car seat manual for specifics.

Secure the car seat's plastic harness ties as well as the vehicle seat belt. This keeps the shoulder straps of the child safety seat properly positioned.

When threading the harness straps, make sure they double back through the buckles. This anchors the straps so they can not pull out in a collision.

Make sure you position the harness straps correctly for the size of your child. Straps should be in the position directly above your child's shoulders in the front facing position and in the middle or lowest slots for rear facing infants. The harness straps should fit snugly—no more than 2 inches (or 2 fingers) of slack offers the best protection. In a crash, baby can receive a severe jolt if the straps are too long. Always adjust the straps to accommodate seasonal clothing.

Make sure the anchor straps are secure with the harness clip. The harness clip should be positioned even with the child's armpits.

Dress your baby in clothing with legs, and avoid bundling baby in a blanket. A blanket, bunting, or sack sleeper prevents you from correctly positioning and keeping the shoulder harness snug. For extra warmth place a blanket over baby after being correctly secured.

Make sure all straps are straight and intact. Twisted or frayed belts can not provide optimal protection in the event of an accident or sudden stop.

Always correctly secure the car seat with a seat buckle. If the seat does not fit tight, secure it with a metal locking clip or supplemental belt.

A heavy-duty, 2 3/4 inch or longer locking clip can be used to shorten a seat belt that is too loose. Make sure you use a heavy-duty locking clip. It is made of stronger metal than the regular 2 1/2 inch locking clip that comes with your car seat. Heavy-duty locking clips cost about $7. You can purchase them from Kolcraft (car seat manufacturer) or most Ford, Toyota, Mazda, and Nissan car dealerships.

During hot or sunny weather, always check the temperature of the car seat and buckle before placing the child in the seat. A blanket thrown over the seat when not in use can help prevent scorching temperatures. A hot buckle or vinyl pad can burn baby's tender skin.

Do not tend to your child while driving. If your child needs your attention, pull over as soon as possible and stop the car before taking baby out of her seat.

Keep groceries and other potentially harmful items away from a child's reach and where they cannot hit the child in case of a crash.

Low Weight Infants

In addition to the previously listed safety tips, premature infants and those weighing under 7 pounds may need special attention when riding in a car seat. These guidelines, from the American Academy of Pediatrics, do not substitute for medical care and advice from your infant's physician. Furthermore, there may be variations in recommendations for your infant based on individual circumstances.[7]

For correct harness fit on a small baby, the distance from the crotch strap to the seat back should be 5 1/2 inches or less. The distance from the shoulder harness to the seat should be 10 inches or less.

Car seats with shields in the front should not be used because baby's face or chest could hit the shield in a crash.

Some models of car seats can be adapted with padding to help prevent gaping shoulder straps and/or slouching. Rolled up cloth diapers or receiving blankets can be placed along baby's head or side or between her legs and the crotch strap to make the seat fit better. There should be no thick padding or blankets placed behind baby's back. This does not allow for an adequate fit in a collision.

Infants born more than 3 weeks early may have trouble breathing in the semi-reclined position. Your doctor will recommend the proper position for your baby to ride in. Your doctor should test your baby for this before leaving the hospital. She will tell you if your baby needs to lie on her back or tummy. Ask your hospital about special car beds designed for this purpose.

If baby's head flops forward when riding in the reclining position because the seat is too upright, you may need to wedge rolled up newspaper, towels, or a cloth roll under the car seat (at its base below baby's feet) so baby is at a 45 degree angle.

For information on car seats for low weight infants write:

Department C-Cars, American Academy of Pediatrics, PO Box 927, Elk Grove Village, IL 60009-0927; 708-228-5005

Smart Parents Do

Shop around before buying a car seat. Try fastening and unfastening the restraint. Look for a model that makes traveling hassle free. There are more rewarding parenting activities than wrestling with the car seat at each use.

Real Parents Say...

I enjoyed my infant car seat, especially when I had two other children to watch. Convenient—you can let baby sleep, and because the seat is not exposed to outdoor temperatures, the liner is never too hot or cold when putting baby in it.

—Anne, mother of five

Pick a model you are most likely to use properly every time. Most safety experts rate the five-point harness the safest but are quick to stress, only if it's used correctly each time.

Make sure the child safety seat fits properly in your car. All models are not designed for all cars; especially imported models.

Save your receipts and buy at a store with a reputable return policy. If you feel a car seat is unsafe for any reason, return it.

Mail in your car seat registration immediately This allows the manufacturer to contact you in the event of a recall.

Buy an infant car seat for baby's first few months of travel. It's more comfortable for baby and doubles as a carrier and baby seat both in the house and at the store. Infants tend to sleep a lot and most parents agree that those extra moments of sleep are well worth the money spent.

If you frequently drive two vehicles consider buying two car seats. The money spent will be worth avoiding the hassle of constantly removing and installing the car seat, especially if parents take turns with day care transportation.

If your child is premature or has a special medical condition such as cerebral palsy or spina bifida, there are car seats designed for children with special needs. Contact your local physician or nearest children's hospital for specific information in your area.

Keep the instruction book with the car seat so it's handy when you need to readjust the straps or if someone else, like grandma, is using your car to pick up baby.

Treat your convertible car seat with Scotchgard if it has a fabric lining. This will save on the life of the seat and make cleaning mashed Teddy Grahams and Cheerios much easier!

Budget Helpers

Borrow or buy used car restraints with extreme caution! If you are considering this option, check the following:

- ✿ **The car seat has never been involved in an accident.** Even a low impact crash can cause damage, making it unsafe.

- ✿ **There are no cracked, broken, or missing parts.**

- ✿ **The instruction book is intact.**

- ✿ **The seat was manufactured after January 1, 1981.**

- ✿ **Check if the car seat has ever been recalled** by contacting the National Highway Traffic Safety Administration at 1-800-424-9393 or 202-366-0123.

- ✿ **There are no frayed or broken straps or belts.**

- ✿ **All the latches and harness straps secure correctly.**

- ✿ **If you have any doubts about the car seat, do not purchase or use it for your baby.**

Watch for sales. This is a fantastic way to save 10 to 40 percent. Sometimes stores offer great deals when the manufacturer changes to a new fabric design!

Discount stores, Toys R Us, and outlet stores have top brands at hard to beat prices.

Borrow from your local hospital. Many hospitals have infant seats available for rent, especially if baby arrives early. Again, inspect the car seat for any cracks, defects, or broken parts before using.

Midas Muffler and Brake Shop has a public service campaign, titled "Project Safe Baby." Through this program you can get a basic Century car seat for $42. After you are finished using the seat you can return it for a $42 credit toward services at Midas. For more information call 1-800-621-0144 or 312-565-7500 or contact your local Midas dealer.

Check with your insurance company. Some companies offer car seats at no charge if parents attend a parenting and safety seminar.

Check for state programs: for example, the state of Kansas has a program that allows parents to purchase Cosco car seats at greatly reduced prices as an incentive to begin teaching children the importance of buckling up. Contact your State Department of Public Safety or similar bureau for possible programs or to suggest the development of one.

Other Travel Tips

Babies quickly teach parents to be prepared for the unexpected. Whether you are traveling around town or across the country, you may want to equip your vehicle with the following items.

Soft, colorful toys with no sharp edges and soft books that occupy baby on any journey. Rotate these periodically to retain child's interest.

Children's cassette tapes are great for interacting with your child. Parents' and childrens' favorites include the Wee Song cassette series, lullaby tapes, interactive tapes, and stories on tapes. And don't forget Barney or similar tapes that feature popular songs for every season.

Sun protectors for the window to reduce UV radiation, heat, and glare. Purchase these at discount or hardware stores. The films that adhere directly to the windows work best.

Infant mirror placed next to the rear view mirror allows the driver to safely see the infant without turning his head. Make sure the mirror does not create any blind spots in your front window.

Pack **baby wipes, paper towels, and a small trash bag** for unexpected cleanups.

A towel underneath the car seat keeps the vehicle cleaner and supports the seat if it tilts too far toward the rear.

Provide **easy finger foods** like graham crackers for quick snacks.

Have someone sit close to baby and talk or sing to her on longer trips.

Plane Travel

Air travel with an infant or young child can be a pleasant adventure if you plan ahead. Though airlines currently do not require infants and young children to travel in approved safety seats, it *is* recommended. Steps to hassle-free travel include:

Call ahead—let the airline know when you make your reservation that your baby will be traveling with you. Use a car seat that meets all required standards.

If you plan to take along and use a child safety seat, you must purchase a separate ticket for your baby. Your safety seat must also have a label indicating it meets federal standards.

Parents traveling with young children are usually invited to board the plane first. Take advantage of this opportunity to get your child properly situated.

Make sure you pack a carry-on bag with several feedings, diapers, wet wipes, toys, and books.

Encourage your baby to suck on a bottle of water or pacifier during take off and landings to relieve ear problems related to pressure changes.

From day one, remember to correctly buckle your child in her car seat—even on the shortest of trips. May all your travels be safe.

Car and Travel Safety

Guide to Baby Products by Sandy Jones with Werner Freitag, 4th edition, Yonkers, NY: Consumer Reports Books, 1994.

Midas Muffler and Brake Shops **"Project Safe Baby."** Call 800-621-0144 or 312-565-7500

To inquire about recalls or report a safety concern, or for the free brochures "A Shopping Guide to Child Safety Seats," "Protect Your Child With a Child Safety Seat," and "Are You Using It Right?" call or write: The National Highway Traffic Safety Administration (NHTSA) at

NEF-ID, 400 Seventh St. SW, Washington, DC, 20590; 800-424-9393 or 202-366-0123

Auto Safety Hotline: 800-424-9393 (in DC metro area dial 202-424-9393). Call this number if you think your auto or safety seat may have a safety defect.

For a free list of car seats that meet the current federal motor vehicle standards, write: The American Academy of Pediatrics, *Family Shopping Guide,* PO Box 927, Elk Grove Village, IL 60009-0927. Call 708-228-5505

Other Information

Automotive Safety for Children Program (for special needs information): Riley Hospital for Children, 702 Barnhill Drive, S-139, Indianapolis, IN 46202-5225; 317-274-2977

National Easter Seal Society (for special needs information), KARS/Special Kars Program, 230 West Monroe, Suite 1800, Chicago, IL 60606; 312-726-6200

Highway Safety Research Center Contact if you have special problems with child car seats and seat belts. Call or write: CB #3430, 134 1/2 East Franklin Street, University of North Carolina,

Chapel Hill, NC 27599-3430; 919-962-2202

National Safe Kids (consumer calls & informational brochures), 111 Michigan Ave., Washington, DC 20010-2970; 202-884-4993

National Seat Belt Coalition (consumer calls on child car seats and seat belts), 1019 19th Street, NW Suite 401, Washington, DC 20036-6263; 202-296-6263

National Safety Council (Consumer Calls, Informational Brochures, & Statistics), 1121 Spring Lake Drive, Itasca, IL 60143-3021; 708-285-1121

Operation Baby Buckle (Safe American Foundation—gives away child car seats via health departments, etc.), PO Box 14145, Atlanta, GA 30324-1145; 404-497-6168

SafetyBeltSafe USA (consumer questions on child safety seats & brochures in English and Spanish), 123 Manchester Blvd., Inglewood, CA; 310-673-2666 or 800-745-SAFE and 800-745-SANO (in Spanish)

Shinn and Associates (child car seats, special needs seats, bike helmets, and Buckle Bear injury prevention materials), 2154 Commons Parkway, Okemos, MI 48864; 800-955-8870 or 517-349-5575

The Willapa Bay Company *Safe Ride News*, 726 Belmont Place East, Seattle, WA 98102; 206-328-1424

R
e
s
o
u
r
c
e
s

CHAPTER SIX

Baby's Basic Wardrobe—
Clothing for the First Year

*"Parenting, at its best, comes as naturally as laughter.
It is automatic, involuntary, unconditional love."*
—Sally James

It is your first holiday gathering since your baby has arrived and you are excited to don his new three-piece, coordinated outfit. Fastening those micro-sized buttons and snaps has to be one of your most significant accomplishments to date. Especially when you consider that your son ran out of patience 10 minutes ago and has been squirming ever since.

Just as you secure the final snap, you hear it—that explosive sound that can only mean one thing. Why, oh why, does your darling baby always soil his diapers after you have finished dressing him?

Suddenly content, your son looks at you with twinkling eyes that seem to say, "Gotcha! Now you have to change me. This makes us even for the hassle you put me through by

Necessity Checklist

✿ **6 Onesie-style T-shirts.** Size small.

✿ **2 drawstring kimono-type gowns.**

✿ **3 or 4 sleepers**

✿ **1 or 2 blanket sleepers**

✿ **4 to 6 pairs of socks**

✿ **1 or 2 hats**

✿ **12 cloth diapers**

✿ **12 or more washcloths**

✿ **sweater/jacket/snow-suit/bunting**—depending on climate

Nursery Checklist

✿ **5 receiving blankets**

✿ **1 or 2 mattress pads**

✿ **2 fitted crib sheets**

✿ **1 set of bumper pads**

✿ **1 blanket or quilt**

dressing me in those uncomfortable, 'special-occasion' clothes."

As you reach for a clean diaper, you also grab a soft, cotton, one-piece play outfit. No fancy bow tie or matching socks with this last-minute choice. Baby is happier with comfort instead of fashion, and changing took less than 3 minutes!

Baby clothing! It's the first thing parents, especially moms, think of purchasing once they discover they are pregnant. And it's easy to be tempted to buy lots of items because darling baby clothes, in every color and style imaginable, seem to pop up everywhere once the pregnancy test comes back positive. This chapter will help you make smart clothing choices that are comfortable on both your baby and your budget.

Recent studies estimate that you will spend between $9,000 and $14,000 on clothing your child from birth to age eighteen.[1] Depending on where you choose to purchase your child's clothing, this figure could be conservative. That translates into over a $20 billion dollar children's clothing industry. Following the tips in this chapter can help you trim clothing expenses. Any savings can be a tidy addition to baby's college savings account.

Though you may be lured to stock up on soft sleepers, bright outfits, and cute socks, it is best to buy only the basics and wait until your last baby shower or the majority of baby gifts have arrived to purchase many items. Babies grow very fast. You may discover your baby wears an outfit only a few times before it no longer fits .

When shopping for baby clothes, look for items that are easy to care for, soft, and simple to change.

The Basics

Buy only minimal basic items to start. The gifts you receive, amount of laundry you plan to do, and your family's work schedule will all affect the amount of clothing needed. Following is a suggested list of clothing to get you started.

✿ **6 Onesie-Style T-Shirts.** A "Onesie" is a brand-name one-piece undershirt that snaps at the crotch. Baby's tummy stays covered and there's no bunching under the arms. These T-shirts can be worn year-round. The short sleeve style is usually sufficient. Buy no more than three of the extra small or newborn size. Even though they stretch, baby will outgrow these fast. Most babies wear the small and medium sizes the longest. If baby likes these tees you may eventually want to have more of a particular size to decrease on washing. Buying white T-shirts in packages of three or six is the most economical. Some parents prefer to use cotton T-shirts that tie on the side until baby's umbilical cord falls off. The Onesie-style shirt can be used during this period, also. Just make sure you thoroughly clean the cord area and allow it to air dry before redressing baby.

> ### Real Parents Say...
>
> By my third child I realized how wonderful Onesie T-shirts were. They didn't get all crunched up in their armpits and seemed most comfortable for baby.
>
> —*Lois, mother of three*

✿ **2 Drawstring, Kimono-Type Gowns.** These "sacks with arms" make diaper changing a breeze, especially during the first weeks when you are doing this ten or more times a day. Start with two and see if you and baby like them. Try to find gowns with an elastic bottom. If the garment has a drawstring it can be a choking hazard. It is best to remove the string as a safety precaution. Buy in neutral colors for either a boy or a girl.

✿ **3 or 4 Sleeper or Creeper One-Piece Outfits.** Baby will live in these for the majority of the first 2 to 3 months. Consider buying mostly light colors to simplify laundry. Save your receipts. You may get these as gifts and need to return some. Medium size, though a bit big at first, can usually be worn for the longest length of time. Look for snaps down both legs for easy changing.

✿ **1 or 2 Blanket Sleepers.** If you live in a cold climate, you may want to try these heavier weight sleepers to keep baby warm at night. Buy one to start and see how baby likes it. Look for styles with the cloth feet—they breathe better than the plastic footed styles. Newborns to 6-month-old babies aren't walking, so they don't tend to wear the feet out.

✿ **4 to 6 Pairs of Socks or Booties.** Look for socks or booties made of 100 percent cotton that allow feet to breathe. Check so the elastic around baby's ankles is not tight and does not cut into baby's skin. When baby starts to toddle, purchase socks with nonslip soles or let baby go barefoot. Buying all white socks makes washing and folding easier.

✿ **0 Shoes.** Baby's feet change shape during the first months and need plenty room to grow. Babies use their toes to grip the floor and maintain their balance. Therefore, barefoot is best until baby learns to walk. If you feel your child's feet need protection, look for a nonskid, soft-type bootie that doesn't restrict his foot.

✿ **1 or 2 Hats or Bonnets.** The weight of the hat will depend on the season. Sun hats are needed any time baby is in the sun because a baby's skin can burn easily. For a winter hat, look for a style that covers baby's ears. If the hat is wool or a wool blend, make sure it has a lining that will not scratch.

✿ **12 Cloth Diapers.** Whether you decide to diaper with cloth or disposable diapers (see Chapter Seven for diapering needs), you will need a dozen cloth diapers to serve as lap pads, burp cloths, nursing sup-

port, and changing pads. These handy do-it-all diapers will be strategically placed around your house
for about the first six months. Two diapers will go
with you on every journey. Soft, absorbent diapers
make super window washing and eyeglass cleaning
cloths later on.

✿ **12 to 24 Washcloths.** Extra washcloths are a must for
bathing and cleaning up after baby. If you plan to
use washcloths for diaper wipes instead of disposables, you may need a total of four to five dozen,
depending on how often you plan to do laundry.
Check discount stores for packages of twelve. Buy
white. They are the easiest to bleach and wash.

✿ **0 to 2 bibs.** Unless your baby drools a lot, you won't
need bibs until you start to introduce solids at 4 to 6
months. Avoid buying the small drooling bibs and
opt for the full size feeding bibs from the start. Bibs
are also easy to make.

✿ **Snowsuit, Bunting, and Mittens.** These items are a
necessity for babies living in cold climates. The trick
is buying one size to last you all season. If you have
a September baby, a size 12 month will be large in
November, but probably still fit in March; for a
baby due in December or January, a 6 to 9 month
size should work fine. If you plan to use a bunting
make sure it has an opening in the crotch area that
allows you to secure the car
seat belt properly.

✿ **1 Sweater or Jacket.** One sweater
or lightweight jacket is
needed for cool weather outings. Most hooded jackets
are now made with elastic
instead of drawstrings. If you
have a style with a draw-

Smart Tip

When it comes to dressing
baby, dress as you would. If
you need a jacket, so does
baby. Be careful not to overdress baby in too many layers in either hot or cold
temperatures.

string, keep the hood drawstring short, remove it, or replace it with elastic. Long drawstrings can be a strangulation hazard. Look for fabric that washes easily. Hoods are nice for days when you forget the hat.

Clothing to Avoid

✿ **Clothes Sized 0 to 3 Months.** Because babies typically double their birth weight in the first four months, these small sized outfits often get worn only once or twice.

✿ **Sacque Sets.** A sacque set is a shirt and diaper cover. Though it looks cute, it pulls up every time you pick up baby. One piece outfits usually offer more comfort.

✿ **Hooded Bath Sets.** They are a nice luxury, but you can easily get by with a large, soft bath towel to wrap baby in and a hand towel for drying. Either way, baby gets dried off after a bath. And since everyone in the house can use an extra towel, it is one less item to pack away when baby reaches 9 to 12 months of age.

✿ **Synthetic Fabric** (except sleepwear; see page 98). Clothing made of synthetics such as polyester tends to look ragged and worn after a few wearings. Even though they cost more, all-cotton clothes wash better, last longer, and look nicer.

Buying Baby's First Shoes

After baby has learned to walk, usually between 9 and 15 months, you may want to shop for shoes. Baby's feet can grow three to four shoe sizes in one year, so check fit every 2 months. The main purpose of baby's first shoes is one of protection, not support. When fitting baby's shoes, check for the following:

- ❀ 1/4 to 3/8 inch room in front of toes is OK for growth. Make sure the shoe is snug enough to stay on baby's foot.
- ❀ Heel does not slip out.
- ❀ Sole is flat with no elevation in the heel.
- ❀ Sole is flexible. This makes walking easier. Hard soles can be uncomfortable.
- ❀ Adequate width across the ball of the foot.
- ❀ Toes are not constricted. Check this while baby is standing.
- ❀ Look for a lightweight shoe. Heavy shoes tire young walkers.
- ❀ Because shoes mold and shape to baby's feet, avoid hand-me-downs.

What Size Clothing Do I Buy?

Choosing baby clothing sizes can be confusing because garments are labeled differently. Some manufacturers provide sizing information by small, medium, or large definition. Other clothing comes in sizes indicated in months from zero (also labeled as newborn) to 24. And finally, some companies choose to size garments by pounds.

Newborn size (or zero months) will fit for only 2 months or less. These little sizes are really cute, but avoid buying many because baby will outgrow them quickly. If you have a 9- or 10-pound baby (Bless you!), newborn size may not fit at all.

Infants can spend their first months in clothing sized small or 3 to 6 months. Bigger doesn't hurt, just

Real Parents Say...

The small, newborn sized clothing is outgrown so quickly. Baby really seems to stay in one clothing size after 9 to 12 months of age. My children usually wore sizes 6 to12 months above the month tag on the clothes. Lee, OshKosh, and other brand names seemed to run truer to the actual size printed on the clothing tag.

—Evie, mother of two

roll up the sleeves until they grow into the outfit.

Here's an approximate rule of thumb for figuring clothing sizes. For baby's first 12 months, multiply age in months by two and round up to the nearest size.

Baby's Age	Approximate Size to Buy
Newborn	3-6 months
3 months	6-9 months
6 months	12 months
9 months	18 months
12 months	24 months

The above guide is only an estimate. However, just when you think you have this figured out, you'll find your 6-month old actually wears a 6-month size from one manufacturer. Some companies, for example HealthTex, will list baby's weight in pounds on the sizing ticket. This method of sizing seems to be the most accurate.

Taking the outfit out of the package and comparing it to other similar sized outfits can help in selecting sizes, also. Check the garment tag for the type of fabric. Remember, 100 percent cotton may shrink with repeated washings. Therefore, you may want to purchase items made of 100 percent cotton in one size larger.

Sleeping Safely

For a safe sleep, choose flame-resistant clothing. Though cotton clothing may be more comfortable and durable for baby garments, all baby sleepwear must be flame-resistant. Most flame-retardant sleepwear is 100 percent polyester. Some manufacturers now make sleepwear from chemically treated cotton. Make sure you follow the manufacturer's laundry instructions. Some manufacturers recommend that flame-resistant sleepwear be washed inside out and in a mild detergent. Soap can wash out the flame retardant.

The federal law says all garments sold as children's sleepwear must stop burning when they are removed from a fire. If you find synthetics and chemically-treated material less than comfortable, remember that pure cotton ignites in a flash.

Flame-retardant sleepwear is necessary when both you and baby are sleeping. When baby naps and you are awake during the day, regular clothing is fine.

Wash and Wear

Because your baby's skin is sensitive, it's best to use a very mild laundry detergent for the first 6 months. Ivory Snow, Dreft, or a detergent that's perfume- and dye-free is a good option. Wash baby's clothing separate from yours for the first months. Avoid using fabric softener. A fabric softener could cause a rash.

Laundry Tips

- ✿ Wash all clothing, blankets, and linens before using. Washing will remove sizing and other fabric chemicals from garments and decrease the chance that baby will develop an allergic rash.
- ✿ Treat stains immediately with a stain remover.
- ✿ If you have soft water, you may be able to use a quarter to a third less detergent than directed on the packaging.
- ✿ A laundry or lingerie bag is great for washing socks and other small items. It keeps them from getting lost among the rest of the laundry.
- ✿ Never mix bleach and ammonia or any product containing ammonia. A dangerous

Real Parents Say...

A small amount of bleach and water on a Q-tip swab works great on stains. Dab the stained area and rinse immediately.
—*Anne, mother of five*

chemical reaction that produces a toxic gas could result.

✿ If you suspect a laundry soap allergy or sensitivity, try double rinsing the laundry. If this does not work, choose an alternate brand of detergent.

Chapter Seven contains tips on washing diapers and washcloths; however, to remove tough stains and brighten graying or yellowed cotton whites, you might try this:

1. Fill the washing machine to the medium load mark with hot water.

2. Add 1 cup chlorine bleach, 1 cup laundry detergent, and 1 cup automatic dishwasher detergent. Let the machine run a few minutes to thoroughly mix this solution.

3. Place stained baby clothes in washer and allow to soak overnight or for 12 hours.

4. Run machine through the regular cycle.

5. Double rinse to remove any soap residue.

Clothing Safety Tips

✿ **Check clothing carefully to make sure all buttons, ribbons, appliqués, bobbles, and decorative attachments are secure.** These items can be pulled loose by baby and can be a choking hazard. If in doubt, cut off the decorations.

✿ **Clip any loose strings.** Loose strings can also result in choking or get wrapped around baby's toes or fingers, cutting off circulation.

✿ **Check snaps and zippers.** Make sure edges are smooth with no sharp protrusions that could cut or scratch baby.

✿ **Look for hooded items with elastic instead of drawstrings.**

✿ **Choose only flame-retardant sleepwear.**

✿ **Watch baby's skin for any allergic reaction to metal snaps.** If baby is allergic or sensitive to metal, a snap-sized red ring may appear on his skin. A one-piece T-shirt that snaps in the crotch helps protect sensitive areas.

✿ **Avoid constricting arm and leg bands.** Check that coats, sweatpants, and shirts do not leave marks and indentations on baby's skin.

Smart Parents Do

Buy clothing that fastens down the front for easy changing. Some babies do not like to lie on their stomachs while you struggle with back snaps or buttons.

Choose items that snap in the crotch. This makes diaper changing quicker and easier than removing the entire outfit.

Select outfits with snaps along both legs until baby is at least to the age where he can stand and it is easier to pull pants up and down.

Buy one-piece outfits and undershirts. These are more comfortable and keep baby's tummy from peeking out.

Select tops with snaps at the shoulders to make over-the-head dressing an ease.

Keep all clothing tags and receipts in case you need to return an item. Babies grow so fast that sometimes it's hard to buy ahead.

Buy garments made of 100 percent cotton or at least a high percentage of cotton. This clothing is comfy and baby does not tend to sweat in it as much. Clothing made of polyester will often pill and fuzz, making an outfit look tattered after only a few wearings.

Real Parents Say...

Snaps should work easily and there should not be too many, especially on very small baby garments. The baby's not going to escape!

—*Rosemary, mother of six, grandmother of nine*

Spend more money on high quality items that baby will wear often, such as play clothes. Spend less on items he will wear infrequently, such as a Christmas outfit.

Look for clothing with snaps on a reinforced fabric band. This helps prevent the snaps from pulling out of the garment with repeated use.

Look for outfits and shirts with a reinforced band around the neck ribbing. This added feature keeps the neck from stretching out of shape.

Buy clothing in basic colors like yellow, green, and red if you are planning on a second child. These clothes can easily be worn on boys and girls.

Budget Helpers

Save all receipts and clothing tags. You never know when you may need to return an item, and having the proper receipts makes returns easier and more successful.

Buy clothing during the off season. For example, you can save 50 to 75 percent on items such as snowsuits bought in January or February and swimsuits purchased in July or August. Some stores have super sales before their year-end clearance markdowns.

Watch for sales. Baby sales are often in April.

Be a bargain hunter and go to garage sales. Kids clothes, especially infant and early toddler sizes, can often be found in great shape for only pennies. Successful garage sale shoppers scan the newspaper and hit yard sales with baby clothes at opening time. The great buys usually get snatched up fast. Shopping more affluent neighborhoods is another way to hone in on top quality garments at bargain prices.

Let your friends and family know you would be delighted to use hand-me-downs. You can return the favor with tickets to a movie and free babysitting, a homemade batch of cookies, or an outfit for their older child. Most parents enjoy sharing children's clothing. This gives them the satisfaction of knowing their child's outgrown clothes are not just stored away somewhere.

If an item doesn't wear as guaranteed, return it or write the manufacturer. Most are more than happy to correct the flaw or replace the garment in order to retain a happy customer.

Consider sewing your own infant and children's clothing. Quick and easy, basic patterns are listed in the Resource section. Homemade clothing tends to have the strongest seams and can cost less than store-bought clothing. For best savings, choose two to three basic patterns (rompers, T-shirts, and pull-on pants are versatile infant-wear basics). Using the pattern several times keeps costs lower and makes sewing quicker because you can cut out and sew multiple outfits at one time.

Whether purchasing or sewing baby's wardrobe, select prints and fabrics that mix and match. Babies aren't selective as to which end they mess up first. Having coordinated tops and pants means more mix and matching and fewer separate loads of laundry. If most items coordinate you can usually buy less.

Shop outlet stores for infant and children's wear. Savings of 50 to 75 percent on well made, name brand clothing is common. Check the Resource section for mail order outlets and information about stores near you.

> ## Real Parents Say...
>
> Buy well-made clothing. Sometimes the less expensive brands do not hold up well. Some clothing manufacturers have a 1-year warranty as long as you keep the price tag and the sales receipt.
>
> —*Sandy, mother of three*
>
> Invest in one "nice" outfit for pictures, special gatherings, and holidays. Otherwise, use hand-me-downs, garage sales, and gifts.
>
> —*MJ, mother of two*

Watch for clearance sales. Shop clearance sales both early and late. Sometimes clearance items that do not sell at the first markdown price are reduced a second time.

If you find a missing button or ripped seam, ask the sales person for an additional discount. They will often take 10-50 percent off an item if you will fix it yourself.

Take advantage of baby registries. This service helps you avoid duplicate gifts and time spent exchanging items.

Check out discount stores. These stores offer great bargains when it comes to basic sleepwear, booties, and T-shirts with brand names like Carter's, Gerber, and Fruit of the Loom.

Many stores carry their own good quality private label brands at a reasonable price. For example, Honors by Target, Boundary Waters by Dayton-Hudson, and Bright Future by JC Penney offer quality clothes at a great price.

Call stores ahead if you're looking for a specialty item. Comparison shop by phone by asking for style and price information. This can save you time, money, and an unnecessary trip to the store.

Watch for coupons and rebate offers. Just like diapers, manufacturers often offer coupons and money-back incentives for infant wear.

Shop baby megastores, like Li'l Things and Baby Superstore for a wide selection of brands and styles at low prices.

Check out consignment or second-hand thrift shops. The prices are typically higher than those found at garage sales, but you usually find high quality brands in excellent condition.

Consider Kids-R-Us for name-brand clothing like OshKosh, Carters, and HealthTex. Warehouse clubs like Sam's Club are great for diapers and other baby supplies.

Shop from home by mail for convenience. Great mail-order companies are listed in the Resource section.

Outlet Shopping

The Joy of Outlet Shopping Catalog Information Directory of nearly 350 centers with more than 10,000 outlet stores. For a catalog with $100 worth of outlet coupons write: 15950 Bay Vista Drive, Suite 250, Clearwater, Florida 34620-3131; 813-536-4047

VF Factory Outlet Direct For Lee, HealthTex, and other brand name clothing at 50 percent or more off the retail price, check out the VF Factory outlet. For a catalog and information about stores near you: VF Outlet Village, 801 Hill Ave, Reading, PA 19610; 800-772-8336

Carter's Over 90 outlets—call for a location near you; 404-961-8722

Oshkosh Call for location near you; 414-231-8800

HealthTex 45 outlet stores, call for a location near you; 800-772-8336 or 610-378-0408

Baby Guess 800-228-4644 or 213-892-1289

Esprit Not all locations have children's clothing, so ask before you make the trip; 800-777-8765 or 415-648-6900

Ava Kids This Colorado-based manufacturer makes high quality clothing for fancy retailers like Nieman Marcus: 550 W South Boulder Road, Lafayette, CO 80026; 303-673-9300 and 17 Old Town Square, #133, Ft. Collins, CO 80524; 303-493-1900

Kid's Zone 22 outlets; call for a location near you; 918-599-9553

Consignment Shopping

To find a consignment or thrift shop in your area that specializes in high quality children's clothing, check in your local telephone directory or write: **National Association of Resale and Thrift Shops,** Children Resources, 157 Halstead, Chicago Heights, IL 60411 (include a business-sized, self-addressed, stamped envelope)

**R
e
s
o
u
r
c
e
s**

Mail Order for Children's Clothing

After the Stork, 1501 12th St NW, PO Box 26200, Albuquerque, NM 87125; 800-333-5437 or 505-243-9100

Baby on a Budget This mail order company specializes in name-brand bedding at great discounts. Baby on a Budget does not have a catalog. You need to shop other stores first and then call Baby on a Budget for prices. Be prepared to give brand, size, style, and pattern design you are looking for; 800-575-2224

BioBottoms, PO Box 6009, Petaluma, CA 94953; 800-766-1254 or 707-778-0619

Hanna Anderson, 1010 NW Flanders, Portland, OR 97209; 800-222-0544

JC Penney Company Ask for "For Baby," a collection of nursery furnishings and accessories for mom and baby, and "Starting Small" clothing for infant, toddler, and preschool sizes: JC Penney Company, PO Box 10001, Dallas, TX 75301-3114; 800-222-6161

Land's End Ask for both their kids and clearance catalog: Land's End, 1 Land's End Lane, Dodgeville, WI 53595; 800-356-4444

OshKosh Direct, 1112 7th Ave, Monroe, WI 53566-1364

PlayClothes, PO Box 29137, Overland Park, KS 66201-9137; 800-224-4396

Sewing Resources

Check your local fabric or sewing store or write:

Kwik-Sew's Sewing for Baby by Kerstin Martensson or Baby Sleepers—pattern #1903, Kwik-Sew Pattern Co. Inc., 3000 Washington Ave N, Minneapolis, MN 55411-1699

Sewing for Children, Singer Reference Library, Cy DeCosse Inc., 5900 Green Oak Drive, Minneapolis, MN 55343; 800-328-3895

CHAPTER SEVEN

The Diaper Dilemma

"One of the most important things to remember about infant care is: never change diapers in midstream."
—*Don Marquis*

EXTRA! EXTRA! READ ALL ABOUT IT! BABY BORN POTTY-TRAINED! You quickly scan the paper to read about the lucky couple who gets to bypass this messy and time-consuming task. In your first 5 days of parenting, you have already changed more than 50 diapers. You have quickly mastered your diaper changing skills to the point that you can change a diaper in less than 60 seconds—in the dark.

Suddenly, you awake from your daydream. You realize the facts of diapering have not changed, and that you will be doing this task for the next 2 to 3 years.

Fact: Next to feeding, diapering is the second most common new parent activity.

Necessity Checklist

Diapers—Cloth Option

✿ **3 to 4 dozen cloth diapers** (see Resource section for manufacturers of pinless cloth varieties, which are now available.)

✿ **2 or 3 sets of diaper pins.**

✿ **3 to 5 pairs plastic pants or diaper covers** (see Resource section for manufacturers of nonplastic diaper covers.)

Diaper Service Option

✿ **Call diaper service in your area;** many provide the diaper pail.

✿ **May need 2 or 3 pairs of diaper pins.**

✿ **May need 3 to 5 sets of diaper covers.**

continued on next page

Necessity Checklist (continued)

Disposables

✿ **Start saving coupons.**

✿ **2 or 3 packages of new-born disposable diapers**—to take to the hospital.

✿ **1 package of small size disposable diapers**—to take to the hospital. (In case baby weighs 10 pounds!)

Other Diapering Necessities

✿ **3 dozen extra wash-cloths** or 1 package of diaper wipes

✿ **1 package of travel sized diaper wipes** for the diaper bag

✿ **1 small tube of diaper rash ointment** or lotion

✿ **Diaper bag**

✿ **Diaper pail** (necessity if using cloth diapers or cloth washcloths)

Fact: Babies will go through about 6,000 diaper changes by age 3.[1]

Fact: Dad can change diapers with as much skill and expertise as Mom.

Fact: There's a diapering option for every budget.

Fact: Both cloth and disposable diapers affect the environment.

As a new parent, diapering is simply a task which must be done six to ten times a day. There are however, a multitude of choices about what type of diapers and diapering supplies to use. Baby's comfort and environmental safety are two common factors in the diapering decision.

The diaper debate rages on as to which option—cloth or disposable—is safest for the environment and best for baby. As a new parent, you will want to explore the various options and make an informed decision that's best for you and your baby. So for starters, let's look at the four basic diapering options available: home-laundered cloth, diaper service, disposable, and a combination.

Diapering Options
Cloth Diapers, home-laundered

Supplies Needed: 3 to 4 dozen diapers; 2 sets diaper pins or diaper clamps; 3 to 5 plastic pants or diaper covers; diaper pail; laundry supplies (see page 113)

Potential Advantages: Cloth diapers (laundered at home) can be the least expensive option; diapers can be reused; softest on baby's skin; variety of sizes and folding options; pin and pinless options

Potential Disadvantages: Time and labor to wash and fold; need to purchase plastic pants or covers; baby requires more frequent changing; may cause diaper rash if baby is not changed frequently or diapers are not laundered correctly; pin punctures possible; diapers may leak; cost of water and energy to launder

Estimated Cost for First Year: $35 to $70 for traditional cloth and up to $400 for some of the velcro or prefolded types; $240 for water, utilities, and laundry products; $2 to $6 for diaper pins; $24 to $90 for diaper pants/covers. Total: $301 to $736[2]

Cloth Diapers, using a diaper service

Supplies Needed: Diaper pail (some services provide this); 3 to 5 plastic pants or diaper covers (some services provide this)

Potential Advantages: Fresh diapers delivered to your door once or twice a week; all the advantages of cloth with no laundry time and labor. May not be available in all locations

Potential Disadvantages: May run out of diapers before the next delivery; many have only the "pin" option available; diapers may become frayed from harsh laundering procedures; you don't always get your own diapers back; some of the same disadvantages as cloth such as possible leaking, frequent changing needed, and environmental concerns of water and chemical usage

Estimated Cost for First Year: $550 to $800 annually for a weekly supply of diapers; $2 to $6 for diaper pins; $24 to $90 for diaper pants/covers (some services include these). Total: $576 to $896

Disposable Diapers

Supplies Needed: Disposal diapers (of course); lots of coupons for your favorite brand are helpful; diaper pail or wastebasket

Potential Advantages: Variety of sizes; high absorbency, so less frequent changing is needed; convenient, especially when away from home; no pins—no sticks; may keep baby drier; waterproof outer shield for minimal leaks; special features like a cut-out area for the umbilical cord

Potential Disadvantages: Not readily biodegradable; diapers currently take up 2 percent of landfill space;[3] can be the most expensive option; may cause diaper rash if not changed frequently enough; babies can choke on the plastic tabs and linings; odor in trash may be a problem—wastebasket needs to be emptied frequently.

Estimated Cost for First Year: $675 to $885 per year for approximately 2,600 disposable diapers.[2] Note: Diapers may be lower priced with coupons, making it possible to save $60 to $100 per year. You'll also save if you purchase diapers on sale or take advantage of rebates.

> ## " Real Parents Say...
>
> A combination is nice. I prefer cloth for the environment and I also believe it is easier to train a child using cloth diapers rather than disposable.
> — *Wilma, mother of five*
>
> Diapers are a touchy issue these days! Plastic versus detergents. I went for baby dryness and comfort, and a working mom's convenience—disposable.
> — *Kathy, mother of one* "

Combination: Cloth and Disposable

The potential advantages and disadvantages of this final option, as well as costs, vary according to the amount chosen of each type of diaper.

Regardless of which option you choose, you will still need washcloths or diaper wipes to get baby's bottom clean, a supply of diaper rash ointment, a diaper pail or disposal system, and a place to change baby.

Bare Bottom Basics

Butt Wipes

In addition to diapers, you will need something to clean baby's bottom. Cloth washcloths or disposable diaper wipes are the options.

Cloth Washcloths

- ✿ 3 to 4 dozen washcloths needed
- ✿ Pre-soak and wash like cloth diapers (see page 113)
- ✿ One-time washcloth investment
- ✿ A warm wipe for baby's bottom each time

Disposable Diaper Wipes

- ✿ Plan on using about 4,200 single wipes per year. There is a wide variety to choose from on the market including Huggies, Chubs, Baby Fresh, and Wet Ones.
- ✿ Clip and save coupons to cut the cost
- ✿ Make your own (see Budget Helpers in this chapter) or use super thick paper towels moistened with warm water in place of disposable wipes to cut costs.

Powders

Baby powders are not recommended.[4] They can create a "powder cloud" over baby, creating a suffocation hazard if baby inhales the dust and chemicals and it settles in her lungs.

If you must use a powder, use cornstarch-based products. Powder your hands instead of directly powdering baby's bottom to decrease the dust storm. And, never give baby the powder bottle to play with.

> ## Real Parents Say...
>
> After a really "poopy" diaper (which usually happens when you are ready to leave the house), put baby in the tub for a quick bottom bath. This helps get baby really clean and reduces the chances of getting diaper rash.
>
> —*Evie, mother of two*

Diaper Rash Care

Yours will be the rare baby if she makes it through the first year rash-free. Plan on having at least one episode of diaper rash during your baby's first year. The most common cause of diaper rash is leaving a wet or soiled diaper on your baby too long. Once the rash begins it becomes more sensitive to irritation by urine or stool. It is helpful to keep an over-the-counter diaper rash ointment on hand for sudden flare-ups. Because babies respond differently to different ointments, you may want to try sample sizes before buying a full-size tube of a specific brand of ointment.

Parent-Proven Ways to Prevent Diaper Rash Risk

✿ Change baby's wet diapers frequently and soiled diapers immediately.

✿ Allow baby's bottom to be exposed to air whenever feasible. You may want to lay down a few extra towels — just in case.

✿ If your baby develops diaper rash, try an over-the-counter diaper rash ointment or lotion. If the rash does not improve in 2 to 3 days, you should contact your doctor. The American Academy of Pediatrics recommends a bland ointment such as one containing zinc oxide.

✿ Always wash your hands before and after changing baby's diaper.

✿ Never use another baby's prescription diaper rash ointment. Some prescription ointments contain cortisone, a steroid, which should be monitored by a physician if used on an infant.

✿ Vaseline is inexpensive and works great to help protect baby's bottom from wetness. If your baby has a sensitive bottom or if you use cloth diapers, apply a small amount of Vaseline at each diaper change.

Washing Those Dirty Little Diapers

If you've decided to use the traditional wrap 'em in cloth and pin 'em method, plan on doing about two to three extra loads of laundry a week and changing about 10 to 12 cloth diapers per day.

Diapers need to be washed alone—separate from other clothes. Diapers must be washed carefully in hot water, detergent, and bleach to kill bacteria and minimize the spread of germs.

Washing Diapers and Washcloths

- ✿ Rinse soiled diapers in the toilet after changing baby.
- ✿ Soak all dirty diapers and washcloths in a diaper pail, half full of water, until you are ready to launder. To reduce odor, stop bacterial growth, and balance the soaking solution's pH level, add to 3 gallons of water: 1/4 to 1/2 cup detergent and 1/4 cup bleach or vinegar, or 1 teaspoon Borax.
- ✿ Dump diapers (no more than 36 at a time), washcloths, and soaking solution into the washing machine. Set the machine on the rinse or spin cycle to wring out all of the presoaked water.

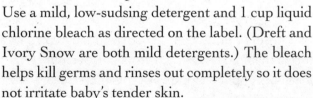

Real Parents Say...

Careful on the bleach. I used so much bleach on Annie's diapers that one day when I was hanging them on the clothesline, I noticed they had large holes in them!!!

—*Julie, mother of two*

- ✿ When that cycle is complete, wash diapers and washcloths in the hottest water possible. Use a mild, low-sudsing detergent and 1 cup liquid chlorine bleach as directed on the label. (Dreft and Ivory Snow are both mild detergents.) The bleach helps kill germs and rinses out completely so it does not irritate baby's tender skin.
- ✿ Do not use fabric softeners on diapers and washcloths. These products tend to build up, decreasing the diaper's absorbency and often irritating baby's skin.

✿ Rinse diapers and washcloths twice in hot water to remove any residues. Add 1/2 cup vinegar to the final rinse to keep diapers soft and absorbent and to help remove any traces of detergent, urine, or bacteria.

✿ Line-dry diapers and washcloths in the sun or machine dry on the highest heat setting.

Diaper Pails

If you use cloth diapers and/or washcloths for bottom wipes, you will need a diaper pail for soaking soiled items. They come in many designs. Some even have deodorizers. Look for:

✿ **A locking lid** so baby can't fall in head first and drown.

✿ **An easy grip handle** for lugging the pail to the washroom.

✿ **A foot-operated pedal** to help keep your hands free for baby and make disposal easier.

✿ **A strong pail handle attachment.** This thing gets heavy!

✿ **A child-resistant deodorizer compartment,** if you choose a model with this option. Children have been known to eat deodorizers and become ill.

Believe it or not, there are even diaper pails on the market for disposable diapers. One such gadget, the Diaper Genie, is designed to take the stink out of stinky diapers. The Diaper Genie costs about $40 initially, plus $5 to $7 for each refill diaper wrap canister for a total cost of $196 per year. You will need refills about every 2 weeks. The system keeps the nursery odor-free by wrapping diapers in deodorized, air-tight plastic bags and storing them in the base of the pail. Just empty once a week.

One budget option to the Diaper Genie system is to purchase an inexpensive wastebasket, a can of Lysol, and plastic grocery bags for wastebasket liners. Take the garbage out three or four times per week, and deposit the remaining $190 in baby's college savings account.

Don't Forget the Diaper Bag

As for this baby necessity, you may want to spend a little extra money and select a high-quality diaper bag. This accessory is going to go everywhere you go for the next 2 years or so. Some parents opt for two bags — a full-size one for trips to day care and overnight stays, and a smaller bag that holds the essentials for short outings. For a great diaper bag, look for:

✿ **A bag that doesn't look like a diaper bag.** Two of you may be toting this thing around so decide together how you feel about a giant Big Bird plastered on pastel pink.

✿ **Sturdy stitching.** Remember this bag needs to be built to carry everything from spare clothing to toys and feeding supplies.

✿ **An adjustable shoulder strap and sturdy handles.**

✿ **Vinyl or washable fabric for easy care and cleanup.**

Other nice features include:

✿ **A changing pad,** for a do-it-anywhere changing station.

✿ **Insulated bottle holders** to keep milk and juice cool on hot days.

✿ **Separate compartments for medicines, lotions, and soiled clothes.**

✿ **Tip:** This book is not about product endorsement, but I think all new parents should know about Land's End's fabulous "Do-It-All" diaper bag. Ours is

> ## Real Parents Say...
>
> Again, common safety sense goes a long way in the diaper pail department. We have used two, 5-gallon pails with tight fitting lids as diaper pails for over 4 years. We keep them in the bathrooms and keep the door shut. That's one room we keep off limits to our kids — it seems to be baby's instinct to play the "tidy bowl attendant!" When the pails get smelly, we bleach them and set them outside for a few hours. There are no deodorizers to worry about and they'll have a multitude of uses when the diapering era is done!
>
> *—Marie & Michael, parents of two*

going on its fourth year and holding up well. It's even got room for the checkbook. Check it out for yourself by catalog. Just call 800-356-4444 or write Land's End, Inc., 1 Land's End Lane, Dodgeville, WI, 53595. You can even order via the Internet at www.landsend.com. The cost is about $29, and it's worth every penny.

What Goes in a Great Diaper Bag?

- ✿ **Extra diapers** (4 to 12 depending on whether you are using cloth or disposable and how long you plan to be away from home)
- ✿ **Spare diaper covers** (2) if you use cloth diapers
- ✿ **Two gallon-size plastic bags** to hold soiled clothing and/or diapers
- ✿ **Travel size, disposable baby wipes**
- ✿ **A full change of clothing** including socks and undershirt. (It always seems the socks get in the messy pants first!)
- ✿ **A pair of pajamas** if you are traveling close to bedtime. Change baby right before you leave for home, and sometimes you can go from car seat to crib without waking baby!
- ✿ **A blanket**
- ✿ **Sunscreen.** Your baby's skin is sensitive and burns easily when exposed to the sun. Be prepared for unexpected outings with a baby-formulated sunscreen.
- ✿ **Hat**
- ✿ **Diaper rash cream**
- ✿ **Body lotion** (if you use it)
- ✿ **Travel size baby bath or soap** for emergency cleanups
- ✿ **A few small toys, teething rings, and soft-covered books** for quick and easy entertainment
- ✿ **Snacks** like Teddy Grahams, vanilla wafers, Cheerios, or oyster crackers in plastic bags

✿ **Your personal belongings,** such as keys, checkbook, wallet, etc.

General Safety Tips for Diapers

Always dump the contents of messy diapers in the toilet if possible. This should also be done with disposable diapers to prevent ground water contamination. (Do not flush disposable diapers down the toilet.)

Store all baby products out of baby's reach. Many products are dangerous if ingested by baby. Remember, baby's number one job is exploration.

Never leave baby unattended on a changing table or station. **NO EXCEPTIONS!**

Use only diaper pins for securing baby's diapers. Safety pins are not safe. The pin can come undone and poke baby's tender skin. The plastic head on diaper pins can become brittle over time; replace all old pins and never use a pin with a cracked head. The head can break and the exposed pin could harm baby.

Do not use dull diaper pins. The extra pressure needed to push pins through layers of cloth can lead to accidental punctures.

Keep diaper pins stuck in a wrapped bar of soap so they slide more easily through layers of cloth diapers.

Keep all disposable diapers out of baby's reach. The outer plastic is a suffocation hazard.

Keep the diaper pail tightly closed and out of the reach of young children.

Smart Parents Do

Avoid stocking up on extra disposable diapers close to a transition stage. Babies grow fast and you may find you have a bag or two that won't fit.

Save sale receipts in case you get a wrong size of disposable diapers. Most stores will gladly exchange unopened packages of diapers.

> ### Real Parents Say...
>
> The Nikky-brand diaper cover worked best for us. It's reasonably priced. The off-brands let the wetness through. Most discount stores carry Nikky diaper covers.
>
> — *Sandy, mother of three*

Try various diapering methods before investing a lot of money in a method that may not work for you. Friends spent over $350 on a cloth diaper system with velcro tabs and special covers before baby arrived only to find out they didn't like or use the system at all.

Buy two packages of newborn diapers and one package of small sized disposable diapers before baby's arrival. Take one package of each along to the hospital. Bringing your own diapers saves on your hospital bill. Most hospitals charge three times the cost for diapers. Keep your receipts. If you have a large baby she may not be able to use the newborn size. The unopened diapers can usually be exchanged for a larger size.

Check with your day care provider as to the type of diapering system they use. Some day cares will only use disposable for sanitation and convenience.

If you're using cloth diapers, prewash them to remove any chemical residues and make the diapers more absorbent. Cloth diapers also make great burp cloths, especially during those first three months.

Budget Helpers

Use coupons when purchasing baby products—especially diapers and baby wipes. Have family and friends save coupons for you. Write your favorite manufacturer. They will often send you diaper and baby product coupons and put you on their mailing list so you receive a regular coupon supply.

Try small packages or samples before stocking up on quantities. Preferences vary greatly from parent to parent and baby to baby. Most hospitals give you product samples when baby is born.

Shop at discount stores like K-Mart, Wal-Mart, Target, Venture, Shopko, or Toys-R-Us for baby products.

Stock up on favorite brands when they are on sale—use coupons for double savings.

Make your own baby wipes. First, cut a roll of soft, absorbent paper towels (such as Bounty) in half. Then, put the paper towels in a large, round, empty, baby wipe container. Mix together: 1 1/2 cups water, 2 tablespoons baby wash (such as Baby Magic Bath), and 1 tablespoon creamy baby oil. Pour mixture over the paper towels. Use like commercial baby wipes.

When using the thick, commercial baby wipes, tear a wipe in half for "wet only" cleanups.

Save your money and don't buy diaper liners. Many parents report they do not work well.

Avoid buying baby products in grocery stores. The prices are usually much higher than discount stores.

Save your money and don't invest in diaper wipe warmers. If you want a warm wipe for baby's bottom, try using a warm washcloth.

Resources

Manufacturers of Pinless Cloth Diapers and Diaper Covers

Biobottoms, PO Box 6009, Petaluma, CA 94953; 800-766-1254

Motherwear, Order Department, PO Box 114, Northampton, MA 01061; 413-586-3488

Bosom Buddies, PO Box 6138, Kingston, NY 12401; 914-338-2038

Natural Baby Co., Inc., 816 Silvia St., 800 B-S, Trenton, NJ 08628; 609-771-9233

Manufacturers will send you samples or coupons for diapers and other baby-related products at the time of this writing. Ask if they have other promotional programs also.

Gerber Baby Products, Customer Relations Department, Fremont, MI 49412

Playtex, House Brands, Inc., 601 Main Street, Suite 500, Vancouver, WA 98660; 800-545-1239

Blistex, Inc., Customer Relations Department, Oak Brook, IL 60521

Kimberly-Clark Corporation (makers of Huggies products), Customer Relations Department, PO Box 2001, Neenah, WI 54957-0058

Johnson & Johnson, Customer Relations Department, Skillman, NJ 08558-9418

Procter and Gamble (makers of Luvs and Pampers products), Customer Relations Department, Cincinnati, OH 45202

Drypers Corporation, PO Box 8830, Vancouver, WA 98666-8830

Scott Paper Co., Customer Relations Department, Philadelphia, PA 19113

Eastman Kodak Company (for coupons toward film, photo developing, photo processing, and other photo supplies), Customer Relations—New Parents Program, PO Box 9023, Paterson, NJ 07509-9023; 800-242-2424

Kendall-Futuro Co., Customer Relations Department, 5801 Mariemont Ave, Cincinnati, OH 45227

CHAPTER EIGHT

Toys on a Budget

"An unbreakable toy is good for breaking other toys."
—John Peers

Attention all new parents. Latest research proves a long-standing theory: toys multiply! Researchers report the degree of multiplication cannot be accurately determined and is directly proportional to the whims of grandparents, aunts, uncles, family, and friends. Proposed theories also suggest holidays, birthdays, and other celebrations are likely variables that cause rapid multiplication of toys.

No, this is not an actual study, but many parents believe this phenomenon is true. Tempting as it may be, hold off on the toy investment for now. Before you know it you will find toys everywhere in your house, even if you do not personally purchase them. Toys do not necessarily need to be expensive. Babies of the '90s still enjoy the time-tested favorite pots and pans (wonderful noisemakers), cardboard boxes (fantastic hideaways) and plastic kitchen storage containers (great for stacking) as well as purchased toys.

Ensuring baby's toys are safe

Necessity Checklist

✿ **Resist buying any toys at first.** Wait to see what you get for baby gifts.

✿ **Inspect all toys for safety.**

✿ **Remove all ribbons, decals, buttons, etc.** that may present a choking or strangulation hazard.

takes priority over making sure he has an abundance of them. There will be plenty of opportunities to add to baby's toy collection. In a few short years your bundle of joy will spot the toy section of every store, memorize Christmas catalogs, and plead for every toy advertised on TV.

Is There More to Play than Just Play?

Play, with or without toys, is one of the most important things your child will do over the next 4 to 7 years. Childhood joy and learning are interwoven in play. Play is essential to a child's development because this is how he will learn life skills.

Play does not need to be structured or school-like for a child to experience learning. It should, however, be fun!

Physical skills, such as crawling, grasping, climbing, and running, are developed through play. Once your child perfects these gross motor skills he will develop increased dexterity and fine motor skills, also. For specific information on how development is enhanced through play or for specific activities to complement skill development refer to a medical parenting manual. Two such resources include the *Mayo Clinic Complete Book of Pregnancy and Baby's First Year* and *The American Academy of Pediatrics Caring for Your Baby and Young Child: Birth to Age Five.*

Language skills develop through play. Whether it's constant cooing between you and baby, or repeating your 10th "Itsy-Bitsy Spider," sophisticated levels of language skill develop through play. Chanting nursery rhymes, singing silly songs, and reading stories are examples of activities that enhance language development. Your child learns from anything and everything at a very young age. This is one reason you want to carefully select television and video programming.

Social skills, emotional well-being, sharing, and bonding abilities develop as your child learns to interact with others through play.

Learning cooperation and negotiation when playing with others is part of your child's early social world. Later, playing games provides added opportunity for social development.

Problem-solving skills are also developed through play. Building with blocks, matching colors, and playing hide-and-go-seek are all foundations for future problem-solving tasks.

It's important to remember there is no magical toy to help your child develop these skills. Children through the ages have used their imaginations to create some of the most wonderful play possible. Remember, Disney-like magic is in the mind and spirit, rather than in the toy. Child's play can be fun and simple; not expensive.

The Gift of You

You are your child's first and best playmate. Not only are you responsible for selecting safe toys for your child, but you can use play to bond and build a special relationship with your baby. There is no instruction manual on right or wrong ways to play. The simplest advice may be to kick back your heels, relax, and recapture your youth. Forget the office, the dishes, and the bills for a while. Relax, have fun, and be a kid.

There are no Robert's Rules for play, but here are a few tips to get you involved.

- ✿ **Observe.** Sit back and watch your child play. This is the easiest way to discover his skill levels and favorite activities.
- ✿ **Follow your child's lead.** All too often as parents we take the role of directing everything from breakfast to bath time to bedtime. When it comes to play, follow your child's lead. Let him be in control and determine the play. Relax—it's fun not to be in charge.

✿ **Be creative.** When you let go of the adult in you, you often find a child. Let the child in you be creative as you give up your adult interpretation of how you have to play with each toy.

✿ **Have fun.** A little play makes the heart merrier. Avoid trying to structure playtime. Children can master many skills without formal schooling in the preschool years. Sing, dance, laugh, and giggle. Baby doesn't care if you are on key or if you have to make up the words. It's more important to feel good about each other and just have fun.

Fun and Simple Games for Baby and You

Toys will keep baby entertained for a short time, but he will probably have the most fun when playing with you. Don't worry if you don't know the exact lyrics to all the "traditional" baby songs—your infant doesn't know them either. His main interest is interacting with you.

If you are new or feeling hesitant about all this baby play stuff, here are a few ideas to get you going.

Dance with Baby. Pretend you can dance like Fred Astaire or Ginger Rogers. Turn on some fun music and dance baby around the living room. Be careful to support baby's neck and back during any dips and swoops.

Sing to Baby. Here's your chance at that singing career you never pursued. Baby will love your lullabies or any melody you wish to try.

"So Big." With baby in your lap or on a floor blanket, lift his hands and arms from a together to an outstretched position all the while saying "so big."

Ride a Bike. With baby lying on a blanket, move his legs like he is riding a bicycle.

Funny Face. Make a face, then watch carefully to see whether your baby copies it. Babies love to giggle and laugh at funny faces.

"The Itsy-Bitsy Spider." As you sing the song, use your hands and fingers to show the spider climbing and the rain falling.

"This Little Piggy." Wiggle each toe as you chant the familiar rhyme.

Horsie. Bouncing your baby on your lap, sing, "Ride a horsie, ride a horsie, all the way to town; Watch out baby, or you'll fall down!" Bounce your baby a little higher on the same word each time. Keep baby's back and neck supported as you bounce.

Bang Bang! Babies love banging. Provide objects that will sound different, such as a wooden spoon, a plastic cup, a plastic pail, and pots and pans if your ears can handle the noise.

> ## Real Parents Say...
>
> All toys can be important, but I think the average child has many more toys than are necessary. Many times they leave the toys to play with boxes, lids, and dishes.
> — *Wilma, mother of four, day care provider*

Up and Down. An easy game. Pick up the objects your baby drops on the floor.

"I'm Gonna Get You!" Slowly and playfully move backward and forward as you approach your baby, saying, "Here I come!" End each "round" with a snuggle or a hug.

Peekaboo. Hide your face, yourself, or a toy for just a few seconds. Say "Peekaboo" when you or the toy reappears.

What's Next? Offer your child a block. When he takes it, offer another. Note if he picks it up with his free hand or transfers the first block to the other hand. Holding two blocks is an accomplishment. Offer him a third block and watch his reaction.

"Pat-a-Cake." Clap your baby's hands together as you sing the rhyme. Be sure to cheer at your baby's first attempts to clap.

The Power of Reading

The best time to start reading to your baby is when he is very young. Some parents even feel it is important to read to baby in the womb! Reading is a very important part of a child's development.

Babies learn right from birth by responding to and interacting with the environment. Be it interaction with people, books, or toys, learning is continuous.

Studies suggest children who are frequently read to become better readers later in life. Even though your baby can't actually "read" books, being read to can still enhance his visual, physical, and emotional development.

Young babies enjoy books that enhance visual stimulation. This can include black and white contrasting objects or large colorful shapes. As baby grows, simple, short nursery rhyme books are fun.

Make reading time fun and special right from the start. Reading should be peaceful, not a tug-of-war. Quiet time just before or after a nap or at bedtime is often an opportune time to snuggle up with baby and a book in a comfortable chair. Turn pages slowly and explore the magic with your child.

When searching for baby books, look for bright pictures and contrasting colors. Words are not necessary in baby's first books. Books with pictures of babies, animals, and colorful objects are popular at first.

As baby grows, books with simple phrases and or touchable objects are great. Soon, you'll be on your way to Mother Goose, Dr. Seuss, and Margaret Wise Brown's *Goodnight Moon*.

Before long, you will have memorized multiple books. Regular reading time is one of the best gifts you can give your baby. Through the world of books you welcome your baby into the fascinating world of sound, rhyme, color, pictures, stories, imagination, and make-believe.

Books for Baby

Undoubtedly, every parent and child will have their favorite books—it's only natural. Babies, like adults, have individual tastes and preferences from the moment they enter the world. Some books may be special only when dad reads while others may be favorites with mom, grandma, or a sitter.

Like other toys and baby products, no book is perfect. If you are looking for a few tried and true favorites, try the following suggestions. Your local library and bookstore are great resources for additional age-appropriate books.

Point-and-Name Books and Simple Board Books

- ✿ *A, B, C, D, Tummy, Toes, Hands, Knees* by B.G. Hennessy; illustrated by Wendy Watson, Puffin
- ✿ *The Baby's Book of Babies* by Kathy Henderson; photographs by Anthea Sieveking, Dial
- ✿ *Baby's Colors* by Neil Rickline, Simon and Schuster
- ✿ *Bumper to Bumper* by Annie Owens, Knopf

Real Parents Say...

We don't mind spending money on books—it's worth it. Hearing the language of good literature is so important. Book lists are available, but remember, all children don't like the same ones.
—Marie, mother of three

Books—a child's most important toy. Start using the library as soon as possible. Very young children love the Dr. Seuss books. The words are all fun. One of our favorites was *Go Dog Go*, second only to *One Fish, Two Fish*.
—Rose and Art, parents of three

Read to even tiny children. It wasn't until I had an infant and was reading to my older children while holding the baby, that I realized how a young child can benefit by being read to.
—Anne, mother of five

Buy some good books and read, read, read.
—Rosemary, mother of six

✿ *Baby's Favorite Walk; Baby's Playtime;* and *Fun with Shapes,* Playskool's Touch 'em Books (washable)

✿ *How Many Animals?* by Denise Lewis Patrick; illustrated by Kate Gleeson. A Golden Book by Western Publishing Company

✿ *Hello Baby* and *Farm Animals,* Macmillan Children's Book Clubs

✿ *Baby Donald at the Playground; Baby Goofy Catches a Fish,* and *Where is Baby Mickey's Red Ball,* The Disney Babies Series, A Golden Book, Western Publishing

✿ *Ernie and Bert Can... Can You? In & Out, Up & Down* by Michael Smollin, Random House/CTW

✿ *The Teeny Tiny Farm,* by Katharine Ross; illustrated by Amy Flynn, Random House

✿ *Ernie's Bath Book* by Michael Smollin, Random House/CTW

Simple Storybooks and Nursery Rhymes

✿ *Pat the Bunny* by Dorothy Kunhardt, A Golden Book, Western Publishing Company

✿ *Baby's Mother Goose* by Alice Schlesinger, Grosset & Dunlap

✿ *Teddy Bear, Teddy Bear* by Carol Lawson, Dian Books for Young Readers

✿ *Wendy Watson's Mother Goose* by Wendy Watson, Lothrop, Lee & Shephard

✿ *Goodnight Moon, The Runaway Bunny,* and *Big Red Barn* by Margaret Wise Brown, Harper & Row

✿ *The Foot Book, Go Dog Go, Dr. Seuss's ABC,* or any other Dr. Seuss book, Random House

Storybooks as Baby Gets Older

✿ *Brown Bear, Brown Bear What Do You See?* and *Polar Bear, Polar Bear, What Do You Hear?* by Bill Martin Jr., Henry Holt and Company

- *The Very Hungry Caterpillar* and *The Very Busy Spider* by Eric Carle, G.P. Putnam and Sons
- *Clap Your Hands* by Lorinda B. Cauley, Scholastic, Inc.
- *Love You Forever* by Robert Munsch, Firefly Books

Basic Baby Toys

A baby learns about the environment by using all five senses. Through play, he will also learn the relationship of cause and effect and the rhythm of repetition. That is why baby insists on playing the same game with you over and over.

Basic Baby Toys from Birth to Age One

- Mobiles and unbreakable safety mirrors
- Rattles and squeak toys
- Nesting and stacking toys
- Tub toys (plastic cups and pitchers, squeeze bottles, etc.)
- Soft balls, especially bright-colored ones
- Pots and pans
- Big cardboard boxes
- Soft-sided, bright-colored blocks
- Singing to your baby
- Lullabye and sing-along cassette tapes
- Musical and chime toys
- Baby gym (the type with four legs that have hanging toys—not a crib gym)
- Push-pull toys
- Picture books—plastic, cloth, and board-type books

Real Parents Say...

The Playskool tape recorder is our favorite. It was useful from birth and our now toddler still loves it.
—*Dan and Chris, parents of one*

Sometimes the simplest toy entertained baby the longest.
—*Marlene, mother of three*

My favorite toy for baby from about four months is a beach ball. They are lightweight and can't hurt baby, lamps, and furniture. They are also colorful and baby loves to crawl after them.
—*Anne, mother of five*

- ✿ Simple pop-up toys
- ✿ Plastic storage-ware, like Tupperware and Rubbermaid
- ✿ Textured toys that make sounds
- ✿ Old magazines to show pictures (for babies 4 months and older — do not leave baby unattended with magazine)

Videos and Television

Television and video can provide baby with both entertainment and education. A word of caution, though, it's easy to let the television become an all-too-handy babysitter. Baby needs a balance between creative play and other forms of entertainment such as favorite videos and TV shows.

Some TV/Video Hints

Preview all television shows and videos before baby watches them. Remember, babies are quick to pick up everything they see and hear.

Watch shows with your child. Play along as Big Bird, Lamb Chop, and Barney sing and dance.

Decide on a TV/video time limit and stick to it. Kids need creative time, imaginative play, and exercise — things they don't get sitting cross-legged in front of the TV for hours at a time.

Rent or borrow videos instead of buying them. Many libraries loan videos and books. This is an ideal way to limit video time and avoid the investment of videotapes. An average video costs $9 to $16. In addition, a videotape is usually only watched on and off for a year or two. Borrow a video and put the saved money into a college fund.

Toy Safety Tips

An infant's environment should be kept as hazard-free as possible. The U.S. Consumer Product Safety Commission estimates that 152,000 children were treated in emergency rooms in 1994 for toy-related injuries. In addition, thousands of children died as a result of toy-related mishaps.[1] Over 2.6 billion toys are purchased each year by parents and other consumers.[2] Though it is against the law to sell a toy that does not pass government testing standards, many dishonest companies do. Three-fourths of all toys sold in the United States are manufactured abroad. In 1990, imported toys accounted for 90 percent of the toy recalls.[3]

This means you, the consumer, must beware. You are the final and most important inspector of your child's toys. Attentive supervision, selective toy purchasing, and regular toy maintenance all help keep your child's play safe. For safety and fun:

Remove all crib gyms and mobiles once your infant reaches 5 months of age or begins to push up on his hands and knees. At this age, these gyms present a strangulation hazard.

Remove and discard all toy packaging. The plastic wrap, sharp staples, and twist ties are all safety hazards.

Store toys on shelves or in open boxes. If you opt for a toy chest look for model with supports to hold the lid in any position or one that has a sliding top, side panels, or removable lid.

Never leave a rattle or toy in the crib with your child. He could get the toy lodged in his mouth.

Rattles should be at least 1 5/8 inches wide to prevent the possibility of choking.

Be sure teethers, pacifiers, and squeeze toys can not become compressed. It could block your child's airway if he got the entire object in his mouth.

Never allow a child to run with a toy in his mouth.

Watch for toys left behind by older children. Though they may be age-appropriate for a toddler or preschooler, they could be potentially dangerous for your infant explorer.

Match all toys to your child's age and ability. You are the final judge on whether a toy is safe for your child. The age recommendation on much toy packaging is for educational, not safety purposes.

Throw away or return any toy if you question its safety.

Report any unsafe toy to the Consumer Products Safety Commission in Washington, D.C., at 800-638-2772 (800-638-8270 for the hearing impaired).

Don't let your child play with a balloon. He could inhale it when trying to blow it up. Immediately pick up and discard any pieces if the balloon pops. Mylar balloons are safer, with adult supervision.

To prevent burns and shocks, use only battery-operated toys until a child reaches age 10. Battery compartments should have a screw closure to prevent baby access to the batteries.

Check all squeeze toys to make sure the squeaker can not detach.

All toys should be constructed of sturdy material. The toy should not shatter or break, even when thrown.

Any strings on pull toys should be 12 inches or shorter. Longer strings or cords present a strangulation hazard.

Check all stuffed animals, dolls, and teddy bears carefully before giving to baby. Make sure eyes and noses are firmly attached; ideally painted on or sewn in place. Remove all ribbons. Do not allow baby to suck on or play with any small bottles, pacifiers, or accessories that come with stuffed dolls. Many are small enough to be swallowed.

Make sure any wooden toy has a nontoxic finish. Check the packaging. If in doubt, do not let baby play with the toy.

Do not allow your child to play with very noisy toys. Noise levels at or about 100 decibels — the sound of a cap gun at close range — can damage hearing.[4]

Look for toys labeled "for children 3 and under." These toys must meet federal guidelines requiring no small parts. This is only a partial safety precaution — you still need to inspect the toy for size appropriateness.

If in doubt about the size of a toy, use the Toys to Grow On No-Choke Testing Tube. The device is designed to help parents weed out toys and other items that may be a choking hazard for baby. Though this device helps parents identify potential choking hazards, it is not a guarantee that a toy is safe or can not be swallowed. As parent, you must still provide close supervision and trust your judgment about safe and unsafe toys. See the Resource section for information on where to order a No-Choke Testing Tube.

Use a cardboard toilet paper tube as another way to determine toy safety. If the toy in question fits inside the tube, it is too small to be safe for baby. Longer and wider toys (without sharp edges or loose parts) that can not fit inside the tube are usually safe for baby to play with.

Carefully check over older toys, especially those you may have played with as a child or find at friends' or relatives' homes with older children. Many of these toys are smaller than is safely recommended. Also, years of storage can cause toys to deteriorate and break easily.

Before Buying Any Toy...

Infants respond to toys that stimulate their senses. As you're selecting or receiving toys, keep in mind, you will want a variety so baby can learn about shape, color, texture, and sound. When picking out those first toys, choose toys that:

- ✿ have pieces too large to swallow,
- ✿ have no sharp points,
- ✿ are nontoxic,
- ✿ are brightly colored,
- ✿ are lightweight for handling,
- ✿ can be used at a variety of stages,
- ✿ are sturdy, well-made, and have no removable parts.

Fisher Price Stacking Rings and Fisher Price Baby's First Blocks, both with colorful shapes, are great toys for the first 18 months, especially because they can be used at a variety of development stages. Baby loves to play with individual shapes and blocks, and as time goes on he learns to match and place shapes through the slotted canister lid or place rings on the stacking spool.

Smart Parents Do

Rotate toys. It is amazing how toys acquire a "newness" if they've been out of sight for a few days. Divvy up toys and rotate them every couple weeks.

Eject the rejects. At holiday, birthday, and other gift giving times, return any duplicate toys. Return any toys you feel are unsafe.

Divide and conquer. Place toys and books in a variety of rooms around your house. This makes each room a special play adventure.

Take out a toy loan. Check out the local toy lending library in your area. This is a great way to get toy variety. Membership is usually about $10 per year. If your community does not have one, consider helping organize one or set up your own toy lending program with parents who have children about the same age.

Inspect toys regularly for cracks, and broken or loose parts. If a toy appears broken, toss it out or contact the manufacturer about a replacement.

Wash and sanitize toys regularly. If baby has a sensitivity to dust allergies, wash favorite stuffed toys often. Toys that baby chews on should be washed and rinsed with boiling water or run through the dishwasher one or more times per week. Wash stuffed toys in a pillowcase and on a gentle cycle.

Have a heart when giving away toys it appears your child no longer uses. If in doubt, store potential giveaways for a few weeks before shipping them off to charity.

Hold back gifts for a while. If your child gets oodles of toys for a birthday, put a few in storage. It will be a big treat to have a "new" toy several months from now.

Budget Helpers

Take advantage of a community toy library. Membership fees are minimal, and just like a book from the library, you can check out toys for a period, play with them, and return them. You get lots of variety at almost no cost. See the Resource section to locate or start up a toy library in your area.

Look in your kitchen cupboards before spending money on toys. Babies love to bang on pots and pans with wooden spoons, stack nested measuring cups, and use funnels and large plastic cups for bathtub toys. As a bonus, you just wash the toys and return them to their original use when baby's done playing with them.

Make homemade toys. A string tied to a spool, a box castle, and a cardboard crown are all easy to make.

Real Parents Say...

I really try to buy brand name toys like Fisher Price and Little Tikes because they are made well. I find these brands last the longest and are the best deal for my dollar. Inexpensive brands seem to be made poorly and break easily.

—*Lois, mother of three*

Allow baby to explore. Put things away that they can't explore. Talk with your child a lot. Your local extension office has lots of free information on age specific activities for children.

—*Linda, mother of three*

Buy toys and most books in wholesale and discount stores whenever possible. Avoid baby specialty shops and bookstores where prices are 10 to 50 percent higher.

January and July are great months to stock up on Christmas, birthday, or special occasion toys. These are slow seasons for toy sales and bargains often appear immediately after and before the holiday marketing campaigns.

Shop garage sales and consignment shops for great buys. Inspect things extra closely because the toys have been used. Disinfect all used toys before allowing your child to play with them.

Take advantage of all the wonderful play equipment at your local park and recreational facilities. Most communities offer lots of opportunities for outdoor fun at little or no cost. Plus, your baby gets fresh air, sunshine, and exercise.

One of the most delightful things about having children is experiencing the miracle of their development, watching the delight, innocence, and expression as they capture the newness in each experience, and sharing in the laughter of their play. So, do as Robert Fulghum suggests, and "live a balanced life—learn some and think some and draw and paint and sing and dance and play and work some every day some."[5] Enjoy your child and the special gift of play he brings into your life.

> ## Real Parents Say...
>
> Limit toys when your child is young. They love simple things: brown paper bags, shiny bowls, and hiding in cupboards. All are perfectly safe. Save the toy money for college funds.
>
> —*Rose, mother of three*
>
> Garage sale toys can be a great buy. When you see a very worn toy at a garage sale, keep this in mind when shopping for new items that this is a toy kids seem to play with a lot.
>
> —*Anne, mother of five*

Books, Brochures, and Pamphlets

Games Babies Play by Vicki Lanski, The Book Peddlers, 18326 Minnetonka Blvd., Deephaven, MN 55391; 612-475-3527

The Best Toys, Books, and Videos for Kids by Joanne and Stephanie Oppenheim, Harper Collins Publishers, Inc., 10 E. 53rd St., New York, NY 10022

For excellent brochures such as "Which Toy for Which Child: A Consumer's Guide for Selecting Suitable Toys;" "For Kids Sake," and CPSC Fact Sheet Number 47: "Toys," call or write: **U.S. Consumer Product Safety Commission,** Washington, DC 20207; 800-638-2772

Other Information

For information on a toy library near you or how to get one started in your area, send a SASE to: **USA Toy Library Association,** 2530 Crawford Avenue, Suite 111, Evanston, IL 50201

For questions or concerns about the safety or age appropriateness of a toy or game, contact: U.S. Consumer Product Safety Commission (CPSC), Washington, DC 20207; 800-638-CPSC (800-638-2772) or 800-638-8270 for the hearing impaired

To order a No-Choke Test Tube send $1 to: Toys to Grow On, PO Box 17, Long Beach, CA 90801; 213-603-8890

For the "Toy Manufacturers of America Guide to Toys and Play" write: The American Toy Institute, Inc., 200 Fifth Avenue, Suite 740, New York, NY 10010

Zero to One (newsletter for new parents, $5 per year), ISU Extension Publications Distribution, 119 Printing and Publications Building, Iowa State University, Ames, IA 50011

Catalogs

R
e
s
o
u
r
c
e
s

Sometimes it's difficult to find toys and safety accessories designed for infants and very young children. Listed below are catalogs that carry these items.

Constructive Playthings, 1227 E. 119th St., Grandview, MO 64030; 800-832-0572

Growing Child (newsletter and developmental/educational products), 22 N. Second Street, Lafayette, IN 47902-0620; 800-338-2624

The Livonia Catalog, 306 Hebron St., Henderson, NC 28739; 800-543-8566

One Step Ahead, PO Box 46, Deerfield, IL 60015; 800-344-7550

The Right Start Catalog, Right Start Plaza, 5334 Sterling Center Drive, Westlake Village, CA 91361; 800-548-8531; Fax 800-762-5501

Music for Little People, PO Box 1460, Redway, CA 95560; 800-727-2233 or 707-923-3241

Hand in Hand Professional (mainly educational toys) Catalog Center, Route 26, RR 1 Box 1425, Oxford, ME 04270; 800-872-3841

The Great Kids Company (mainly educational toys), PO Box 609, Lewisville, NC 27023 or 800-533-2166

JC Penney, Inc., c/o Little Tikes, 2180 Barlow Road, PO Box 2277, Hudson, OH 44236-4108

CHAPTER NINE

Feeding Made Simple

*"When you are dealing with a child, keep all
your wits about you, and sit on the floor."*
—*Austin O'Malley*

You lay half-awake in bed and listen proudly to your baby cooing in the next room. Oh, how you would love to catch a few more minutes of sleep. You glance at the clock—7:58 a.m.—and instinctively know it is time to get up. The morning feeding ritual is about to begin.

Baby's giggling turns impatient as she signals her need to be held and fed. As you hop out of bed, you smile with pride and confidence at how your feeding skills have developed during these first few months with your daughter. You can hardly remember all your recent fears and worries about how to feed her. As with other aspects of parenting, you learn as you go. Understanding basic infant feeding principles as well as developing a trusting feeding relationship with your baby are keys to healthy, fun-filled mealtimes.

Necessity Checklist

✿ **Bottles.** Start with two until you are sure of the style baby prefers.

✿ **Formula** (if this is your chosen feeding method).

✿ **Bibs**

✿ **Sippy cups/tippy cups.**

✿ **Three baby-sized feeding spoons** (at about 4 months).

✿ **Nursing bras** (optional; two to four)

✿ **Nursing pads**

✿ **Breast pump** to express milk (optional).

✿ **Bottles or storage bags** to hold expressed milk.

Nutrition during baby's first years builds the foundation for a healthy body for years to come. Your baby received her first nutrition from mom during those months of pregnancy. Good nutrition during pregnancy was your first gift to your baby.

At no other time in baby's life will you be so tuned into her hunger as during the first 6 to 12 months. Initially, every cry may sound like a starvation wail, but soon you will be able to determine the difference between a hunger howl, a holding pang, or an "I am wet" summoning. You may experience days when baby's stomach seems like a bottomless pit, followed by days when she appears to be on a hunger strike. Feast or famine — learn to trust baby's hunger and fullness cues and you will all be happier eaters.

What and how much baby eats during the first year affects her mental and physical growth and development. It also establishes habits that can be the cornerstone for a lifetime of healthy eating. Because babies learn primarily by example, now is a great time for you to evaluate your own eating habits. Does your eating promote a healthy mind and body or will you be enrolled in a cardiac rehabilitation program by age 55? Your baby will do as you do and not as you say, so now is the right time to concentrate on making healthy eating choices.

There is no right or wrong way to nourish baby during her first months of life. You and your partner need to select an option that works best for you. No other aspect of early parenting generates quite as much advice as infant feeding. Be confident in your ability and shrug off comments like, "Don't you think you should quit nursing since you are going back to work?" or "Do you think she's getting enough to eat?" or "When you were little, we put cereal in the bottle to make you sleep better."

Milk is baby's first food. It offers complete nourishment for your baby's early months of life. Your choices in the milk department are breastmilk, formula, or a combination of both. The American Academy of Pediatrics recommends breastmilk or formula be provided until age 1. Breastmilk and/or formula is the only food your baby will need until she is 4 to 6 months old. At that time you will introduce her, and your dining room floor, to the world of solid foods.

Following are lists of breast, formula, and combination feeding tips. Whichever method you chose, these tips can help you feel more successful with your feeding experience.

The Choices: Breastfeeding

Breastmilk completely satisfies your baby's nutritional needs during her first 4 to 6 months. It is the most appropriate food for baby's developing systems. As baby's growth and nutritional needs change, so does the composition of your breastmilk.

In addition to being a healthy food choice, breastfeeding is economical. Formula currently sells for more than $50 a case, so a 6-month supply could cost over $300.

The costs of breastfeeding are reflective of your increased calorie needs and any supplies (breast pump, bottles, etc.) you may need if you choose to express breastmilk during the day. Breastfeeding uses approximately 600 calories a day above your normal energy requirements. This additional energy will come from a combination of fat stored during pregnancy and now converted to energy, as well as foods in your diet. Your grocery bill, however, will typically not increase significantly compared to formula costs.

Besides being an optimal economical choice, breastfeeding offers a multitude of other advantages:

- ✿ **Special bonding time with baby.**
- ✿ **Helps the uterus contract** and return to its normal size more quickly.
- ✿ **Uses extra calories** and can help your body return to its pre-pregnancy weight. However, dieting during breastfeeding is not recommended. It is difficult for your body to produce an adequate milk supply on an insufficient diet. If you are concerned about your

weight, avoid excessive high-fat foods, eat no more than your appetite, and take a brisk 20- to 30-minute walk two to three times a week to help you regain your pre-pregnancy shape.

✿ **Convenience**—Breastmilk is always ready and at the right temperature. No bottles to prepare, nothing to sterilize. As breastfeeding becomes more accepted in our culture, women find it easier to nurse baby almost anywhere.

✿ **Colostrum, a yellowish fluid and the first milk to be produced, is packed with antibodies and other protective substances.** These antibodies help your baby ward off illnesses and infections.

✿ **Breastmilk is rich in infection-fighting white blood cells that help destroy bacteria.** Breastfed babies often have fewer respiratory, intestinal, and ear infections.

✿ **Breastmilk is easier for babies to digest than formula.** Because of this, breastfed babies tend to have fewer gastrointestinal problems and they also like to nurse often.

✿ **Breastmilk stimulates maturation of baby's intestinal tract** and decreases the risk for developing food allergies later in life.

✿ **Breastmilk does not stain baby's clothing like formula does.**

Contrary to common myths, most new moms can breastfeed. Breast size does not determine breastfeeding success. Early in pregnancy, your body starts changing to prepare for breastfeeding. Changes in breast size and shape later in life are not due to nursing. Rather, these changes are influenced by heredity, number of pregnancies, and the aging process itself.

Breastfeeding Success Tips

Have an "I Can Do It" attitude. A positive, persevering attitude helps get you through the challenges of breastfeeding.

Educate yourself about breastfeeding. The more you know about nursing a baby, the more relaxed and confident you will be. See the Resource section at the end of this chapter for books, brochures, and organizations you can refer to for help.

Relax. The more relaxed you are, the easier it will be. Both you and baby will be more comfortable and content if you are calm.

Make sure both you and baby are in a comfortable position when nursing.

Vary your positions for holding baby when nursing. This helps prevent sore nipples and promotes adequate emptying of breast ducts.

Ask your doctor about supplementing baby's diet with vitamin D and iron. Some doctors also recommend a fluoride supplement to help with the development of healthy teeth. If you have fluoridated water, be careful of over supplementing baby's diet with fluoride. Because iron in breastmilk is easily utilized, a breastfed baby usually does not need an iron supplement until about 6 months of age.

Avoid supplementing baby's intake with water unless directed by your physician or health care provider. Baby can get adequate fluids from breastmilk. Supplementing with water can cause inadequate nutrition and poor weight gain. In addition, baby will tend to nurse less, which does not allow mom to build up an adequate milk supply.

Real Parents Say...

In addition to being a fulfilling experience, breastfeeding helped me get back into my pre-pregnancy clothes quickly. A word of caution, it can be wearing on your body, so eat well and get as much rest as you can. My doctor encouraged me to take the rest of my prenatal vitamins while I was nursing, also.

—Evie, mother of two

Allow time for both you and baby to adjust to the newness. In a few weeks, you will both have your routines established.

Select a good breast pump for times you are away from baby and need to express milk. Breast pumps that attach directly to a feeding bottle are convenient. Avoid pumps that resemble the old fashioned bicycle horn. These tend to be very inefficient and impossible to clean. Consider renting an electric pump from a reputable medical supplier. Manual breast pumps cost $15 to $40. Mini electric pumps cost about $80 and $50 per month to rent. All these options are still less costly than formula feeding. As an added bonus, your baby gets the benefits of breastmilk.

Expressed breastmilk with colostrum can be kept in the refrigerator for 24 to 48 hours; whole milk will keep up to 72 hours. If you are planning to freeze the milk, do so immediately. Ideally, you should use frozen breastmilk within 1 month, but you can freeze it in the top of your refrigerator freezer for up to 3 months and in the deep freeze for up to 6 months. Breastmilk should be frozen at least as hard as ice cream. Rotate your supply of breastmilk in the freezer. Use the oldest first. Sometimes when breastmilk is frozen for an extended period it becomes off-flavored. Discard any bad tasting milk.

> ## Real Parents Say...
>
> Breastfeeding was very easy and convenient for me. It was easy on our baby's digestive system and our baby never had any problems with constipation. Breastfeeding was especially nice at night. I never had to prepare or warm up bottles.
>
> *—Martha, mother of one*
>
> I enjoyed breastfeeding very much. It is a neat bonding experience and both our children were relatively free from illnesses and ear infections.
>
> *—Marie, mother of two*

Freeze breastmilk in amounts to be used at one feeding. This prevents you from thawing too much at one time and having to throw it out. Thawed breastmilk should not be refrozen.

Breastfeed your infant every 2 to 3 hours to establish an adequate milk supply.

Plan to nurse your baby 8 to 12 times a day at first. By 4 months of age or sooner baby will probably cut back to four to six feedings per day. Expect to nurse more often when baby is going through growth spurts and calorie needs are high.

"Breast on Request" is a great motto. This helps baby learn to trust her hunger and satiety cues. Forget about the feeding schedule. Appetite depends on physical and biological needs. Just like babies don't dirty diapers on schedule, neither do they get hungry at a set time.

Nurse your baby on the fullest breast first at a feeding. Some women prefer to alternate which breast they begin on at each feeding. A safety pin clipped to your bra is an easy way to help remind you which side to nurse on first.

Breastfeeding twins and triplets can be done. A feeding schedule is sometimes helpful in this situation. Support from other parents and professionals who have successfully breastfed more than one infant at a time is also beneficial. Eating well and getting extra rest is a must for mom. Consider contacting a lactation consultant or joining a breastfeeding support group.

Nutrition and Health Tips for Breastfeeding Moms

Get plenty of rest. Your body needs lots of energy to produce enough milk for your growing baby. If possible, sleep when baby sleeps. This is especially important during the first 4 to 6 weeks.

Drink plenty of fluids. Trust your thirst sensation. You will need to drink at least six to eight cups of liquid each day to maintain an adequate milk supply.

Avoid caffeine-containing beverages. Caffeine passes from mom to baby via breastmilk. Babies are not very good at eliminating caffeine from their bodies so it tends to build up over time. This can cause baby to be more irritable. Common caffeine-containing beverages include coffee, soft drinks, cocoa, chocolate, and tea.

Eat a balanced diet by choosing foods from each of the food groups. See the Food Guide Pyramid on page 160 for healthy eating guidelines.

Avoid alcohol. Remember, what you drink, your baby drinks, too.

Check with your doctor before taking any medications. Many medications can be passed to baby via breastmilk.

Occasionally, your baby may be sensitive to a specific food in your diet. If you suspect baby is fussier or gassy after you have eaten something, limit your intake of that food for the time being. Slowly reintroduce the food into your diet in small amounts. Watch baby for any intolerances.

Do not diet. Do not restrict calorie intake, especially for the first few months of brestfeeding. Your body requires extra energy for breastfeeding. Dieting or restricting your food intake may cause your milk supply to become inadequate and leave you feeling constantly tired and run down.

Getting Dad Involved

Some parents choose not to breastfeed because mom feels strapped with 100 percent of the feeding responsibility or dad feels left out of the feeding picture. Addressing these and other concerns and implementing strategies to include dad in the feeding routine can create a successful breastfeeding experience for all family members.

Remember, parenting involves shared duties and responsibilities. As with any other job, the work is easier and more fun when two people do it rather than one. Feeding baby is no exception. Here are some tips for involving dad:

When bottlefeeding is desired, have dad offer baby the bottle. Most breastfed babies prefer to nurse. When mom offers a bottle, baby often becomes confused and upset. Having dad offer the bottle is a wonderful solution.

For nighttime feedings, encourage dad to pick up baby when she cries. After mom nurses baby, take turns putting her back to bed. This routine involves both parents with those middle-of-the-night feedings. It also helps prevent mom from getting resentful about "going it alone" at midnight feeding time.

Alternate getting up with baby at night. Mom can express breast milk on alternate days that dad is responsible for night duty. This allows each parent to get a full night's rest periodically.

Encourage dad and baby to have special bonding time, too. For example, have dad rock baby after she has nursed.

Take turns doing all those other baby care duties like baths, changing diapers, and dressing.

Mom, do not criticize the way dad takes care of baby. Avoid grabbing baby out of his arms the minute she whimpers, redoing the diaper, or commenting on clothing choices. These acts or comments scream "You're not doing it right!" and discourage new fathers. Baby will benefit from dad's involvement; she won't care if the diaper is on "just right." Remember, dad may be uncomfortable with all these new duties, too. He, like anyone else, will be more eager to continue to participate with words of praise and encouragement.

Make introducing solid foods a special time for dad. Encourage him to feed baby her first cereal, drink from her first cup, and gum her first graham cracker.

Listen to dad's frustrations with feeding. Remember, mom is the breastfeeding expert and dad is the bottlefeeding expert.

> ## Real Parents Say...
>
> My biggest challenge with our breastfed daughter and son was getting the milk ready quickly when they were hungry. I thawed and warmed the milk at the same time by running hot water over the frozen, bagged milk. Once we got our routine down, we were all happy campers. It was much easier with our second child.
>
> —*Dave, father of two*

Follow baby's lead and use a bottle and nipple combination that she prefers. Different babies prefer different bottle feeding systems.

Store frozen milk (two ounces initially and more as baby grows) in regular bottles or the disposable bottle feeding bags (e.g., those that fit into the Playtex Nurser or similar system). These disposable bags are sterilized and make thawing milk easy, which helps speed up preparation time. Breastfed babies are not used to waiting for lunch. Help dad come up with a system to quickly get the milk thawed or warmed when baby gets hungry.

If You Do Experience Breastfeeding Problems. . .

A wide array of information and support about breastfeeding is available in books, from organizations, or through your hospital or physician's office. Here, remedies are suggested for some common problems.

Sore or Cracked Nipples

Possible Cause: Improper positioning or baby not being fed on demand and sucks too vigorously when fed.
Try: Nursing frequently and for shorter periods on each breast. Change position of baby on breast. Try using the football hold or nurse lying on your side.

Possible Cause: Using soap or antiseptic on your nipples.
Try: Discontinuing the use of soap or antiseptic.

Possible Cause: Leaking causing bra flap to stick to nipple.
Try: Moistening bra flap with water before lowering bra to nurse baby. Dry flap or put on a clean bra after nursing.

Possible Cause: Using a plastic liner in your bra or nursing pads, which may result in inadequate drying.
Try: Using a clean handkerchief, thin cloth diaper, or washable nursing pad instead of the plastic or disposable types.

Possible Cause: Baby may have thrush and/or your nipples are infected.
Try: Washing nipples with baking soda and water. Rinse with water and pat dry with a very soft cloth.

Possible Cause: Not allowing your nipples to dry before replacing bra flaps.
Try: Exposing nipples to air and sitting next to a bare light bulb, sunlamp, or hairdryer set on the lowest setting. Lanolin, ointments, and breast creams may aggravate the problem, so consult with your doctor or lactation consultant before using them.

Insufficient Breastmilk

Possible Cause: Mother not nursing often enough to stimulate milk supply.
Try: Nursing frequently—every 2 to 3 hours until milk is well established.

Possible Cause: Offering only one breast at each feeding.
Try: Nursing frequently, using both breasts at each feeding.

Possible Cause: Baby is not emptying at least one breast at each feeding.
Try: Encouraging baby to nurse longer. Express milk at the end of feedings.

Possible Cause: Offering bottle too often.
Try: Nursing only for the first few weeks. One bottle a day is too often when you are trying to establish your milk supply.

Possible Cause: Baby is experiencing an appetite spurt.
Try: Nursing frequently for 2 to 3 days to increase milk supply. This is common around 2 to 3 weeks, 5 to 6 weeks, and 3 months.

Possible Cause: Baby is given solid foods too early.
Try: Waiting until 4 to 6 months to give solid foods. Solids reduce the vigor of baby's sucking and consequently reduces supply.

Possible Cause: Mother is taking diuretics, antihistamines, cortisone, or birth control pills.
Try: Avoiding all medications possible. Check with your doctor before taking any medications and breastfeeding.

Possible Cause: Excessive activity or stress, resulting in an exhausted mom.
Try: Getting plenty of rest and eating a balanced diet.

Breast Engorgement
Possible Cause: Incomplete emptying of at least one breast at each feeding.
Try: Using both breasts at each feeding and nursing frequently. Apply moist heat to breasts before feeding to encourage let-down.

Possible Cause: Nursing from only one breast at a feeding.
Try: Nursing from both breasts at each feeding.

Possible Cause: Skipping a feeding or going too long without nursing.
Try: Nursing or expressing milk frequently.

Plugged Duct or Breast Infection
Signs of a breast infection include: mother has a fever, aches all over, breasts are tender, red streaks appear on the breast, the breast may feel hard and/or warm to touch, and it may be uncomfortable to nurse baby. Be aware that you can get mastitis (inflammation of the breast, usually caused by infection) anytime you are breastfeeding, not just during the first few weeks.

Possible Causes: Insufficient rest; undiagnosed, untreated infection in an infant; undiagnosed, untreated mastitis in mother.
Remedy: Call your physician or health care provider immediately for antibiotics. Go to bed and rest. Apply moist heat and attempt to keep sore breast empty. The milk will not harm baby. Change positions of baby when nursing. Slowly massage your breast(s) from your armpit to the nipple area. Drink plenty of fluids.

Fussy Baby

Possible Causes: Baby is not allowed to nurse long enough at each feeding; baby is experiencing appetite spurts; general periods of irritability not associated with hunger; mother's use of cigarettes, coffee, tea, or other nicotine- or caffeine-containing products is too great; mother is taking diuretics, antihistamines, cortisone, birth control pills, or other medication; mother may be menstruating.
Try: Nursing on demand and allowing baby to use your breast as a pacifier. This will satisfy baby's need to suck as well as stimulate milk production. Extra skin contact with your baby may be important. Try carrying baby in a front carrier.

Possible Cause: Mother may not be having let-down.
Try: Taking a hot shower and massaging breasts before nursing.

Exhausted Mother

Possible Cause: Baby is sleeping too long between daytime feedings and then nurses all night.
Try: Gently encouraging baby to nurse more during the day.

Possible Cause: Mother is not able to rest whenever she can.
Try: Laying down whenever baby does. Give yourself some personal time every day such as taking a bath while someone else watches the baby.

Possible Cause: Inadequate diet and intake of fluids and/or too much exercise or activity.
Try: Eating and drinking to match your appetite. Nursing requires extra calories and nutrients. Do not attempt to diet or follow a low calorie eating plan while nursing. Keep exercise moderate.

Baby Has Skin Rashes or Discomforts
During Breastfeeding or Weaning

Possible Cause: Insufficient rinsing of baby's sheets and clothing.
Try: Rinsing all laundry and avoid using fabric softeners. Use a mild, dye- and perfume-free detergent.

Possible Cause: Drugs or medications being taken by mother.
Try: Talk with your doctor before taking any medications.

Possible Cause: Sensitivity to food in mother's diet.
Try: Limiting your intake of the specific food, if you suspect a sensitivity; however, know that babies are rarely bothered by food in their mother's diet.

Possible Cause: Weaning too rapidly.
Try: Weaning slowly, if possible, eliminating one feeding at a time. If rapid weaning is necessary, allow baby to nurse just long enough to relieve discomfort, but not long enough to stimulate milk production.

Formula Feeding

Some parents choose the formula option for feeding baby. The advantages can include:

- ✿ Freedom for mom from being baby's sole food source.
- ✿ Anybody can feed baby. This enables other family members to have more opportunities to bond with baby during feeding time.
- ✿ Convenience.
- ✿ No need to worry about mom's diet or any medications she may be taking.
- ✿ You know exactly how much formula baby is taking.
- ✿ Because formula takes longer to digest, bottlefed babies do not need to be fed as often as breastfed babies.

✿ You can still experience feelings of closeness during feeding times similar to someone who is breastfeeding. Rocking, cuddling, softly stroking baby's hair, and gazing into baby's eyes enriches the experience.

Formula Feeding Tips

Discuss formula choices with your doctor. Once you have decided on a formula, avoid switching brands. Each type is slightly different, so it is best for baby to stay with one formula unless an intolerance develops.

Most physicians recommend formula with added iron. This helps prevent iron deficiency anemia in baby.

Always use sterilized bottles and nipples. You can sterilize feeding bottles by running them through the dishwasher or placing them in boiling water for 5 minutes. Pacifiers and nipples should only be in boiling water for 2 minutes. The high temperature breaks down the rubber nipple and could cause it to break or tear. Silicone and vinyl nipples hold up better. If the water in your home is chlorinated, you can wash the bottles in hot tap water and detergent, and then rinse with hot tap water. Always wipe off the top of the formula can with a clean, wet cloth before opening. Make sure the can opener is clean, also.

Formulas can be purchased in ready-to-feed, concentrate, and powder forms.

Ready-to-feed formulas, as the name suggests, require no mixing so they are very convenient. However, they are also the most expensive type of formula, and opened containers should be discarded after 24 hours. To use, just pour the formula into a sterile bottle, warm, and serve.

Formula concentrates mix easily with water and have a moderate price, but you must follow preparation directions carefully and use the exact amount of water and formula. Like other types of formula, it should be discarded 24 hours after preparation. To use, mix equal amounts of concentrate and sterile water, then warm, and serve.

Formula powders are the least costly type of formula. They are also lightweight, easily portable, and have a long storage life in powdered form. Mix the powdered formula with warm, sterile water to prevent lumps from forming. Formula made from powder should be discarded 24 hours after it is prepared. Powders come in individual packets or cans. To use, follow the directions very carefully. Reconstitute using sterile water; warm, and serve.

Some doctors recommend a fluoride supplement to help with the development of strong teeth. Check if your water (bottled or city-treated) is fluoridated before giving a supplement. Most cities add fluoride to the water supply. Also, check the product label for fluoride if you are using bottled water. Too much fluoride could be harmful to baby.

Never put baby to bed with a bottle. Baby could choke on the milk. Also, the milk or formula tends to pool in baby's mouth and can impair the development of healthy teeth.

Use vitamins and minerals only if your doctor recommends them. Formulas are specially developed with added nutrients.

If your baby is experiencing diarrhea, check with your doctor. You may need to consider an alternate formula.

Only give breastmilk or formula in baby's bottle. Juice and other liquids are best given in a cup. This

> ## Real Parents Say...
>
> The choice of bottle and nipples depend on baby. All three of my children were different.
> *—Sandy, mother of three*
>
> Formula is expensive! Get as many coupons as you can.
> *—Evie, mother of two*
>
> I truly liked powdered formula the best. Less waste, less cost, and very convenient.
> *—Linda, mother of three*

prevents teeth from being overexposed to juices or sugars that can contribute to tooth decay.

Combination Breastmilk and Formula Feeding

For years women have been presented with the options of either breastfeeding or formula feeding. New parents sometimes feel forced into making an all or nothing decision about breastfeeding at or before baby's birth.

Unfortunately for many women, breastfeeding and the workplace may not mesh well. Facing the dilemma of no place or time to express milk during the day, many women quit nursing earlier than they want or never attempt to breastfeed.

Combination breast and formula feeding is an option for those women who enjoy the advantages of nursing and need some of the conveniences of formula feeding. As with full-time breastfeeding, baby nurses when mom is at home. During work hours, your baby receives formula. Mom and baby usually adapt to the new routine within a week or so.

Combination breastmilk and formula feeding may cut full-time formula feeding costs in half. Baby still receives the benefits of breast milk. Mom's body continues to use the extra calories stored during pregnancy. And, combination feeding helps ease some of the anxiety and guilt that mom may feel if she returns to work and quits nursing at the same time.

Tips for Success with Combination Breast and Formula Feeding

If possible, wait to switch to combination feeding until your milk supply is well established. This is usually optimal after 6 or more weeks of breastfeeding. If you need to do this sooner, try to breastfeed baby as often as possible when you are home. Because of the extra energy demands of breastfeeding, you still need to get extra rest.

Try to establish a routine of when baby nurses and when she receives a bottle. This will make the transition go more smoothly, keep milk supply adequate, and help prevent breast engorgement.

Trust your body and believe combination breast and formula feeding can work for you. Relax and give you, your spouse, and baby time to adjust.

Have someone else offer baby the bottle. Doing this keeps baby from becoming confused with feeding methods.

Initially, and after a weekend with baby, you may need to express a small amount of milk at skipped feeding times. This will prevent breast engorgement and keep you more comfortable.

Is My Baby Getting Enough to Eat?

There is no crystal ball or magical device to tell you that your baby is eating enough. However, there are some common signs to look for:

Once your milk comes in if you are breastfeeding, or if you are formula feeding, your baby should wet six to eight times and have several small bowel movements each day. This is usually a good indicator of adequate fluid and nutritional intake.

Most babies lose up to 10 percent of their birth weight during the first week (that's 11 to 12 ounces in a 7 to 8 pound baby). If baby is eating adequately, that weight is usually regained by two weeks of age. After that, you can expect your baby will gain approximately 1/2 to 1 ounce each day for the first 3 months.

There are no exact amounts to feed baby. Each baby is different. Many child nutrition experts recommend feeding on demand and letting baby determine the amount and length of time for each feeding. Baby's intake will change as she goes through varying developmental and growth stages. (The exception to this rule is with premature infants and babies who take a longer time to learn the knack of breastfeeding. Once baby is nursing properly and your milk supply is adequate, let baby determine the feeding schedule.)

Introducing Solids

Breastmilk or formula is the nutrition of choice for baby's first 4 to 6 months. Until then, baby's digestive system is not mature enough to adequately handle solid foods. Some studies indicate that when solids are introduced too early, it can lead to the development of food intolerances, allergies, and possibly childhood obesity.

It seems everyone, often including grandma, can hardly wait to feed baby her first "real" meal. But waiting is what's ideal for baby until she is ready to eat solid foods.

Cherish your infant a little longer and wait until she gives you the developmental cues that she is ready to enter the food zone, such as:

- ❀ She watches with curiosity while you eat or begins to grab for food.
- ❀ She is no longer satisfied with breastmilk or formula and seems hungry for more food, especially between or shortly after feedings.
- ❀ She is at least 4 to 6 months of age.
- ❀ When given solids, she does not reflectively push foods out of her mouth with her tongue. This is an indication

Real Parents Say...

I continued breastfeeding after starting back to work. It works despite any discouraging words you might hear. I always felt nursing was more special after I was away from my baby for awhile. It eases some of the guilt and provided an opportunity for both of us to feel really close.

—Rose, mother of three

Sometimes baby has a hard time adjusting to the bottle. Mine adjusted best when I was not around. Remember, your baby will eventually eat when she gets hungry enough.

—Marie, mother of two

that she is losing her tongue-thrust reflex and is ready to try new foods.

✿ Teeth appear.

✿ Baby demonstrates good head, neck, and upper body control while sitting.

Baby's nutrition is important to her development. Here are some basic guidelines for introducing solids:

Offer an iron-fortified rice cereal mixed with formula or breastmilk as a first food for baby. One to two tablespoons is an ample serving for those first meals. If baby resists the cereal, wait and try again another day.

Gradually increase the amount of cereal offered to four tablespoons and then move on to other cereals.

When offering those first foods, rice cereal is usually recommended as the starter. Then, foods should be introduced slowly to allow baby a chance to experience new tastes. Introducing one food at a time allows you to monitor if your child has any reaction to a specific food. Add a food item and wait 3 to 5 days before adding another food.

Watch for allergic reactions or intolerances to foods. Reactions could include diarrhea, vomiting, a rash, or wheezing. Foods that infants are sometimes sensitive to include citrus fruit, citrus juice (like orange and grapefruit), fish, eggs, peanut butter, and cow's milk.

If you introduce a food and baby does not like it, wait a while and try again at a later date. The more familiar baby becomes with a food, the more likely she is to eat it.

When introducing solids into baby's diet, focus on balance. Portion sizes and specific types of foods don't need to be exact. Offer a variety of food choices and your child will receive the nutrients she needs for a healthy body.

Introduction of solids is recommended as follows:

Age	Food
4 to 6 months	Iron fortified infant cereals (rice, oatmeal, mixed)
5 to 7 months	Strained vegetables, cracked, dry cereals
6 to 8 months	Strained fruits and juices
7 to 9 months	Strained meats
8 to 12 months	Strained or mashed hardcooked egg yolk, soft table foods, and ground or finely diced meat

Check commercial baby food labels for salt and sugar content. Some products have more sugar than fruit. Avoid cobblers and desserts. These tend to be loaded with sugar.

Always serve juice in a cup. Giving fruit juice in a bottle can allow it to stay in contact with baby's teeth too long. It may cause tooth decay known as Nursing Bottle Syndrome. Also, since juice is sweeter than milk, it may be difficult to get baby to take milk from the bottle if juice is also offered in a bottle.

Make mealtime fun. Be creative with food and offer foods baby can easily handle herself. Finger foods like crackers, cold cereals, triangle-shaped sandwiches, and mini muffins are great choices.

Feed baby before she gets overtired or overhungry. You will both have a more enjoyable experience.

Expect an occasional mess. Let baby hold a spoon. Offer her finger foods like cut up bananas and crackers when possible. Babies love to touch their food and discover the texture. Cover the floor with a feeding mat, keep a wash cloth handy, use a large bib, and relax. The only way baby can master her feeding skills is with practice.

Keep baby's mealtime short. Once baby is finished eating, allow her to nap or play. Long, drawn-out meals typically end with a fussy baby, frustrated parent, and messy floor. There is plenty of time in the future for formal dinners and Miss Manners etiquette. As your child gets older, mealtime can be extended.

How Much Food Is Enough?

Children, like adults, need a balanced diet for energy, growth, and good health. Your eating habits will far exceed any rules you set about when and where to eat. Your child will observe you closely; if you serve and eat balanced meals, it is likely that your child will do the same. It is impossible to expect your youngster to try a variety of vegetables if you refuse to eat anything besides peas and carrots.

The Food Guide Pyramid provides a simple eating guide for children as well as adults. Remember, this is only a guide. Your child's hunger is the most important indicator of how much she wants and needs to eat.

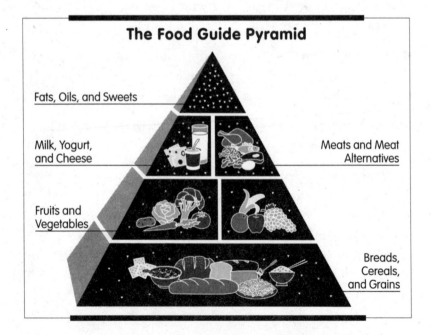

The Food Guide Pyramid

Fats, Oils, and Sweets

Milk, Yogurt, and Cheese

Meats and Meat Alternatives

Fruits and Vegetables

Breads, Cereals, and Grains

Serving sizes for young children and toddlers are less than those for adults.

Food Group	Toddlers (12 to 36 months)	Preschoolers (3 to 6 years)
Meat & meat alternatives	2-3 servings daily (1 serving=1 oz)	2-3 servings daily (1 serving=1 1/2 oz)
Fruits and vegetables	5 or more servings daily (1 serving=2 Tbsp)	5 or more servings daily (1 serving=1/4 cup)
Breads, cereals, and grains	6 or more servings daily (1 serving=1/4 to 1/2 slice or 1/4 to 1/2 cup)	6 or more servings daily (1 serving=1/2 slice or 1/2 cup)
Milk, yogurt, and cheese	3-4 servings daily (1 serving=1/2 cup)	3-4 servings daily (1 serving=3/4 cup)

Safety Tips

To keep baby safe from burns, choking, and food-related illnesses:

Do not heat baby's bottle in a microwave oven. Microwaving overheats milk in the center of the bottle. Even if the bottle feels comfortable to your touch, hot spots in the milk can scald the inside of baby's mouth.

When introducing solids and feeding young children, avoid giving any foods that are round. These types of foods can lodge in baby's throat and cause choking. Carrot coins, hot dogs (always cut lengthwise), peanuts, nuts, popcorn, raisins, hard candies, grapes, peas, celery, fruit with skin, peanut butter, and mini bagels are examples of foods that could cause choking.

Serve only quality, fresh food to your child. Never give your child a food that may be old, stale, or tainted with harmful bacteria. Food poisoning can be very dangerous to a child. If you are ever in doubt about a food, throw it out. This is an important precaution to prevent foodborne illness.

Refrigerate food when not in use, especially meats, milk, dairy products, fish, poultry, and eggs.

Never give honey to a child under 1 year of age. Honey contains a bacteria that is harmless to adults, but can cause botulism (a fatal form of food poisoning) in children.

Cook all food thoroughly. Only serve well-done meat to your child.

Heat leftovers to 165°F for at least 10 minutes. This time and temperature kills most harmful bacteria that may be present in leftovers and could cause food poisoning.

Keep leftovers in your refrigerator for no more than 3 days.

Use foods before their expiration date.

Do not use commercial foods if the container is bulging or the product seal is broken.

Serve prepared baby food from a dish, not a jar. The unused portion in the dish should be discarded. The unused portion in the jar should be used within 24 hours.

Discard any prepared, opened formula that is not used within 24 hours.

Always wash your hands before preparing food and anytime after you have handled raw meat or eggs. This helps prevent the spread of salmonella and other bacteria that contribute to food illnesses.

Keep your kitchen area clean. Use an antibacterial agent or soap and water for washing off countertops and cooking surfaces. Bacteria has a harder time growing in a clean area.

Never let your baby or young child consume foods that are uncooked or contain raw eggs. Make sure all meats that you serve your child are cooked to the well-done stage. This is an important precaution to prevent foodborne illness.

Have your water tested for lead. Some water supplies or homes with old pipes can introduce lead into baby's drinking water. Lead can be harmful to baby's growth and development.

To prevent fluoride toxicity, check with your doctor before giving fluoride drops to your child if your water is fluoridated. Too much fluoride can cause mottling of baby's teeth.

Goat's milk is very low in folic acid. It should not be given to baby before 6 months of age. Check with your doctor first.

Smart Parents Do

Supplemental water is usually not necessary for baby. Whether breastfed or bottlefed, baby usually does not require additional water during the day. The exception to this may be in very hot weather or if baby has a fever.

Feed baby on demand instead of following a strict schedule. Feed her based on *her* schedule, and let her eat until she tells you that she is full. Before you know it, baby will settle into his or her routine.

When baby cries, identify the cause of the cry. Babies are not hungry every time they cry. Your child may be wet, tired, bored, or in need of some cuddling. Check for these things before automatically offering milk or food.

Feed baby breastmilk or infant formula until age 1. Cow's milk lacks adequate amounts of vitamin C and iron. It also is difficult for babies to digest. The high protein and mineral content can stress an infant's kidneys and lead to dehydration.

Give regular, whole cow's milk from age 1 until at least age 2 unless your physician specifically states otherwise. Babies need fat in their diets to maintain normal weight gain. Whole milk helps the body absorb vitamins A and D. Also, skim and low-fat milks have a higher content of protein and minerals and can be harder for baby to digest; they also stress the kidneys.

Budget Helpers

Breastfeed if possible and you can save over $300 in formula cost during the first 6 months alone.

If you use formula, ask your physician, nurse-midwife, or hospital personnel for formula samples. They often receive cases of samples from formula companies and are happy to pass these on to patients.

Use coupons, coupons, coupons. If you use commercially prepared baby foods or infant formulas make a commitment to using a coupon with every purchase. Shop on double coupon days if possible.

Ask friends and family to clip and save coupons for you.

Write formula and baby food companies and ask for coupons and to be put on their mailing lists. They often send you great coupons, gifts, and rebate information.

Save those labels and your receipts. Companies often offer rebates or free formula and baby food if you send in receipts and labels.

If you have time, make your own baby food by blending or grinding cooked or canned fruits and vegetables. Pour the blended product into ice cube trays or small sandwich bags. Freeze for up to 2 months. Thaw, reheat, and serve.

Instead of traditional baby food, give baby table foods mashed to a consistency she can tolerate. Mashed bananas, regular applesauce, mashed pears, mashed potatoes, squash, and crackers all make acceptable foods for the first year. Using these regular foods the rest of the family eats can help keep your food costs down. Table foods also tend to be lower in sugar and sodium content.

Check out Toys-R-Us or wholesale discount warehouses like Sam's Club for baby food. They often have great prices.

Invest in only one or two baby bottles until you determine which style baby prefers. Some babies like the Playtex-style nurser, others prefer Evenflo, and still others prefer the traditional straight nipple and bottle style. Initially, one or two bottles will be enough, preventing you from purchasing a style baby does not like. Save your receipts in case you need to return unused bottles.

Buy feeding spoons, sippy cups, bibs, and other feeding supplies at a discount store or Toys-R-Us. These stores tend to carry products at a lower price than the baby specialty shops.

If cost is a significant factor and you choose not to breastfeed, consider making your own formula. Many parents do, and the cost is about one-third of that of purchased formula. However, the formula is nutritionally deficient and you must speak with your doctor

> **Real Parents Say...**
>
> I made a lot of my own baby food. I purchased 1-gallon cans of peas, beans, peaches, and pears (in water or juice pack), blended each, and froze it in small jars or ice cube trays. Then I stored the frozen food in freezer bags. It worked well for me and saved us some money, too.
> —*Karen, mother of four*

about giving iron and vitamin C supplements to baby. Also, making your own formula takes extra time and more sanitation precautions. If you choose to make your own formula or use it in combination breast-bottle feeding, the American Academy of Pediatrics recommends:

1. Check with your doctor before making your own formula.
2. Supplement baby's feedings with vitamin C and iron.
3. Have baby checked regularly to ensure normal growth and development.
4. Follow the recipe exactly every time you make the formula.

The recipe for a homemade infant formula is included in *The American Academy of Pediatrics' Caring for Your Baby and Young Child: Birth to Age Five* (see Resource section). The recipe for the homemade formula is not included here because you should carefully discuss the option with baby's physician before considering it.

"Graduate" type baby foods like miniature or baby carrots and 2-inch hot dogs in a jar are costly. If baby can eat these foods, she is probably ready to master an assortment of table foods.

Nursing shirts and even nursing bras may not be necessary. The nursing top selection is similar to the maternity selection. Save your money and choose comfortable clothing that pulls up easily or buttons down the front. Forget zipper backs for now! Many women choose nursing bras for convenience. Expect to pay two times what a normal bra costs!

Nursing pads are necessary for the first few months. You can purchase either cloth or disposable. Try writing Curity, Gerber, Evenflo, and other baby care companies and asking for samples of their nursing pads. This allows you to try different brands before you buy a large box of a brand that doesn't work for you!

Creating a Healthy Feeding Environment

Feeding and eating can and should be a fun experience for the entire family. Granted, there will be days when your patience is tested to the limit, but overall dining together should be enjoyable.

As your child's primary teacher, it is your role to help her develop a healthy relationship with food. There is a growing epidemic of eating problems in our country ranging from the life-threatening eating disorders of anorexia and bulimia to all-time high levels of obesity. Many of these food-related problems involve misconceptions and struggles with food. To help your child develop a positive attitude and relationship with food:

Teach your child that all foods are good in moderation. Avoid labeling foods "good" and "bad."

Offer small amounts of food to your child at a time. Too much food on a plate can be overwhelming to a young child. Encourage her to sample everything and let her know it is okay if she does not like everything she tries.

Provide a predictable eating routine. As parent, you play an important role in deciding when mealtime is and what foods will be served; your child determines how much she will eat. See the Resource section for additional resources.

Examine your own eating and exercise habits. Do you make healthy food choices? Do you enjoy eating? Do you offer and eat balanced meals or are you a TV and TV dinner junkie? Are you overly concerned about your weight and looks? Do you make comments about people's size? Do you incorporate a regular walk, bike ride, or other form of physical activity into your family routine or do you promote the couch potato image? Remember, your child observes you at all times. She will learn many of her lifetime habits from you.

Schedule "kids' choice" night. Let your child select the supper menu once a week. You may need to offer suggestions to balance it out, but your child will enjoy being involved during meal preparation time.

Avoid the "clean plate" rule. For starters, clean plates do not save starving children in a faraway country. More importantly, it teaches your child not to listen to her body's cues about eating when she is hungry and stopping when she is full. The clean plate rule simply seems to make overeating more likely in the future and sets up parent-child food struggles. Rather, teach your child to take moderate portions and ask for seconds if she's still hungry.

Do not use food as a reward or punishment. Food is fuel for the body. Discipline using food only sets up control struggles over food later in life. Discipline your child using timeouts or other techniques. Avoid sending your child confusing messages about food by keeping food choices and discipline issues separate.

Do not use food as a means of comfort or as a way of avoiding feelings. All too often food, chocolate and sweets for example, is used to comfort hurt feelings. Talk with your child about her feelings. Teach her to express her feelings instead of hiding them around food.

Encourage water instead of soft drinks as a thirst quencher.

Give your child healthy food choice options. A Happy Meal from McDonald's now and then can be fun. However, these meals can be purchased with milk instead of a soft drink. Choosing milk can make the meal a healthier lunch and there is no reason a two year old even needs to know soda is an option.

Mealtime should be fun. Encourage your young child to participate in making the meal, setting the table, and helping with the dishes.

Be adventurous and routinely try new foods. If your child sees you willing to sample new things, she will follow your lead. Practice trying a new food or recipe each week. This allows your entire family to share in the tasting of new foods.

Avoid dieting. Dieting has become a national obsession. Studies indicate 95 percent of all diets do not work; in fact, most people regain more weight than they lose. Dieting is not uncommon among eight and nine year olds. This early focus on weight and body size often leads to a lower sense of self esteem, especially in girls. Set a good example for your child by focusing on healthy food and lifestyle choices instead of encouraging dieting in your home.

Breast Pump and Breastfeeding Supplies

Medela Inc., PO Box 660, Mettenry IL 60051-0660; 800-435-8316

Engnell's Mother's Touch One Hand Breast Pump; 708-519-7730

Books

The Complete Book of Breast Feeding by M. Eiger and S. Olds, Workman Publishing, New York

The Nursing Mother's Companion by K. Huggins, Harvard Common Press, Boston

Nursing Your Baby by K. Pryor and G. Pryor, Pocket Books, New York

Breast Feeding Today: A Mother's Companion by C. Woessner, J. Lauwers, and B. Bernard, Avery Publishing Group, Garden City Park

Breast Feeding and the Working Mother by D. Mason and D. Ingersoll, St. Martin's Press

Breast Feeding: Getting Breast Feeding Right for You by M. Renfrew, C. Fisher, and S. Arms, Celestial Arts, Berkeley, CA

The Womanly Art of Breast Feeding, LaLeche League, 9616 Minneapolis Ave, Franklin Park, IL 60131

How Should I Feed My Child: From Pregnancy to Preschool by S. Nissenberg, M. Bogle, E. Langholz, and A. Wright, Chronimed Publishing, Minneapolis

How to Get Your Kids to Eat...But Not Too Much by Ellyn Satter, Bull Publishing Co., Palo Alto, CA

Child of Mine: Feeding With Love and Good Sense by Ellen Satter, Bull Publishing Co., Palo Alto, CA

Caring for Your Baby and Young Child by The American Academy of Pediatrics, Bantam Books, New York

The Mayo Clinic Complete Book of Pregnancy and Baby's First Year, William Morrow and Company, New York

Breast Feeding: The Art of Mothering, A book and video set, by The American Academy of Pediatrics, PO Box 927, Elk Grove Village, IL 60009-0927; 800-433-9016

**R
e
s
o
u
r
c
e
s**

Brochures

For a great informational pamphlet on infant feeding: **"Airplane, Choo-Choo, and Other Games Parents Play,"** National Dairy Council, 6300 North River Road, Rosemont, IL 60018-4233

"Expressing Breast Milk" and other pamphlets on nursing: Childbirth Graphics Ltd., 1210 Culver Road, Rochester, NY 14609

"Starting Solids," National Association of Pediatric Nurse Associates and Practitioners, 1101 Kings Highway North, Suite 206, Cherry Hill, NJ 08034-1931

"Thinking About Breast Feeding?" Lactation Associates, 254 Conant Road, Weston, MA 02193-1756

"Broccoli or Brownies," Flintstone Vitamins, 444 N. Michigan Avenue, Suite 1600, Chicago, IL 60611

Organizations

The American Dietetic Association, National Center for Nutrition and Dietetics, 216 W. Jackson Blvd., Chicago, IL 60604; 800-366-1655

The American Academy of Pediatrics, 141 Northwest Pt. Blvd., Elk Grove Village, IL 60007-1098

For information on food and safety regulations, drugs, pesticides, and cosmetics, contact: **Food and Drug Administration,** Office of Consumer Affairs, 5600 Fisher Lane, Rockville, MD 20857; 301-443-3170

For information about good eating during pregnancy and childhood, contact: **National Dairy Council,** 6300 N. River Road, Rosemont, IL 60018-4233; 800-426-8271

For information on child and preschool nutrition programs as well as food and nutrition databases, write: **U.S. Department of Agriculture, Food and Nutrition Information Center,** National Agricultural Library, 10301 Baltimore Blvd., Beltsville, MD 20705; 301-504-5917

Breastfeeding Support

To locate a lactation consultant, call your local hospital or write: **International Lactation Consultant Association;** 201 Brown Avenue, Evanston, IL 60202-3601; 708-260-8874

For breastfeeding counseling contact: **Nursing Mothers Counsel, Inc.,** PO Box 50063, Palo Alto, CA 94303; 408-272-1448

For mother-to-mother support and breastfeeding resource materials write: **LaLeche League,** 9616 Minneapolis Avenue, Franklin Park, IL 60131; 800-LaLeche or 800-525-3243

Lactation Associates, 254 Conant Road, Weston, MA 02193-1756

Newsletters and Nutrition Columns

Pineapple Press (food and nutrition subscription newsletter for parents), PO Box 2171, Sausalito, CA 94966; 415-381-7774

The Washington Parent (nutrition in the 90's column), 5604 Bent Branch Road, Bethesda, MD 20816

For Coupons, Samples, and Information

Earth's Best, Inc., PO Box 887, Pond Lane, Middlebury, VT 05753

Heinz Baby Food, PO Box 57, Pittsburgh, PA 15230-0057; 800-USA-Baby

Gerber, 445 State Street, Freemont, MI 49413; 800-4-GERBER

Ross Laboratories (maker of Similac), Columbus, OH 43216

Mead Johnson (maker of Enfamil), Evansville, IN 47721

Nestle Food Corporation (maker of Carnation products), Glendale, CA 91203

Evenflo Products Company, 771 North Freedom Street, Ravenna, OH 44266; 800-233-BABY or 800-356-BABY (in Ohio)

Playtex Family Products, PO Box 1400, Dover, DE 19901; 800-222-0453 or 800-624-0825 (in New Jersey)

The First Years, Avon, MA 02322-1171; 800-533-6708

Resources

CHAPTER TEN

The Medicine Chest—
Knowing When to Go to the Doctor

"Parenthood remains the greatest single preserve of the amateur."
—Alvin Toffler

As a parent, you will occasionally encounter health situations where your child needs to be seen by a physician. Sometimes it is for well-baby checkups, and at other times it is due to illness. As you get to know your baby you will also be better able to judge when he is ill and needs a physician's care. (You may choose to have your baby's care provided by a family practice physician, pediatrician, physician assistant, nurse practitioner, or other health care provider. For simplicity, I have referred to this care giver as baby's physician.)

Never take any unnecessary chances with your baby's health. This chapter is not intended to replace the medical advice of a physician. If you feel uncertain or uneasy about your baby's health, contact your physician. Don't feel silly or guilty about asking questions or seeking medical advice; your baby is your most precious responsibility.

Your physician realizes new par-

Necessity Checklist

- ✿ Thermometer
- ✿ Fever-reducing medication
- ✿ Oral electrolyte replacement solution
- ✿ Bandages
- ✿ Antibiotic salve
- ✿ Baby's illness record or some method to track illnesses
- ✿ Health records
- ✿ Bulb syringe

ents are less experienced with baby care and is available to assist you. He or she can help you learn about baby's health, growth, and development as you begin your exciting parenting journey.

A good pediatric reference book is also a valuable and handy resource. The American Academy of Pediatric's *Caring for Your Baby and Young Child: Birth to Age Five* and *The Mayo Clinic Complete Book of Pregnancy and Baby's First Year* are excellent resources. Complete and comprehensive, these books cover everything from developmental skills to common childhood illnesses. Written by the nation's leading child experts, these books also include baby care guidelines and helpful health tips.

A reference manual does not replace your physician's care and advice, but it can help you distinguish between a case of the chicken pox or the measles, identify important times to seek medical attention, and provide simple, safe advice for treating mild illnesses. It is a good idea for every household with small children to have one of these types of manuals.

When to Go to the Doctor

At one time or another, you and baby will make a trip to the doctor. It is sometimes hard to know when to wait and when to go for medical care. Before you leave the hospital, or at a well-baby check, ask your doctor about situations in which you should seek medical attention. He or she can also advise you on common child illnesses to expect, as well as basic treatments. In addition, you may want to refer to one of the pediatric guides mentioned earlier for signs of illness. These are symptoms or conditions that indicate your baby may need to be seen. Remember, contact baby's physician any time you feel uncomfortable about the way your child is acting or feeling.

Medical Records

Keeping accurate records of your child's illnesses, injuries, doctor's visits, and immunizations is very important. Even though your medical clinic does this for you, you should keep your own set of records. You never know when you may need the information.

If you move, you may need to have your records transferred. When your child enters school, you will need proof of his immunizations. A second set of your child's health history can prove a convenience, as well as a backup, in case original records are accidentally destroyed or lost.

Another reason to keep up-to-date health records is to assist your physician when your child becomes ill. Remember, even the best trained, skilled physician cannot know your child like you do. Information you provide is helpful to your physician in making an accurate diagnosis and recommending the best treatment.

Your child's health is an important responsibility. Keeping good records will make your job easier. The importance of these records should not be underestimated. Computer programs and other record-keeping systems are listed in the Resource section at the end of this chapter.

In addition to long-term health records, it is best to write down information whenever you notice baby is not acting himself. Because you never know when the common cold could turn into a bad case of bronchitis, it's best to always write down any abnormal signs or symptoms.

A calendar or note pad both work well for tracking baby's illness. Even brief notes like cranky, eating less, and developed runny nose with yellow mucus, can be helpful for recalling how the illness began. Once again, the more information you can provide to your physician, the better he will be able to treat your baby. Tracking baby's symptoms can also be helpful in deciding when to go to the physician.

Immunizations and Well-Baby Clinics

Some of your child's physician visits will be for health checks instead of illnesses. Before you leave the hospital with your bundle of joy you will probably be encouraged to make a well-baby appointment with your baby's physician. Most insurance companies cover these routine checkups. Ask your insurance agent about this benefit. Well-baby checks are important because they:

Allow your baby's physician to monitor your baby's growth. If there is a deviation from normal growth and development, it can be found early. The sooner a potential growth problem is detected, the greater the chance it can be corrected.

Provide a time and/or reminder for baby's immunizations to be given.

Provide a time and environment for education. Your baby's physician can tell you what growth and development stages to expect and how to safeproof your home to prevent accidents.

Allow an opportunity for you to have your infant health questions answered. Between visits, keep a list of questions you wish to talk with your baby's physician about. This enables you to make the most of your appointment. This is an educational opportunity to learn about any child health concerns you may have.

> ### Real Parents Say...
>
> If watching baby receive his shots is too traumatic for you, have your spouse take baby for his shots. It will be easier for everyone involved. I cried so much with our daughter's first shots that I terrified her more than the shot did.
>
> —*Anne, mother of two*

A typical well-baby schedule includes visits at 2 to 4 weeks, 2 months, 4 months, 6 months, 9 months, 12 months, 18 months, 2 years, and once a year thereafter. Frequency may vary with each individual physician. Premature infants may require more frequent checks initially.

Immunizations—More Than an Ounce of Prevention

Baby shots are probably harder on many parents than on baby. Discuss any concerns about the shots with your baby's doctor. Many outbreaks of fatal or debilitating childhood illnesses such as polio and smallpox have virtually been eliminated by immunizations. Babies stay healthier and have less chance of dying from a childhood illness because of these routine vaccinations.

The benefits of baby shots far outweigh the risks, so it is necessary to have your child immunized. In addition, your child must have proof that his immunizations are current before he can enter most school systems.

To make your baby's shots a safer experience:

Discuss baby's health status with your health professional before the shots are given. Let him or her know if your child has had a recent cold, flu, or infection; is not developing properly; has a history of seizures; has a history of reactions to previous shots (or a sibling with previous reactions), or has any immune problems related to cancer, AIDS, medications, or other therapies.

Discuss with your doctor the option of giving your baby a dose of pain reliever like acetaminophen (Tylenol) 30 minutes before receiving the immunizations. For some babies this helps decrease any pain and discomfort associated with the shot.

Make the immunization process as calm and nontraumatic as possible for your child. Babies are very perceptive. If you are tense and nervous, baby will be tense; if you are relaxed, baby will be more relaxed, too.

Watch baby carefully for at least 2 days following his immunizations. It is not uncommon for your child to develop a slight lump where the shot was given. However, if you notice any of the following symptoms, contact your physician or emergency room immediately.[1] If baby:

✿ has a rectal temperature of 105°F (39.4°C) or above. Some vaccine manufacturers recommend contacting the doctor if baby's temperature rises to 103°F (38.7°C). Ask your health professional before you leave the clinic. Ask your doctor for specific guidelines for children under 6 months of age.

✿ has an unusual, high-pitched cry

✿ sleeps much longer than usual and is hard to awaken

✿ cries for 3 hours or more at a time

✿ collapses or becomes blue, pale, limp, or unresponsive

✿ experiences seizures or convulsions (usually resulting from a high fever)

The Sabin (polio) vaccine is one virus that passes into baby's stools for several days. This can infect a nonimmunized individual who comes in contact with the stool. Because of this, it is important to wash your hands carefully after changing baby.

If your child is allergic to eggs, notify your baby's physician or health professional before receiving the MMR (measles, mumps, rubella) vaccine. The vaccine is manufactured using eggs and could cause a reaction in your child.

Keep your immunization records up to date. Record any reactions to the shot. Take these notes with you to your next scheduled immunization appointment.

What to Do When Baby Has a Fever

Very few babies get through their first year without having a fever. A fever is often the body's natural response to an infection. A fever is not an illness. Rather, it is usually a positive sign that the body is fighting some type of infection. Fevers can also be caused by overdressing baby, baby's reaction to a hot room, or by baby not drinking enough fluid.

Average body temperatures vary from person to person (including baby to baby). A rectal temperature above 100°F

(38°C) may indicate a fever. If you suspect your child is ill or has a fever:

1.Observe baby. Is he or she happy and playful or cranky and fussy?

2.Take baby's temperature if you still suspect an illness. The pioneer hand-to-forehead method is not accurate and extremely difficult to relay to the doctor on the telephone. For a child under the age of 3 or 4, it is best to take a rectal temperature.[2] If baby has been active, have him rest quietly for 15 to 30 minutes before taking the temperature. Running, playing, and other activity can raise baby's body temperature.

3.Contact your child's physician if you have any concerns about the fever. Your child may need to be seen if:[3]

- ✿ A rectal temperature of 100.2°F (37.9° C) or greater in a baby 3 months of age or younger.
- ✿ A rectal temperature of 101°F (38.3°C) in a child 3 to 6 months of age.
- ✿ Your child runs a fever (no matter how mild) for more than 3 days.
- ✿ Your child shows signs of delirium (sees objects that are not there), confusion, or hallucinations.
- ✿ Your child experiences convulsions, twitching, or shaking with fever.

Your baby's physician will discuss with you ways to bring down the fever. Do not give baby aspirin to treat a fever. It has been associated with Reye Syndrome, stomach upset, and gastrointestinal bleeding. Therefore, most doctors recommend acetaminophen (like Tylenol or Pandol) if medication is indicated to bring down a fever. You may also want to refer to a pediatric reference guide for other treatment tips.

It is very important that you tell your doctor or nurse how you took your baby's temperature. For example, you may call and say, "Doctor, Katie's temperature is 103°F rectally."

An oral temperature of 98.6°F is considered normal. However, this is simply an average. Normal for your baby may vary slightly. A rectal temperature tends to run about one degree hotter and an armpit temperature one degree cooler than the reference oral temperature. You can use this chart to help make conversions when reading literature and medication bottles.

Temperature Conversion Reference Chart

Oral					
°F	98.6	100	101	102	103
°C	37	37.8	38.3	38.9	39.4
Rectal					
°F	99.6	101	102	103	104
°C	37.5	38.3	38.9	39.4	40
Axillary (Arm Pit)					
°F	97.6	99	100	101	102
°C	36.4	37.2	37.8	38.3	38.9

What Type of Thermometer Should I Buy?

Having a sick child is worrisome for any parent. Anxiety and frustration only seem to heighten as you attempt to take baby's temperature. Obviously, manufacturers have figured this out and have tried to remedy the problem with a recent array of temperature-taking gadgets.

Now available with the traditional oral and rectal thermometers are the highly technical digital varieties—ear, forehead, and even pacifier models. So, which is best? It simply depends on you, baby, and how much money you want to spend to take baby's temperature.

Oral Thermometer Used to take temperatures by mouth. Available in the traditional glass style ($1 to $3) or the newer digital versions ($10 or more). Oral thermometers are difficult to use until child is about age 4 or 5 and can hold the thermometer under his tongue.

Rectal Thermometer Similar to the oral thermometer, only the end is short and stubby to protect against breaking in the rectum. This type of thermometer ($1 to $3) is easy and most accurate to use with a baby or young child. To use:

1. Coat the end with petroleum or KY jelly or cover with a prelubricated plastic shield.
2. Shake down glass thermometer to below the 96°F (36°C) mark or clear the digital thermometer.
3. With child lying on his stomach, insert the thermometer 1/2 to 1 inch—no deeper—into the anal opening.
4. Hold in place for 2 minutes (or until reading appears for the digital style).

Axillary/Armpit Thermometer Use an oral thermometer to take temperature under the armpit. This method is OK to use in a pinch, but it is less accurate than the oral or rectal method. (However, some days you just take what you can get!)

To use:

1. Shake down glass thermometer to below the 96°F (36°C) mark or clear the digital thermometer.
2. Place bulb in middle of armpit against bare skin; hold child's arm against his side.
3. Wait 3 minutes for accurate reading.

Ear or Tympanic This thermometer allows your child's temperature to be taken quickly, by inserting the tip of the thermoscan into the ear canal.

The device, which resembles a rectal temperature, must be positioned properly so it gives an accurate reading. Practice on your child

Real Parents Say...

Always completely shake down the thermometer before using. We called the emergency department one evening when our warm, but not fussy, infant was running a 103°F temperature. Upon instructions (from a very calm doctor) to recheck her temperature, we realized we had not shaken down the new thermometer. We chalked the experience up to lessons learned and one of our many "new parents' most embarrassing moments."

—*Marie and Michael, parents of two*

when he is well so you can obtain an accurate reading when your child is ill.

Cost: $100 to $120. For more information, call Thermoscan at 800-327-8367.

Forehead Thermometer An inexpensive plastic strip is placed on the child's forehead for 1 minute until a reading appears. As with the armpit method, it works in a pinch. It is inaccurate, but it can at least give you a ballpark range if baby is running a temperature.

Pacifier Thermometer A thermometer designed like a pacifier, which needs to remain in the mouth for 5 minutes. Cost: $15. For information, call Dubby at 800-531-5486.

Preventing Dehydration

Babies and young children can quickly become dehydrated without an adequate fluid intake. Vomiting and diarrhea are the two most common causes of dehydration in young children. Both conditions can lead to rapid fluid loss. (Another, less frequent occurrence, failure by baby to nurse properly, can also cause dehydration in infants. For helpful breastfeeding tips, see Chapter Nine.)

Dehydration can best be prevented by making sure your child gets plenty of fluids during times of illness, fever, vomiting, diarrhea, and play in hot weather. You should suspect dehydration and contact your physician if your child:[4]

- ✿ urinates less frequently (wets fewer than six diapers per day)
- ✿ plays less than usual
- ✿ has a sunken soft spot (anterior fontanel)
- ✿ has a parched dry mouth and possibly dry lips
- ✿ has fewer tears when crying

If you notice any of the following symptoms of severe dehydration, have baby seen by a doctor immediately:[5]

✿ a change in your child's behavior such as listlessness
      or extreme fussiness
✿ sunken eyes
✿ excessive sleeping with difficulty awakening
✿ wrinkled skin
✿ cool, discolored hands or feet
✿ goes several hours without urinating

Encouraging adequate fluids is the best way to prevent dehydration. Your physician will advise you how to best handle the situation. Though good nutrition choices are important, fluids in any form, even pop or popsicles, should be your main goal when baby is ill. As a guide, a child needs a minimum of 1 to 1 1/2 ounces of fluid per pound of body weight each day. For example, an 11 pound baby needs a minimum of 15 ounces of fluid per day. If fluid losses such as vomiting, diarrhea, or excess perspiration from a high fever have occurred, more replacement fluid is necessary.

Fun Fluids

When your child is sick, you may need to be creative to entice him to take extra fluids. Some kids will easily drink Pedialyte and other electrolyte replacement formulas. Others are more particular and prefer the bubble gum, orange, and punch flavors available. Still others need a more clever disguise.

If you are having a hard time getting fluids into a fussy baby or child, give these tasty liquids a try:

✿ Start with popsicles, and later offer juice bars. Avoid
      the sugar free varieties for now. Your child needs
      the calories to get well.
✿ 7-Up, Slice, or Sprite are often easily tolerated.
✿ Sugar water made with 1/2 teaspoon sugar in 4
      ounces of water
✿ Flavored gelatin before it sets up (while it's still liquid)

- Pedialyte or other electrolyte replacement solution, or rice water
- Pedialyte or other electrolyte replacement solution mixed with 7-Up, Cherry 7-Up, Slice, or Sprite
- Clear soup broth
- Gelatin in a variety of flavors. Its cool, slippery texture is easy for a child to eat
- Diluted mild fruit juices like apple, grape, peach, pear, and apricot. Mix 2 to 3 ounces of water with 4 ounces of juice
- The thick syrup from canned fruit can sometimes help alleviate nausea and vomiting symptoms. Peach, pear, and fruit cocktail juice are the most effective. Avoid pineapple and other acidic juices. For children under age 2, give 1 teaspoon of fruit syrup every 15 minutes until nausea and vomiting subsides. If symptoms persist for more than 90 minutes, discontinue and call your physician.
- Sherbet or fruit ices
- Ice cream, ice milk, or frozen yogurt if vomiting or an upset stomach is not a problem
- Continue to breastfeed even if baby is vomiting or has diarrhea. Breastmilk is easily digested and baby needs the fluid.

Sudden Infant Death Syndrome (SIDS)

Every new parent at one time or another quietly checks to make sure their sleeping child is breathing. As a new parent, you may feel like you are doing this every minute.

Sudden Infant Death Syndrome (SIDS) awareness among new parents is high. SIDS is defined as a medically unexplained death of a baby under the age of 1. This mysterious phenomenon claims the lives of approximately 6,000 sleeping babies in America each year.[6] Preemies and infants with respiratory problems or nervous system disorders may be at a higher risk.

Though no one knows exactly how or why SIDS strikes, experts suggest these safety measures to reduce the risk.[7]

Discuss with your physician whether baby should sleep on his tummy, back, or side. Substantial research indicates placing a baby on his back or side reduces the risk of SIDS. Premature infants with breathing problems, infants who vomit often and infants with upper airway obstructions are exceptions. Be sure to discuss proper positioning with your physician.

Choose a firm mattress. Do not lay baby on a lamb's wool pad, fluffy comforter, or waterbed. Each of these items is a suffocation hazard.

Do not place pillows in baby's crib, cradle, or bassinet.

Avoid overheating baby's room or overdressing baby in sleepwear. Studies have found an increased risk of SIDS when the room is too warm or baby is overclothed. Keep the temperature in baby's room so it feels comfortable to you.

Do not smoke and do not allow smoking in your home. Studies indicate the risk of SIDS increases for infants whose mothers smoked during pregnancy as well as for infants whose mothers smoke around them.[8]

Breastfeed if possible. Breastfeeding helps ward off infections and may consequently reduce the risk of SIDS.

Seek good, early prenatal care. Women who receive prenatal care are less likely to deliver low birth weight babies, which can be a risk factor for SIDS.

Use a safe crib. (See Chapter Four on crib safety.)

Try to plan pregnancies at least one year after baby's birth. This allows mom adequate time to fully recover. A healthy baby starts with a healthy mom.[9]

Though there is no guarantee your child will not be afflicted by SIDS, these prevention tips can make baby's sleep safer. And, yours more peaceful.

Safety Tips

Every child will have an accident now and then. You can not prevent every one, but you can make your baby's environment as safe as possible. Listed here are some tips to prevent medical-related accidents.

Never leave a child unattended in a closed car, even for a few minutes. Also, be careful not to overdress baby in hot, humid weather. Each year, babies needlessly die from heat stroke.

If a child's body temperature rises to 105°F due to climate, the temperature must quickly be reduced. Fanning, sponging with cool water, and movement to a cool place can all help. Seek emergency attention immediately.[10]

Dispose of all outdated or unused medications by flushing them down the toilet.

Keep all medications and alcohols locked and out of baby's reach. This includes mouthwashes.

Rinse medicine droppers for at least 1 minute with hot water before placing it back in the medicine bottle. If the dropper is shared between children, boil it in water for 2 to 3 minutes before replacing it in the bottle to prevent the transfer of germs.

Keep all liquid medicine in the refrigerator. The cold temperature slows the growth of bacteria.

Make sure all medication and vitamin bottles have child-resistant caps. Do not allow your child to play with the medicine. As few as 6 iron pills can be toxic to a child.

Smart Parents Do

Take a course in first aid and infant and child CPR. Knowing what to do in an emergency situation will help you react more intelligently and calmly.

Stock up on standard medical supplies including pediatric acetaminophen liquid (such as Tylenol or the generic equivalent) or pediatric ibuprofen (like Motrin), a thermometer, rubbing alcohol, a diaper rash ointment, bandaids for small cuts, a bottle of oral electrolyte maintenance solution (such as Pedialyte or generic brand), and saline nose drops and/or a bulb syringe for unplugging stuffy noses. Check with your doctor before giving pediatric ibuprofen.

Give your child the physician recommended dose of pain reliever, such as Tylenol or the generic equivalent, 30 to 60 minutes before he receives an immunization shot. Check with baby's physician first.

Look for acetaminophen suppositories. They are much easier to give to a protesting baby than liquid drops between clenched teeth. If you need to halve the dose, make sure you cut the suppository lengthwise. Cutting the suppository in the other direction can result in an overdose or inadequate dose. During manufacturing, the medicine is poured into molds and is sometimes unevenly distributed throughout the suppository.

Real Parents Say...

Always have your area poison control center telephone number available. Keep a bottle of syrup of ipecac in your home, also. Only administer this when directed by your physician or poison center. It saved me a trip to the hospital emergency department.

—Lois, mother of three

If your child has to take an antibiotic, it is often beneficial to also give him 2 to 4 tablespoons of yogurt per day to prevent diarrhea and yeast infections. Antibiotics can destroy some of the body's natural bacteria, and yogurt is helpful in restoring them.

Avoid caffeine-containing beverages, especially if your child is experiencing vomiting or diarrhea. Caffeine is a diuretic and actually causes the body to get rid of fluid. This can increase your baby's chance of becoming dehydrated.

Prevent illnesses by encouraging good handwashing before people hold baby, before and after diaper changing, and any other time it is necessary. Try and keep your child's exposure to flu bugs and illnesses minimal.

Breastfeed as long as possible. The antibodies transferred in breastmilk from mom to baby help keep baby healthier and more resistant to infections.

Budget Helpers

Check with your local county or public health department about the availability of well-baby immunizations. Physician's offices typically charge $40 to $90 for shots while public health fees may range from $7 to $15. This lesser charge at the public health agencies is because they often receive the vaccines for free and only need to charge for administrative costs.

Select or ask your pharmacist for generic medications. You can often save half the cost of prescription drugs as well as over-the-counter acetaminophen and oral rehydration formulas.

Use coupons and stock up on acetaminophen, bandages, antibiotic salves, and rehydration products when they are on sale. Look at expiration dates and choose products that will not expire for months.

Phone first before making a hasty trip to see the doctor. Speak directly to a nurse or your baby's physician. A phone call can sometimes save you an unnecessary, expensive office visit.

Use your physician's clinic and night and walk-in clinics as often as possible, especially for cases like the flu or an ear infection. Avoid using the emergency department unless it is necessary. An emergency room visit will cost you double the charges and you will often have a long wait.

This is by no means the complete guide to baby's health. Your baby's physician is the expert where any health issues are of concern.

Expect baby to be sick some time during the first year. Be prepared, relaxed, and observant. Most of the time a little extra TLC, sleep, and lots of fluids will make recovery quicker and more comfortable. If you feel at all uneasy about baby's health, call your doctor. There is no such thing as a silly question where your child's health is concerned.

R
e
s
o
u
r
c
e
s

Books

Caring for Your Baby and Young Child: Birth to Age Five by The American Academy of Pediatrics, Bantam Books

The Mayo Clinic Complete Book of Pregnancy and Baby's First Year, William Morrow and Company, New York

The American Medical Association Family Medical Guide, Random House

The Mayo Clinic Family Health Book, William Morrow and Company, New York

Health Newsletters

Harvard Health Line PO Box 380, Department PAR, Boston, MA 02117

Mayo Clinic Health Letter 200 First Street SW, Rochester, MN 55905; 800-333-9037

University of California at Berkeley Wellness Letter University of California at Berkeley, School of Public Health, Berkeley, CA 94720

Consumer Reports on Health 800-234-2188

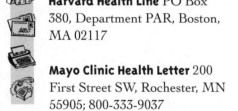

Computer Software Programs

Medical Drug Reference Parsons Technology, One Parsons Drive, Hiawatha, IA 52233; 800-223-6925

The Complete Guide to Symptoms and Illnesses and the Medical Dictionary and **Family Health Guide** from HealthSoft, 4Home Productions; 800-909-4168

Sudden Infant Death Syndrome (SIDS)

SIDS Alliance 800-221-SIDS

Sudden Infant Death Syndrome Institute 800-232-SIDS

For more information about infant sleep position, call 800-505-CRIB or write **Back to Sleep,** PO Box 29111, Washington, DC 20040

CHAPTER ELEVEN

Babyproofing Your Home

"If you can't open a childproof bottle, use pliers or ask your child."
—Bruce Lansky

As you climb the steps of your split-level home, you expertly shift the groceries in your arms and unlatch the child-safety gate with one hand. Gently closing the gate, you head for the kitchen. Skillfully opening the safety latches on the cupboards, you put away the dish soap and groceries.

As your 6 month old crawls into the kitchen, you automatically place all the plastic grocery bags into a locked cabinet. Your daughter gives you a big grin as she scrambles to "her" drawer filled with plastic lids and containers. Watching her, you effortlessly remove the electrical safety plug, plug in the can opener, and open a can of peaches to go with dinner. Task complete, you unplug the appliance and replace the safety device.

Gazing at your daughter, you realize how much having a baby has changed every aspect of your life.

Necessity Checklist

✿ **Smoke detectors** on each floor, ideally outside each bedroom also. Check that they work properly each month.

✿ **Consider checking your home for lead, radon and carbon monoxide.**

✿ **Fire extinguisher.**

✿ **Outlet covers** and/or plugs.

✿ **Cupboard and drawer latches and safety locks.**

✿ **Safety gate(s)** especially if you have two or more stories in your house.

continued on next page

Necessity Checklist (continued)

✿ **Do a crawl through your house.** Check each room from baby's point of view. Move the plants, crystal and family heirlooms.

✿ **Move everything up,** out of baby's reach. Lock all medicines and chemicals.

✿ **Remove all poisonous plants.**

You know your days of babyproofing have just begun. But you don't mind the minor inconveniences that have almost become second nature. They seem a small price to pay to keep your child safe from household hazards.

As a baby grows, every piece of furniture, plant, and family keepsake will be subject to exploration. This means one thing—learning how to babyproof. Babyproofing is something most parents do naturally and continuously as baby grows. Babyproofing, in a nutshell, is going through your home and removing, modifying, or locking up anything that might be dangerous to baby.

Though there is no such thing as being too safe where your baby is concerned, some parents may go overboard and become lost in the details of securing every cupboard, cabinet, and drawer. They feverishly purchase items like refrigerator locks and TV radiation detectors. To make their homes completely hazard-free, they overcompensate. To avoid this, rely on your common sense as you begin babyproofing your home.

Remember, your house still needs to be a home, a place where people can socialize, share experiences, and enjoy life. It can be safe for baby without becoming a locked prison camp. You do not need to buy every safety device on the market. Overzealous babyproofing can cost a fortune. Smart shopping, common sense, and following the tips in this chapter can help you babyproof your home without spending a small fortune on safety products or a babyproofing service.

Safety Awareness and Attitudes

All the babyproofing in the world can not substitute for expert adult supervision. You can be sure that even in a professionally babyproofed home your youngster can still find things to get into. You may have every outlet covered, cabinet locked, and mini blind cord secured only to find your infant chewing on the hidden lamp cord he casually rolled over. Because you cannot predict the day your child will first roll, crawl, pull up on the furniture, or walk, you need to start babyproofing at month four or sooner.

The best way to babyproof is to look at things from baby's point of view. So, get down on your tummy and then all fours. Look at everything. When you see something that could be a baby hazard remove it or modify it if possible. As baby grows, you will need to move to higher levels of security. A newborn isn't going to get into the medicine cabinet for example, but by age 18 months, she could easily scale the toilet and sink to reach the Tylenol!

While you are crawling around, look for things baby could destroy, such as videotapes and ceramic vases. If it is sacred, move it to higher ground. According to the National Safe Kids Campaign, every day more than 38,000 children in the United States are injured seriously enough to require medical treatment, totaling nearly 14 million or one out of every four children.[1] Nearly 6,700 of these injuries will result in death, and more than 50,000 will result in permanent disabilities.[2] Motor vehicle accidents, falls, drownings, fires and burns, suffocation, poisonings, and choking are among the leading causes of these unintentional injuries and deaths.[3]

Adopt the motto, "Home Safe Home," and make your child's world safe at every turn. Approached sensibly, this philosophy should be in the front of your mind every time you make a baby purchase, alter your home, or put away the cleaning supplies.

> **Real Parents Say...**
>
> You can't be too careful with a baby around. Still, the least expected things can be dangerous like tables, chairs, and piano benches.
>
> —*Rosemary, mother of six*

Household Safety—Room by Room

There is no right or wrong way to babyproof your house. It is simply a matter of looking at everything from a curious baby's perspective. Following are lists of room-by-room safety tips to get you started making your home safe for baby.

General

Cover all outlets. You can purchase individual outlet plugs or covers at local hardware stores or in the baby section of most discount stores.

Use safety gates where appropriate—especially at the top and bottom of stairs. When baby is learning to crawl, it's time to block doorways and stairwells. Only use gates that have the JPMA (Juvenile Products Manufacturers Association) safety seal. Check the gate carefully for sturdiness and a proper fit. Avoid accordion style gates where baby's head could get trapped. Make sure the gate slats are no more than 2 3/8 inches apart. For specific safety guidelines on gates, see Chapter Four.

Keep basement and other stairway doors closed at all times. A lock on these doors can also help deter an investigating toddler.

Cut all blind and shade double cords. Since 1981, at least 140 children have been strangled when they became caught in window covering cords.[4] Also, look for new breakaway tassels, such as Gerber Break-Thru Window Blind Cord Tassels and Hunter-Douglas Break-Thru Mini Blind Safety Tassels. Check discount stores, supermarkets, or window covering stores.

To cut double blind and shade cords:

1. Cut the double cord above the tassel.
2. Remove the extension buckle.
3. Secure separate tassels to each cord.

For free tassels check your local JC Penney, Sears, Home Depot, Wal-Mart, Pier One Imports, Montgomery Ward, Builder's Square, and Maher's stores or call the Window

Covering Safety Council hotline at 800-506-4636.

Attach wall covering cords to floor mounts or wall brackets to keep them out of your child's reach.

Put window guards on any window you plan to open (except emergency fire exits). Don't rely on screens. The weight of a child can easily push through a screen. Open windows from the top when possible. Keep windows locked when not in use.

Do not position furniture beneath windows. This creates the opportunity for a serious fall.

Never leave your child unattended around a fireplace.

If you have hardwood floors, don't let baby run in socks, which are slippery on wood floors and can result in falls.

Never leave a bucket of water in any room. This could be a drowning hazard for an investigating youngster.

Keep all pet food, dishes, water, and litter boxes away from baby. Your best option is to keep all pet paraphernalia in a separate room. Food and water present a choking hazard, and some pets might get jealous of an eager toddler approaching their food dish.

Make sure all rugs have skid-resistant backings so they don't become a tripping hazard.

If you smoke, keep all tobacco products, ashtrays, and ashes out of baby's reach. Tobacco is acutely poisonous. Because of the health hazards of secondhand smoke, avoid smoking anywhere near your baby.

If possible, move furniture with sharp edges out of baby's path. Coffee table corners can cause injury if your child falls against them.

Make sure all furniture is sturdy. As baby starts to pull up to things, wobbly, unstable furniture could topple over. Secure shelves and bookcases to the wall.

Keep all alcoholic beverages out of baby's reach. Alcohol (including mouthwash) can be very toxic to a young child.

Keep floors picked up regularly. At baby's level, it's easy to find dropped jewelry, loose screws, pieces of food, and broken parts. These choking hazards can quickly end up in baby's mouth.

Don't let any appliance cords dangle off the edge of a counter or shelf. Babies love to grab and pull dangling objects.

Avoid ironing near baby. If you must iron with baby present, never leave baby or the iron unattended.

For safe use of baby equipment, see Chapter Four.

Secure floor lamps behind other furniture so baby can not pull them over.

Safety mark glass doors or secure them open so your child can not run into them. If you have swinging doors, consider removing them until your child is older. You may also want to move glass-front bookcases, glass-top coffee tables, and lamps with glass shades out of baby's main play area.

Repair loose railings in your home.

Secure the shower curtains and drapery rods so baby can't pull them down with a mighty tug.

Kitchen
Put all cleaning supplies and poisons in upper, locked cabinets.

Use safety latches on cabinets with glassware.

Keep garbage covered with a child-resistant lid. Take broken glass, sharp can lids, and other cutting hazards out to the trash can promptly.

Keep the dishwasher locked. It's a combination poisonland and stepping stool for baby.

Don't add dishwasher soap until you're ready to start the machine. Remove any soap residue after the washing cycle. Don't leave any chemicals around for baby to get into! Dishwasher detergent is dangerous if baby ingests it.

Unplug all appliances when not in use so Junior is not found playing Julia Child when you are not around.

Keep all knives and sharp utensils in a drawer with a safety latch. Be careful that knife blocks are not accessible to your child. Consider storing them on a high shelf.

Use placemats instead of tablecloths when possible. Babies are known for pulling on things. Unless you want the table cleared in a hurry, skip the linen.

Keep stools, chairs, and children's playchairs away from the counter and stove.

Turn all pan handles in on the stove. Use back burners whenever possible. Don't leave your child unattended in the kitchen when food is cooking.

Teach your child when he is little that the stove is hot. Children can learn early that they are not to touch the burners.

If purchasing a stove, select the type with control knobs toward the back of the appliance. Otherwise, remove stove control knobs when not in use.

If possible, lock the oven door whenever the oven is on.

Keep matches out of reach and out of sight. Teach your child not to play with matches.

> ## Real Parents Say...
>
> By 16 months, our son had mastered plugging in small appliances! We were on constant alert to keep every outlet covered at all times.
> —*Marie and Michael, parents of two*
>
> Children can learn the meaning of "no" at a young age. It is very important that baby learns from early on not to touch the stove, plug in appliances, wander into the street, and a multitude of other safety "no-no's."
> —*Julie, mother of two*

Always use hot pads to lift hot pans. Never use a towel, which is a poor heat protector and can easily catch on things. Know where baby is whenever carrying anything hot.

Avoid storing medicines on the counter or on windowsills.

Don't hold baby while cooking.

Keep all foods, especially hot items, away from counter- and table-top edges.

If you are drinking hot liquid, avoid holding baby at the same time.

Keep all appliance cords out of baby's reach. One tug and a hot appliance can land on baby.

Bathrooms

Store all medicines, including vitamins and topical ointments, in safety containers. Just six iron tablets can be toxic to a child. Remember, bottle caps are child-resistant, not childproof. Rocket scientist babies can often open these devices by age 2, so keep medicines up high and locked up.

Clean the medicine cabinet regularly, and dispose of all outdated medications by flushing them down the toilet.

Separate your medicines and vitamins from baby's. This helps prevent accidentally giving a wrong medicine when it is needed in the middle of the night.

Store bathroom cleaners up high and in locked cabinets.

Keep mouthwash and toothpaste out of baby's reach.

Always unplug and store hair dryers, curling irons, and hot rollers out of baby's reach. Keep electrical outlets covered.

Operate all electrical appliances away from water. They can cause a shock if they fall into the sink or bathtub.

Lower the temperature on your hot water heater to 120°F or less for baby-friendly bathrooms. To check the tap water, run hot water for 3 minutes. Use a meat or candy thermometer to check the temperature. It should be 120°F or less. If it's too hot, turn down the water heater, talk with your landlord, or install an anti-scald device.

Always test the water temperature with your hand or a thermometer before putting baby in the tub. The water should only be warm to the touch and not leave your skin pink or red.

Consider installing anti-scald devices on water faucets your child has access to. Even if your water heater is turned down, a running dishwasher, washing machine, or flushed toilet can cause other water faucets to run hotter than usual.

Keep all razors out of a child's reach.

Never leave a young child alone in the bathtub—no exceptions. It only takes a few inches of water for drowning to occur. Also, baby can slip and fall easily in the bathtub. If the phone or door-bell rings, take the time to take baby with you or don't answer.

Consider no-slip strips in the bottom of the bathtub. Some parents also use a cushioned spout cover to prevent baby from bumping her head.

Get in the habit of always closing the toilet lid. This will help detract the curious toddler with an affinity for water. Babies can lose their balance and fall in.

Keep the bathroom door shut tight when not in use. If baby masters the doorknob, consider a simple hook on the outside of the door. This allows you to lock baby out when the bathroom is not in use.

Make sure all doors can be unlocked from the outside in case baby accidentally gets locked inside.

Bedrooms

Don't let your infant sleep with a pillow in her crib, cradle, bassinet, or carriage. It could be a suffocation hazard. Among children under age 1, suffocation is the leading cause of unintentional injury-related death.[5]

Don't let your baby sleep on a waterbed. Babies have been known to suffocate and/or become wedged between the mattress and the frame.

Remove all medicines from dressers, chests, nightstands, and changing tables.

Keep all perfumes, cosmetics, and contraceptives out of reach.

Keep all jewelry out of reach.

Check for any flaking paint on ceilings, walls, windowsills, woodwork, cribs, and other furniture.

Outside the House

Keep baby out of the garage or basement when possible.

When mowing the lawn or cutting hedges, never let your child play in the mowing area.

Do not let your child ride on or operate a rider mower.

Clear the area to be mowed before mowing.

Mow only during the day, not at night or dusk when visibility is poor.

Keep all oil, gasoline, antifreeze, charcoal, lighter fluid, pesticides, and other products locked up and on high shelves in your garage.

Keep all power tools unplugged and out of baby's reach.

Make sure rakes, shovels, garden tools, and hand tools are secured high enough so a toddler can't reach the handle and pull them off the wall.

Scan your yard regularly for wild mushrooms. Some can be poisonous. Teach your child not to eat them or any other yard plant.

Always observe your child around water. A 5-gallon pail filled with water to wash the car and a swimming pool both present a drowning risk to a toddler.

Don't assume a child can swim just because she has had swimming lessons.

Other Safety Issues

Bicycle Safety

530 children and adolescents die each year from injuries sustained while bicycling.[6] Exercise extreme caution when placing a young child in a bicycle carrier seat. The added weight on the bicycle can make it more unstable and increases braking time. Pull-along bicycle carriers are roomier for baby, allow for more control for the driver, keep baby closer to the ground, and tend to be safer overall. Check out your local bike shop or bike catalog or the Right Start catalog for styles and models. The following tips can keep both you and baby safe.

Always use a bike helmet. Studies show helmets reduce the risk of head injury by as much as 85 percent.[7] A child's helmet costs between $20 and $30. Parents also need to set a good example for their child by wearing a helmet each time they bike.

Ride with caution and at a reduced speed.

Ride only on bike paths, in parks, or on quiet streets. Avoid busy roads.

Make sure the carrier or trailer is securely strapped to the bike.

> ## Real Parents Say...
>
> We enjoy our bike carrier that can be pulled behind our bike. It easily seats two and is easier to balance than the bicycle carrier seat styles.
>
> —*Dave and Anne, parents of two*

Only a very competent cyclist should carry or pull a young passenger.

Place reflective stickers on your bike and trailer or carrier to alert motorists to your presence. These show up during both the day and night.

Lead

Lead ingestion can be very harmful, especially to young children. Lead poisoning is often caused by eating lead in bits of dirt contaminated with lead or lead paint, breathing lead in the air, and drinking water from pipes lined or soldered with lead. Lead poisoning can cause learning disabilities, a slowed mental and physical development, stomach and intestinal problems, diarrhea, anemia, hearing loss, headaches, behavior problems, and even death. Lead can also cause abnormal fetal development in pregnant women.

In 1978, the government limited the amount of lead allowed in paints to .06 percent. However, about three-quarters of the nation's housing built before 1978 (approximately 64 million dwellings) contains some lead-based paint. When properly managed and maintained, this paint poses little risk. However, 1.7 million children have blood levels above safe limits, mostly due to exposure to lead-based paint hazards.[8]

While lead-based paint, dust, and soil are the most common lead hazards, other lead sources also exist. Drinking water can contain lead if you have plumbing with lead or lead solder. Other sources include old painted toys and furniture, lead crystal, and lead-glazed pottery or porcelain, and hobbies that use lead, such as making pottery or stained glass and refinishing furniture. In addition, the worksite can be a source of lead exposure if you live near lead smelters or other industries that release lead into the air, or if you work with lead on the job.

The U.S. Consumer Product Safety Commission has determined that vinyl miniblinds purchased prior to October 1996 can present a lead poisoning hazard. More than 25 million of these blinds came into the United States containing lead to stabilize the plastic. Over time the plastic deteriorates from exposure to sunlight and heat to form a lead dust. The amount of lead varies from blind to blind. Safe blinds should now be in stores. They will be labelled "New Formulation," "No Lead Added," or "Non-Lead Vinyl Formulation." Replace your old blinds.

If you suspect your house has other lead hazards, here are some tips to minimize the risks.

Have your child tested for lead between the ages of 9 months and 1 year and possibly again at 2 years.

If you live in a rural area or in an older home, have the lead level in your drinking water tested.

If you think your plumbing might have lead in it, run the water for 15 to 30 seconds before drinking, especially if you have not used your water for a few hours. Use only cold water for drinking; lead leaches into hot water more readily.

Wash your child's hands often, especially before she eats and at nap- and bedtime.

Keep play areas clean. Wash bottles, pacifiers, toys, and stuffed animals regularly.

Keep rooms, doors, and windowsills free of paint chips.

If redecorating, remodeling, or painting an older home, keep the area well ventilated. Do not let your child sleep or play in the area until the project is done.

Remove lead paint before repainting, if possible. Move out or tightly seal off the area during the renovation process. It is best that removal of lead paint be done by a professional or at least with expert guidance.

If you are unable to remove the paint, keep your home as clean as possible to reduce the dust. Wet mop and wash all bare surfaces with a high phosphate compound. Check your local hardware store.

Be sure to include foods containing iron and calcium in your diet. These minerals can help reduce lead absorption and may make your child less susceptible to lead poisoning.[10]

Poison Control: Chemical and Medicine Safety

In 1995, more than 125,000 children under the age of 1 and 1,070,000 under the age of 6 years were exposed to something poisonous.[11] Accidental poisonings are most common with the use of household cleaning chemicals and medicines. Keeping all chemicals and cleaning solutions locked up and out of baby's reach is your first and best line of poisoning defense.

Poison Prevention Tips

Keep all medicines and household chemicals locked up and out of baby's reach.

Check with your physician before giving any over-the-counter medicine to a child younger than 2 years old.

If your child is taking a prescription medicine, check with your physician before giving any other medications.

Keep all medications and chemicals in their original containers so you know exactly what the product is in case of accidental ingestion. You will also need product or medication information when you call your physician or poison control center.

Keep all colognes, perfumes, mouthwashes, and cosmetics on high shelves out of baby's reach.

Store all medicines and chemicals in high cupboards. By age 1, many children can "pick" a child safety latch quicker than you think.

Never tell a child medicine is candy.

When giving your child medicine, keep the remaining medicine out of her reach.

Make sure all medicines and vitamin-mineral supplements are in child-resistant containers. Iron tablets and other vitamins can be toxic to young children, even in small amounts.

Only purchase cleaning compounds with child-resistant tops.

Post the number of your local poison control center or emergency department next to every telephone.

Keep a bottle of both syrup of ipecac and activated charcoal accessible. Only administer this to your child if directed by a poison control center, physician, or emergency room personnel.

Keep purses containing medicine up high. Keep all medicine in child-resistant bottles.

When visiting someone else's house, especially an elderly person who is on medication, be very observant for pills, chemicals, or plants within your child's reach.

Share safety tips with grandparents before baby goes to stay for a day.

Contact your local poison control center early on in your pregnancy or during baby's first months at home. Ask them to send you poison information specific to your area. This may include information on the water supply, poisonous snakes, or animals in your area. Your poison center may also send you poison stickers for your phone, markers for chemical bottles (like Mr. Yuk or Mr. Ug) and guidelines for handling poisoning situations. Check the front of your phone book for a poison center in your area.

Discard any leftover prescription medicine when the illness has passed. The safest way to discard medicine is to flush the unused portion down the toilet.

Do not take medication in front of your child. She may try to imitate you later.

Check the label every time you give your child medication to be sure you are giving the correct dose. Mistakes are often made at night, so be sure to turn on the lights.

Read all labels on household products. Try to find the least toxic ones for the job.

Never put a poisonous or toxic product in a container once used for food. A hungry child or unaware adult could accidentally taste or eat the product.

Be careful when disposing empty chemical bottles. Even an almost empty bottle of toilet bowl cleaner in the bathroom wastebasket can be a hazard to a curious crawler. Make sure empty cleaning chemical bottles are disposed out of your child's reach.

What to Do in Case of Poisoning

Prevention is your best defense against medicine and chemical poisoning. Supervision and locking up dangerous products are important steps in keeping baby safe. First aid, CPR courses, and easy-to-find phone numbers are other key safety steps. In general, call your local poison center first if you suspect your child has ingested or inhaled something dangerous. In the event of exposure to a toxic substance, stay calm, and act quickly to get the appropriate treatment.

If your child is unconscious, having seizures, or has stopped breathing, call 911 or your local emergency ambulance number. Otherwise, contact your local poison control center, physician, or hospital emergency department if you suspect any poisoning. If the number is not available, call 911.

Poison centers are open 24 hours a day, seven days a week. When you call them you can get an immediate response and save valuable time in getting treatment for your child. If possible, have the product container with you when you call, so you can provide detailed information about the suspected poisoning.

Remember, if you are in doubt about anything your child may have eaten, call your poison control center. There is no such thing as a dumb question when it concerns your baby's safety and well-being.

Plant Safety

You don't need to become a horticulturist, but before you bring baby home, be sure you know the name of every plant in your home. Household plants have become one of the nation's leading poisonous products ingested by children. Baby can be quick to grab a leaf of any plant and stuff it in her mouth. If a plant is poisonous, it could harm your baby. Besides being potentially toxic, plants are a choking hazard.

Know the name of all your household plants. Write the name of the plant, whether it is toxic or not, and your local poison control center telephone number on the bottom of each plant pot. The poison control center can not accurately identify plants over the telephone. This system eliminates any confusion in an emergency.

Get rid of or keep all poisonous houseplants out of your child's reach.

Store all bulbs, seeds, plant food, and fertilizer on a high shelf or in a locked cupboard.

Never eat any part of an unknown plant or mushroom.

Teach your child to never put any part of a plant in her mouth. This includes nuts, seeds, berries, stems, leaves, and bark.

Do not rely on cooking to destroy the toxic substances in plants.

Do not use products prepared from "nature" as medicine or tea for young children without checking with your doctor.

Learn to identify the poisonous plants in your neighborhood.

Any plant can cause an unexpected reaction when ingested. Always check with the poison control center if your child has eaten or you suspect she has eaten part of a plant.

Do not assume a plant is not toxic just because birds or animals eat it.

Keep all water premixed with plant food in a high, locked area.

If you can not identify a plant in your garden or yard, contact your nearest garden and landscape center.

Toxic Plants

Following is a list of toxic plants (poisonous or possibly poisonous). They contain a wide variety of poisons, which may cause symptoms from a mild stomachache, skin rash, or swelling of the mouth and throat, to involvement of the heart, kidneys, or other organs.

Always check with your local poison control center no matter what type of plant has been ingested. Any plant can cause an unexpected reaction in certain individuals. Contact your local poison control center for information about plants not on the following list.

Acorn	Anemone	Angel Trumpet Tree
Apple Seeds	Apricot Pit-Kernels	Arrowhead
Avocado Leaves	Azaleas	Betel Nut Palm
Bittersweet	Buckeye	Buttercups
Caladium	Calla Lily	Castor Bean
Chinese Lantern	Creeping Charlie	Crocus, Autumn
Daffodil	Daphne	Delphinium
Devil's Ivy	Dieffenbachia	Elderberry
Elephant Ear	English Ivy	Four o'Clock
Foxglove	Ground Ivy	Hemlock, Poison
Holly Berries	Horsetail Reed	Hyacinth (bulbs)
Hydrangea	Iris	Ivy (Boston, English)

Jack-in-the-Pulpit	Jequirity Bean or Pea	Jerusalem Cherry
Jessamine (Jasmine)	Jimsonweed (Thorn Apple)	Jonquil
Lantana Camara	Larkspur	Laurels
Lily-of-the-Valley	Lobelia	Marijuana
Mayapple	Mescal (Peyote)	Mistletoe
Monkshood	Moonseed	Morning Glory
Mushroom	Narcissus	Nephthytis
Nightshade	Oleander	Peach Seeds
Periwinkle	Philodendron	Poison Ivy
Poison Oak	Pokeweed	Poppy (except
Potato-Sprouts	Primrose	California Poppy)
Ranunculus	Rhododendron	Rhubarb Leaf
Rosary Pea	Star-of-Bethlehem	Sweet Pea
Tobacco	Tomato-Vines	Tulip
Water Hemlock	Wisteria	Yew

Reprinted with permission from: Minnesota Regional Poison Center, St. Paul, Minnesota 55101.

Fire Safety

Among children ages 1 to 4, fires and burns are the leading cause of unintentional injury-related death.[12] Smoke is the major killer with most fire-related deaths. Fire prevention demands a few easy steps.

1. Purchase essential safety equipment

Smoke Detectors. Have a minimum of one smoke detector on each level of your home, including the basement. Ideally, there should be a detector in the hall outside each sleeping room. Look for a detector with a "UL" rating label, which indicates it meets the industry standards. Replace the battery at least once a year; pick an anniversary or daylight savings time date. Check your smoke detector monthly to see if it is working properly.

Fire Extinguishers. Choose an all purpose fire extinguisher labeled "ABC." Know how to operate the extinguisher. There is no time to read directions when you are trying to put out a fire. Keep an extinguisher close to your kitchen, on each floor in your home, in the garage, and in other fire-prone areas. Always remember, get everyone to safety before attempting to put out a fire. Belongings can be replaced, lives can't. Replace or recharge fire extinguishers after every use.

Fire Ladders. A window escape ladder is a must if you live in a two-story house or second story or higher apartment. Ideally, the escape ladder is stored close to the window.

2. Remove fire hazards

Outside Your Home. Clean the chimney, roof, eaves, and gutters to clear leaves, grass, and branches away from the exterior of your home where they could be a fire hazard.

In the Kitchen. Keep the stovetop free of grease, which can easily catch fire. Keep curtains, towels, and pot holders at least three feet away from the stovetop. In the event of a fire, cover the pan with a lid or pour baking soda over it if it is containable. Never use water, salt, or flour on a fire—it could actually cause it to spread.

In the Basement. Get rid of oily rags, old newspapers, and rubbish. Keep all flammable liquids in the garage.

Around the Rest of the House. Avoid overloading outlets. Do not use extension cords with heavy load appliances like toasters, hair dryers, or computers. A heavy load appliance is one that generates heat. Replace frayed extension cords. Keep fireplaces clean and use a screen to prevent sparks from setting your family room on fire. Keep all space heaters and heating devices at least three feet away from all cribs, beds, curtains, furniture, and paper. Keep halogen lamps a safe distance from curtains. Avoid leaving appliances on when you are not at home. Washing machines have been known to malfunction and start a fire.

3. Fireproof your family

Have an escape plan for each room. Walk through your home and figure out an escape route for each room. Determine a safe place to meet outside your home. This is a quick and efficient way to check that everyone is out of the house.

Make sure your house is numbered clearly. Can you see your house number easily from the street? Remember, this is how the fire fighters will find you quickly in an emergency.

Practice a fire drill twice a year. Practicing getting out of your home enables you to move quickly and calmly in case of a real fire. You may even want to activate the smoke detector so your child knows what it sounds like.

Teach your child about fire safety. Teach your child fire safety from the time she is little. Children learn by example and observation, so removing fire hazards, talking and reading about safety, and practicing fire drill safety are all great ways to teach your young child.

Smart Parents Do

Lower the setting on your water heater to 120°F or lower.

Move heavy furniture in front of seldom used outlets.

Do not leave any plastic bags or plastic packaging around. Baby could easily put the bag over her head or bite off a piece of plastic and suffocate or choke.

Purchase blank outlet plates (usually less than $1) for unused outlets at your local discount or hardware store.

Shop discount stores for outlet covers, safety latches, and other child-proofing devices. Avoid buying the products in baby specialty shops where the cost is usually double.

Check out pet shops and catalogs for safety gates. You can often find safety gates for $5 to $10 less from pet product suppliers than in baby departments and catalogs. See the Resource section for catalogs.

Shop for larger baby safety items in discount stores like Wal-Mart, K-Mart, and Target. These stores will usually save you 5 to 25 percent over specialty shops and hardware stores on things like gates and outlet plugs.

Much of the best babyproofing is free. Crawl on your hands and knees through each room and move any questionable safety hazard to higher ground. Use high cupboards for any cleaning product and chemical storage. Use safety locks or latches to lock up all sharp knives, glassware, and cleaning compounds. Keep baby out of hazard zones like the laundry, sewing, garage, and woodshop areas. Sweep, vacuum, and pick up the floors on a constant basis.

Never leave your child unsupervised.

Assist relatives, friends, and babysitters with babyproofing education and safety awareness.

Real Parents Say...

Childproof the house by placing unbreakable items on the lower shelves and cupboards.
—*Rose, mother of three*

There is no safety item like constant observation.
—*Linda and Ed, parents of three*

Watch fall sales for fire safety equipment.

Check with your local fire department about free or low-cost smoke detectors.

Contact your homeowner's insurance agent. You may qualify a for premium discount if you have specific fire- and safety-proofing devices in your home.

Catalogs

The Safety Zone, Hanover, PA 17333-0019; 800-999-3030; fax: 800-338-1635 (outside the U.S. call 717-633-3370)

Perfectly Safe, 7245 Whipple Avenue NW, North Canton, OH 44720; 800-837-KIDS; fax: 216-494-0265

R.C. Steele (wholesale pet equipment company—check out their pet gates at a fraction of the cost of child safety gates), 1989 Transit Way, Box 910, Brockport, NY 14420-0910; 800-872-3773;

Safety by Design, PO Box 4312, Great Neck, NY 11023; 516-488-5395

The Right Start Catalog, Right Start Plaza, 5334 Sterling Center Drive, Westlake Village, CA 91361-4627; 800-548-8531; fax: 800-762-5501

Hand in Hand, Route 26, RR 1 Box 1425, Oxford, Maine 04270-9711; 800-872-9745

Safety First, 210 Boylston St., Chestnut Hill, MA 02167; 800-962-7233

One Step Ahead, 950 North Shore Drive, Lake Bluff, IL 60044; 800-274-8440

Brochures

To request copies send a stamped, self-addressed, business sized envelope

"Safe and Sound for Baby" and **"Crib Safety Alert,"** The Juvenile Products Manufacturers Association (JPMA) Public Information, Two Greentree Centre, Suite 225, Box 955, Marlton, NJ 08053

"Home Safety," Fisher-Price's Family Alert Program; 800-635-2440

"Household Hazardous Waste Wheel" (lists hazardous home chemicals and less toxic, alternate solutions). For more information, contact: Iowa Department of Natural Resources, Waste Management Authority Division, Wallace State Office Building, Des Moines, IA 50319-0034 or contact the Environmental Hazards Management Institute, 10 Newmarket Road, PO Box 932, Durham, NH 03824; 603-868-1496

"Make Your Day With Safety," Outdoor Power Equipment Institute, Inc., 341 South Patrick

R
e
s
o
u
r
c
e
s

Street, Old Town Alexandria, VA 22314; 703-549-7600

"Tips for Your Baby's Safety" and **"Protect Your Child,"** U.S. Consumer Product Safety Commission, Office of Information and Public Affairs, Washington, D.C. 20207

"Parents Guide to Safety" (send $1 for the 12-page brochure), National Safe Kids Campaign, 111 Michigan Avenue NW, Washington, D.C. 20010-2970

"Protect Your Family from Lead in Your Home," National Lead Clearinghouse, 1019 19th Street NW, Suite 401, Washington, D.C. 20036; (800) 424-LEAD

Books

Baby-Safe Houseplants and Cut Flowers by John and Delores Alber, Story Communications, Inc.; 800-827-8673

Childproof Your Home, Safety First, Chestnut Hill, Massachusetts 02167; 800-962-7233

Other Information

For free information on safety and first aid skills, contact your local **Red Cross.**

Contact your area **poison control center** for poison control information and phone stickers with the local poison center's emergency number. Look inside the front cover of your telephone book where other emergency numbers are listed.

For information regarding lead in your home, contact **National Lead Watch,** 800-532-3394 (800-LEAD-FYI)

Environmental Protection Agency's Drinking Water Hotline Call 800-426-4791 for information about lead in drinking water.

National Lead Information Center of the Environmental Health Center, 1019 19th St. NW, Suite 401, Washington, DC 20036; 202-833-1071; fax: 202-659-1192

CHAPTER TWELVE

Finding the Best Child Care

"I suppose there must be in every mother's life the inevitable moment when she has to take two small children shopping in one big store."
—*Shirley Jackson*

"You Know You Have Found the Ideal Care Giver When..." The title catches your attention as you pick up your favorite magazine. Quickly, you flip through the pages to read the wisdom of other parents. The article begins: You know you have found the ideal care giver when—

- ✿ your child asks to go to day care;
- ✿ your child calls you by his care giver's first name;
- ✿ you find yourself asking for her recipes;
- ✿ the diaper bag comes home fully organized;
- ✿ your care giver gives you a list of items to bring tomorrow; and
- ✿ your baby's missing button is sewn back on his shirt.

As you read, you find yourself wondering if this too-good-to-be-

Necessity Checklist

- ✿ Decide on type of child care arrangement

In-Home Provider

- ✿ Develop job description
- ✿ Advertise position
- ✿ Screen candidates by telephone
- ✿ Interview
- ✿ Complete necessary employer paperwork

Away-From-Home Provider

- ✿ Obtain a list of potential child care centers or family-based providers

continued on next page

Necessity Checklist (continued)

✿ **Screen providers by telephone**

✿ **Interview and visit sites**

✿ **Select a provider**

✿ **Develop a back-up plan** for sick days

✿ **Find a sitter for brief outings** like a shopping trip, bike ride, or romantic evening

true care giver even exists. Eventually, the time will come when you will need to entrust your child into someone else's care—whether you work away from home or stay at home. Regardless of your needs, an evening out or for a 40-hour work week, you must select a provider carefully.

Parents return to work for a variety of reasons, many of which are financial. Child care is often the second or third largest baby expense for families.[1] Depending on where you live, the availability of child care, and the amount you need, it can cost you as much as 10 percent or more of your annual income. In addition to these costs, quality child care can be very hard to find. Standards for safety and health, as well as enforced regulations for staff-to-child ratios, are few. Consequently, finding the quality, affordable child care that is best for your family rests with you.

Be assured, if you are willing to identify your child care needs and standards, and be persistent, you can find great, affordable care for your child. If you cannot find a child care option that fits your current work schedule, you may need to reconsider your working options. See Chapter 13 on working options.

What Does Child Care Cost?

The cost of child care services can vary greatly. The type of care, hours of care (part time may cost more), where you live, and the age of your child can all affect price. A 1993 study by the Bureau of Census estimated national mean weekly costs at about $50 for family day care (at a neighbor's, for instance), $63 at a child care center, and $68 for an in-home babysitter. Costs, though, have been increasing between 2.5 and 7 percent each year. You'll find that the cost for infant care is usually higher than for toddler and preschooler care. Furthermore, costs tend to be highest in the northeast and in metropolitan areas.

Contact your local Child Care Resource and Referral Network for specific child care information in your area or look for agencies under day care or child care in your telephone directory. The National Association of Child Care Resource and Referral Agencies at (202) 393-5501 may also be able to direct you to a local agency.

Budget Helpers

Child care costs and quality are not always proportional. Your child is your most precious asset and greatest responsibility. Identify the level of quality you want and then search for options within your budget. Ideas for controlling child care costs without compromising care include:

If possible, consider working shifts opposite your spouse or significant other. Keep needed child care hours to a minimum. If you choose this option, make sure to plan time to nourish your relationship with your significant other.

Take advantage of child/dependent care spending accounts if your employer offers them. This type of account allows you to place an amount of your salary (determined by you) into a child care spending account. The money is exempt from social security and income tax. You

Real Parents Say...

I will never forget my first day back at work. It was time to leave and my recently hired in-home sitter was late. The phone rang. It was my sitter, calling to tell me she would not be taking the job.

With my husband 60 miles away at work, I felt anger, panic, and despair at the same moment. Luckily, Grandma came to our rescue. We survived the next few days only to find the two most fantastic child care providers in the world. Looking back, we learned the hard way about the do's and don'ts of choosing a quality care giver.

—*Dave and Anne, parents of two*

may draw the money out of your account to pay for child care expenses.

The tax savings can add up fast. A married couple with an annual income of $50,000 who put $3,000 into a flexible child care account can save between $300 and $900 on taxes. Child care expenses paid through the flexible dependent care account cannot be deducted on your tax return at the end of the year. Also, you must use all the money in the account by the end of the year or you lose it. Sorry, no refunds! However, if you plan conservatively, flexible dependent care accounts can save you money.

Uncle Sam may help out a little, also. You may be eligible for a child care tax credit if you and your spouse are both working or looking for work (assuming your child is 13 or younger).

A tax credit can lower the amount of income you are taxed on. Depending on your income, you may be eligible for a tax credit up to 20 percent of your child care expenses up to a maximum of $2,400 per child.

Check if your employer has voucher plans. Under this type of plan, an employee's child care contributions are deducted before taxes. In addition, employers provide employees with vouchers that entitle the employee to charge part of their child care expenses to the employer. Voucher plans usually allow the employee to select the child care provider.

If your work site does not have such a program, encourage one. According to the Child Care Action Campaign (CCAC), businesses lose an estimated $3 billion a year due to child care-related absences.[2]

Investigate the possibility of employee discounts. Many companies are now negotiating discounts for groups of employees with local providers. Typically, the child care provider or agency will agree to lower its fees by 10 percent. The employer then contributes an additional 10 percent. The only drawback is that employees must use the provider(s) designated by the company.

Keep track of all work-related child care expenses. Any expenses not reimbursed through a dependent care, employee discount, or voucher program may qualify for deductions on your income tax at the end of the year. You will need your care provider's taxpayer identification number or social security number to claim the deductions.

Avoid late fees and charges by being prompt. Some providers charge by the minute when you are late.

Check with your local Department of Human Services or other similar state agency for possible child care funding assistance.

Consider sharing a sitter with other families in your neighborhood, especially if you work part time. This option can really work well, cut costs, and provide socialization for your child. It also works well for the sitter who can earn more money if she has more children.

If you like the idea of a nanny or au pair service, consider sharing the service with a close neighbor or friend.

Swap child care with other parents. This works great for one-day shopping sprees, evening getaways, or afternoon breaks. Every parent relishes a few uninterrupted hours now and then.

Form a child care co-op with other parents. A babysitting cooperative is a group of parents who trade off giving and receiving care for their child or children.

Setting Up a Babysitting Co-op[3]

1.Round up potential members by contacting friends and associates, posting notices at day care, doctor's offices, churches, etc. Size: 10 to 15 families is ideal; minimum of 4 families.

2.Set up a meeting to get acquainted and decide how the co-op will run. Two types of co-ops include:

> Catch-as-you-can approach: Call each other when you need a sitter and track your own hours.

> Centralized approach: Select a coordinator to field requests and log hours. Rotate coordinator duties and/or reimburse the coordinator—in babysitting hours, of course!

3.Decide on a barter system to keep child care hours worked and used equivalent. Some groups exchange poker chips (1 chip=1/2 hour of babysitting), develop coupons, or simply log hours on paper. Determine other group rules.

4.After the group rules have been established, each family receives: a copy of the rules; member names, addresses, and phone numbers; and children's names and ages. Medical release forms, medical histories, emergency contacts, and preferred hospital information is also shared.

5.Get together every 6 months or so to evaluate and make needed changes.

When to Start Looking for Child Care

Your search for quality child care can begin at anytime. First, identify your family's child care needs. How many hours of care do you need each week? How close to work or home do you want your child? What are your typical work hours? What can you afford to spend on child care?

If you plan to change your work status (for example, full time to part time, flex time, or compressed work week) it is best to begin discussing options with your supervisor months before baby's due date. Employers need time to consider and arrange staffing and work distribution changes. See Chapter 13 on other working options.

Interviewing and securing a child care provider is best started by at least the seventh or eighth month of your pregnancy. This allows you time to evaluate a number of options and references without feeling rushed. Do not be surprised, however, if the search takes a few months. Some providers have waiting lists or take a limited number of infants, so it is less stressful if you begin your search early. Occasionally, providers will not hold a spot for you. In this situation, you may need to request your name be placed on a waiting list to be notified when openings occur, or if the provider is an ideal fit for your needs, you may offer to pay to reserve a spot for your baby.

Real Parents Say...

Child care—a major headache. Parents should start with the realization that no one can care for their child like they would. Start by making a list of all the positive aspects and concerns of child care. Make your decision based on what areas you are willing to compromise on. Go part time if necessary. I needed the extra time to do family activity.

—*Rose, mother of three*

Your Child Care Options

There are basically two categories of child care: in-home and away-from-home care. Each has its own potential advantages and concerns, as well as a wide range of costs.

In-Home Child Care

In-home child care may include a sitter, relative, friend, or grandparent who comes into your home to care for your child. The care giver may also perform other household duties such as cooking and light cleaning.

Au pair and nanny care are alternatives to the above in-home options. Nannies are typically child care specialists. They can live either in or out of your home. They are hired specifically to tend to your child. Many nannies have special training in child development, nutrition, and first aid. If Mary Poppins' magic or

Julie Andrews' singing is on your request list, expect to pay $250 or more per week, plus room and board.[4] The salary is higher if your nanny lives outside your home. When using an agency to find a nanny, ask about their agency charges. Many agencies charge $500 to $2,500 just to help you locate a qualified nanny.[5]

Au pair care is provided to your child by an 18 to 25 year old from a foreign country. These young adults do not typically have any specialized training in child care or development. The au pair will usually spend one or more years with you and your family. The concept of au pair care is to exchange services — about 40 hours of child care for a stipend of about $100 per week and room and board.[6] The arrangement allows foreign students to spend time abroad. American au pairs are also available. See the Resource section for referral agencies. Because au pair services are contracted through an agency, you are not usually responsible for taxes. If you hire au pair services independently, you are responsible for taxes and other paperwork as you would be with hiring any other household help.

Potential Advantages of In-Home Care

✿ Your child remains in a familiar environment

✿ No exposure to other children's germs

✿ Limited disruption to baby's schedule

✿ A timesaver of an hour or more per day spent getting baby ready and traveling to and from a child care setting

✿ Care giver comes to your home

✿ Care is constant and available, even if baby is sick

✿ Hours tend to be more flexible and set by the parents

✿ Lots of individual attention for your child

✿ Care giver may provide other light housekeeping and cooking duties

✿ Care giver is typically stable (exception is au pair arrangements), allowing your child and the care giver to develop a positive relationship

✿ You have more control over environment, discipline, and parenting issues

Potential Concerns with In-Home Care

✿ The cost is generally higher than away-from-home care

✿ There are hidden costs like meals for the care giver, heating, electricity, etc.

✿ Your child may have less opportunity to socialize with other children

✿ Backup coverage is needed when your sitter is sick or on vacation

✿ You may have to purchase additional liability insurance. Check with your insurance agent

✿ If you allow the care giver to drive your car, there may be an increase on your auto insurance coverage

✿ Because your care giver is essentially your employee, you must follow some specific state and federal laws, complete and file necessary paperwork, and meet minimum wage and tax requirements.

✿ Child-rearing styles and discipline can be difficult if you and your care giver do not share similar beliefs and values

✿ Your child may develop a strong attachment to her care giver that could be difficult if he or she leaves

✿ Rivalry may develop between parents and care giver if the child and care giver develop a close relationship

✿ You give up a certain amount of family and personal privacy

✿ The care giver is unsupervised

Away-from-Home Child Care

Family child care and care centers are the two basic types of away-from-home care. As with an in-home care giver, each has its own potential advantages and concerns.

Family day care is generally less expensive and more flexible than child care centers. Often, the provider is tending to children of her own, too.

Some family-based operations are formally licensed and registered. Requirements vary from state to state. Licensing regulations can be obtained from your local or state health department. Licensing helps ensure that state-specified child care, health, and safety standards are followed. Referral agencies can often help you find in-home providers that meet set requirements. There is usually a fee for this service, but it can be helpful in securing a quality provider.

Real Parents Say...

If an in-home sitter is your first choice, go to your local clergyman or physician. Ask them if they know of someone who would benefit from a positive relationship with your family and who may need some extra income.

—*M.J., mother of two*

As with any environment in which you leave your child, you must observe, carefully check references, and follow your gut instincts before making the decision regarding the care of your child.

Potential Advantages of Family Day Care

✿ The setting is more home-like; your child can be involved in household activities

✿ Individualized care may be more likely than in formal child care centers

✿ It may be more flexible in accommodating a parent's need to work long hours, care for a child with a minor illness, or arrange to meet a child's special interests

✿ There are playmates, which allows your child the chance to learn social skills and interact with children of various ages

✿ The cost is usually less than in larger, formal child care centers

✿ Bonding and continuity of care with a single care giver is possible

Potential Concerns with Family Day Care

✿ Care giver often works alone. Long days, minimal breaks, and isolation can cause fatigue and stress

✿ If the provider works alone, handling emergencies can be difficult

✿ Inexperienced providers may go out of business in a short time

✿ A backup plan is needed for days when your child or provider is ill, or if your provider has a family emergency or takes a vacation

✿ Some providers may not have the expertise or resources to provide age-appropriate activities for children

✿ Some providers use child care for added income, yet may only give custodial care to the child.

✿ Since your child is exposed to more children, he is also exposed to more germs, which increases the risk for illness and infection

Child care centers, including day cares, corporate day cares, child development centers, and nursery schools, offer more formal child care programs than family child care centers. These centers often care for groups of 10 or more children. Most are licensed. A structured, school-type system is often followed, with children grouped with others their own age. Some programs offer infant care, sick care, drop-in care, and evening or weekend hours.

Low staff-to-child ratios are necessary for quality care. Look for a program with a clear philosophy, goals, a sense of teamwork, and a stable staff.

Potential Advantages of Child Care Centers

- ✿ Many systems are structured to meet your child's developmental needs
- ✿ Most centers have multiple care givers so you are not dependent on one person in times of care giver illness, emergency, or vacations
- ✿ Centers tend to be more closely regulated, allowing for potentially higher safety and health standards
- ✿ A written account of your child's daily experiences is more likely
- ✿ Workers tend to have more formal training in early childhood education and are supervised more closely
- ✿ The environment is totally focused on child care
- ✿ With corporate day care, the company often picks up a portion of the costs
- ✿ Drop-offs, drop-ins, and pickups are convenient with on-site or corporate day care

Potential Concerns with Child Care Centers

- ✿ Since your child is exposed to more children and germs, he has an increased risk of illness and/or infection. A backup plan for sick day care is still needed.
- ✿ There may be strict schedule requirements, less flexibility, and high fees if you arrive late to pick up your child
- ✿ The atmosphere may be more institutional
- ✿ Changing shifts and staff turnover may result in less individual attention between your child and his primary care giver
- ✿ Communication gaps may occur due to multiple providers
- ✿ Good programs typically have a waiting list

Selecting the Best for You and Your Baby

A child needs warmth, love, and security; emotional constancy; and appropriate stimulation and activities. With these needs in mind, knowledge of the child care options available, and your personal needs and budget, you are ready to evaluate potential care givers and settings.

To choose a quality in-home provider, first define the job and the wage. For instance, will cooking or grocery shopping be required? Then, advertise the position. Place notices in local papers, your church or synagogue bulletin, employment offices, senior citizen centers, or area schools and colleges. Talk with friends, relatives, and colleagues. Contact nanny and au pair agencies. Talk with your pediatrician, family doctor, or clergy.

Hopefully, there will be several candidates to interview. Invite them to your home and get to know them. Helpful questions include: What is your idea of a typical day with my child? How do you discipline a child? Tell me how you feel about play? Tell me how you approach feeding: on demand or scheduled? How often do you change diapers? What would you do in case of an emergency? Do you have CPR and first aid training?

Watch the potential provider interact with your child. Does he or she smile, talk with baby, show affection, and handle baby carefully?

If the candidate appears to meet your needs, discuss job specifics, wages, taxes, time off, etc. Ask for at least three references for you to call.

When it's all said and done, trust your instincts. If you feel uneasy about someone, don't hire her. You may also want to try the arrangement on a trial basis before making it permanent. This gives everyone time

> **Real Parents Say...**
>
> Good day care is very hard to find. There is a lack of qualified people and centers with flexible hours. I opted to work part time and opposite hours from my husband after my children were born. We use minimal day care, save money, and have the best care for our children.
>
> —*Lisa and Roger, parents of two*

to adjust. Finally, don't forget to complete the necessary tax and social security paperwork.

Finding a quality away-from-home child care provider requires many of the same steps, except you'll want to visit the day care, both when children are there and when they are gone, if possible. One of the key questions to ask is if the day care is licensed or registered. Ask, too, how long they plan on providing day care services. Finally, before making your decision, remember to call at least three references.

Sick Child Care

If your child is like most others, he will get his share of illnesses. Whenever possible, sick children are best kept at home. Sending a sick child to day care only exposes other children to the illness. As a parent, you can help control the spread of disease by keeping your sick child home. Some agencies or centers provide "sick child care." These facilities are set up to care for your child on days he is not feeling well. Expect the cost to be double that of regular child care.

Keep a child with the following conditions at home or in sick child care:

- Colds, flu, respiratory infections, diarrheal infections, skin and eye infections, hepatitis, or any contagious disease, such as head lice, pinkeye, or bronchitis.
- A child with a 100°F or higher fever or a child who has vomited two or more times in 24 hours.
- A child with any weeping mouth sore should not be sent to child care.
- If a child must take medicine, write out detailed instructions. Include: when, how much, and with or without food. If a child is not contagious and is feeling well, you and your provider should decide if the day care setting is appropriate.

Develop an alternate plan for sick days, whether it includes one parent staying home, sick child care, or asking a friend or relative to help out.

Finding and Keeping a Super Sitter

Periodically, you will want and need to go out for a romantic evening, shop without baby, or visit friends. In these situations, you often need child care providers other than your work-related providers. Look for an experienced babysitter. Avoid hiring someone who is too young to handle emergency situations.

Sometimes family or friends can recommend someone who has worked well for them. If you don't know the babysitter personally, ask for and check references. Excellent care givers for an occasional outing can include:

- ✿ A high school or college student
- ✿ A babysitting co-op
- ✿ Grandparent, friend, neighbor, or relative
- ✿ Someone from your religious congregation

Once you have found a great sitter(s), you will need to acquaint them with your child, his routine, and your home. Here are some pointers for keeping a great sitter.

When using a babysitter for the first time, have him or her come early so that your child has time to adjust to this new person. You may even wish to have the care giver come to your house for an hour or two some afternoon while you are home.

Always take the time to go over your baby's routine, explaining how you do things and where supplies are. Remember, aspects of baby care that are second nature to you may be entirely unknown to someone who doesn't have children or hasn't been around children in some time (even your own parents may need a refresher course). For example, remind the sitter to put up crib rails and to close gates at the top of stairs.

Leave the phone number and address of where you will be. Let the sitter know how long you plan to be gone. Post all emergency numbers (fire, police, doctor, ambulance, poison control center) next to the phone and show the babysitter where they are. Also, provide a list of trusted neighbors, friends, or relatives who can be contacted if you can't be reached.

Leave the babysitter medical authorization form in case you can't be reached in a medical emergency.

Encourage your sitter to take a babysitting and first aid course. You may even offer to pay for this course. Hospitals often offer the course inexpensively.

Provide your sitter with child care information. An excellent resource is "The Super Sitter" booklet. It's packed with play ideas and safety tips. Write the U.S. Consumer Product Safety Commission for your free copy: U.S. Consumer Product Safety Commission, Washington, DC, 20207.

Be on time. Call if you are going to be late. Be willing to pay overtime.

Settle baby before you leave. Try not to leave a screaming child (though during certain development stages, this may not be possible). Avoid long goodbyes. This can heighten baby's fears and anxieties over your departure.

Leave snacks for both your sitter and your baby.

Avoid leaving dirty dishes, laundry, and other household chores for your sitter unless you have discussed this ahead of time.

Refrain from asking your sitter to handle things you don't like to do— for example, bath time.

Smart Parents Do

Respect your care giver and the important work they do.

Be punctual. Call ahead if you are going to be late. If you find yourself habitually late, you may need to reassess your schedule.

Honor the sick policy.

Exchange information regularly with your care giver. This enables both of you to develop continuity of care and mutual respect for one another. Share with your care giver things that your child makes or does at home.

Discuss any problems promptly and constructively.

Show appreciation for your care giver. Caring for small children is rewarding work, but care givers also welcome being told they are valued. A thank you note, gift certificate, or floral arrangement is a thoughtful gesture. Remember birthdays, special events, and holidays.

Be careful not to take advantage of family and friends. Provide payment or some type of compensation for their services.

Inform your care giver of your schedule in advance as much as possible.

Don't create a scene when you leave. Help your child by getting him settled. Say goodbye before you disappear. Your care giver doesn't need a screaming child for the first 15 minutes of each day.

As your child gets older, provide materials for special activities your child can work on during the day or evening.

Allow for a period of adjustment when baby is with a new care giver. Start with 1 to 2 hours of child care so everyone can adjust slowly.

Pay a fair wage. Check with other parents. Ask your sitter his or her fee.

Do not ask for babysitting credit. Pay on time. If you are exchanging child care services, repay promptly.

Abuse and Neglect

Any time you entrust your child into someone else's care, you want to make sure your child is safe and well cared for. Careful child care selection will help ensure a quality provider. Unfortunately, abuse and neglect occur. Paying special attention to your child can help you assess the quality of care. Warning signs of abuse or neglect include:[7]

- ✿ Changes in a child's behavior or appearance
- ✿ An injury that does not have a reasonable explanation or inconsistent account of what happened
- ✿ Hand or belt shaped bruises
- ✿ Burns
- ✿ Infections, bruises, or bleeding around the genital area
- ✿ A child who has been toilet trained for a long time suddenly starts having accidents
- ✿ Your child's diapers are extremely wet whenever you pick him up and you notice minimal diapers are used during the day
- ✿ A child repeatedly gives you accounts of being bit, hit, or mistreated
- ✿ A change in your child's play. For example, a very gentle child starts hitting or yelling at a doll or smashing toys

If a child has been comfortable with his provider or center and suddenly protests going, look for explanations. Do not automatically assume the worst. He may very likely be going through a developmental stage or may miss you during the day. Make special time together when he is the only focus of your attention.

If you suspect abuse or neglect is occurring, have your child seen by his pediatrician or physician. The health care professional can help you take the necessary steps to report your suspicions. In the meantime, remove your child from that specific day care environment.

Finding quality child care is a challenge whether it is for 4 or 40 hours per week. Your vigilance and dedication to checking out providers, as well as matching your needs with their services, is your best insurance for finding quality care. Top-notch child care providers are very special people. Side by side with parents, they help provide our children with skills and values they will build on for the future.

Real Parents Say...

Day care — check it out thoroughly. Drop in unexpectedly. Watch baby's reactions. Check references. I can't stress this enough — your child is your most important asset. You can learn a lot about your child's care by watching baby and care giver's reactions when you leave and pick up baby.

— *Rene, mother of two*

Organizations

To locate a child care resource and referral center near you that helps link providers and parents, call or write: **Child Care Aware,** 2116 Campus Drive SE, Rochester, MN 55904; 800-424-2246 or 507-287-2220

For information on child care and for assistance connecting parents to child care resources, call or write the following agencies:

National Child Care Information Center (also publishes "Child Care Bulletin"), 301 Maple Avenue West, Suite 602, Vienna, Virginia 22180; 800-616-2242

National Association of Child Care Resource and Referral Agencies (NACCRRA), 1319 F Street NW, Suite 606, Washington, DC 20004; 202-393-5501

For information on child care safety, selecting a quality provider, and selecting and setting up a safe child care environment, call the **National Resource for Health and Safety in Child Care** at 703-524-7802

For information on accredited child care centers, call the **National Academy of Early Childhood Programs** at 800-424-2460

For child care and other parenting information or a copy of their "Children's Bulletin," call the **Children's Foundation** at 202-347-3300

For general information about infants, toddlers, and families, call **Zero to Three** at 703-528-4300

For information on legal issues in child care as either a parent or provider, call **Child Care Law Center** at 415-495-5498

For information on companies and organizations to enable them to respond to the challenges of a changing work force, including information on child care and work options, call or write: **Catalyst,** 250 Park Avenue South, New York, NY 10003-1459; 212-777-8900

For information on family day cares, call or write: **National Association for Family Day Care,** 1331-A Pennsylvania Avenue NW, Suite 348, Washington, DC 20004; 800-359-3817

For information on child care for children with disabilities, call or write: **National Information Center for Children and Youth Disabilities (NICHCY),** PO Box 1492, Washington, DC 20013-1492; 800-695-0285 or 202-884-8200

Brochures and Pamphlets

For a list of accredited early-education programs in your area, send a self-addressed, business sized, stamped envelope to: National Association for the Education of Young Children (NAEYC), 1509 16th St NW, Washington, DC 20036-1426

For information on finding good child care, send two stamps and a business sized, self-addressed envelope and ask for information guide #19 "Finding Good Child Care: The Essential Questions to Ask When Seeking Quality Care for Your Child," and guide #20,

"Finding and Hiring a Qualified In-Home Care Giver:" Child Care Action Campaign (CCAC), Dept. N, 330 Seventh Avenue, 17th Floor, New York, NY 10001

For the pamphlet "Guidelines For Parents — Child Care: What's Best for Your Family" or general information on basic require-ments and the new national stan-dards for acceptable child care centers, write: American Acad-emy of Pediatrics, 141 Northwest Point Road, PO Box 927, Elk Grove Village, IL 60009-0927

Nanny and Au Pair Information

The following agencies offer (for a fee) state-by-state directories of placement agencies specializing in live-in care:

International Nanny Associa-tion, PO Box 26522, Austin, TX 78755-0522

Au Pair in America, The Ameri-can Institute for Foreign Study, 102 Greenwich Avenue, Green-wich, CT 06830; 800-727-2437

Au Pair/Homestay USA, World Learning Inc., 1015 15th Street NW, Suite 750, Washington, DC 20005; 202-408-5380

EF Au Pair, 1 Memorial Drive, Cambridge, MA 02142; 800-333-6056

Au Pair Programme USA, 2469 East Fort Union Blvd, Suite 114, Salt Lake City, UT 84121; 801-943-7788

Au Pair Care, One Post Street, 7th Floor, San Francisco, CA 94104; 800-288-7786 or 415-434-8788

EurAuPair, 250 North Pacific Coast Highway, Laguna Beach, CA 92651; 800-333-3804

R
e
s
o
u
r
c
e
s

InterExchange, 161 6th Avenue, Room 902, New York, NY 10013; 212-924-0446

For a complete list of authorized foreign au pair programs, call the **U.S. Information Agency's Office of Exchange Visitor Program Services** at 202-475-2389

Computer Program
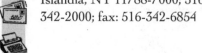
Parents Magazine's Simply Kids: Caring for Your Child Made Easy (Window-based software)
Available at computer stores or write: 4 Home Productions, One Computer Associates Plaza, Islandia, NY 11788-7000; 516-342-2000; fax: 516-342-6854

CHAPTER THIRTEEN

Take This Job and Keep It, Share It, Downsize It, or Leave It

"Contributions to the common good are not measured in dollars, hours, or labor. They are measured in love."
—Della White Steele

Today, 77 percent of all women are employed outside the home before becoming pregnant. Three-fourths of these will return to the working arena after the birth of their babies.[1] The pressures on the working family and need for work-life balancing skills has never been greater.

Many parents feel there are limited options to working outside the home. Often, jobs are necessary for insurance benefits and day-to-day financial security. However, all parents need to take time to evaluate their attitudes, priorities, and role of the work they do in relation to their new family situation. Personal views and attitudes toward work, societal contributions, parenting roles, and responsibilities will influence your children. If you feel your work has purpose and meaning, whether you're a stay-at-home mom or dad or a corporate manager, your child will develop a healthy attitude about the contribution of work to society. However, if you grumble as you leave for work, feel undervalued at home, or perceive a

Necessity Checklist

✿ **Complete a personal inventory** (page 239)

✿ **Assess your financial standing**

✿ **Evaluate your options**

✿ **Make the best work decision for your situation**

paycheck as your total value indicator, your child will be set up to develop a similar outlook on working.

As a parent, you must first seek to find the balance between work outside the home and your parenting goals. Assess your values, expectations, and goals both on the home front and in the workplace. Reviewing this personal inventory before contemplating financially feasible work options will improve your chances of long-term happiness.

Too often this personal financial assessment process is done in reverse with the first question being, "What work situation can we afford?" Personal values and integrity take a back burner in this process, rendering parents susceptible to continuous guilt—guilt about not spending enough time with baby, not contributing financially to the household, lack of promotions at work, and on and on.

Many parents find that once they listen to their inner voice and act on their values, the financial aspects of working options often seem secondary. When you have less money to spend, you simply make do with less.

What to Do When Baby Makes Three— A Personal Inventory

As you contemplate your new role as a parent, take time to think about your expectations. Identify your beliefs and then determine how important those beliefs are to your overall goal of being a good parent. In some situations, you may need to alter your beliefs for the sake of reality. Avoid setting your expectations of yourself too high or at unattainable levels.

For example, if you believe a "good" mom makes her children a balanced breakfast every morning, but you leave for work at 6 a.m., you may end up feeling inadequate when you leave the house without providing breakfast. By understanding your belief, you can identify all possible options to make it happen or you can change your expectation.

Challenging this belief may include exploring a flexible schedule at work, setting out cold cereal the night before, engaging your spouse in breakfast preparation, or providing a special brown-bag breakfast for your child to eat at day care. It may also call for changing my personal standards to include a light breakfast on work days and a full breakfast on days off.

Each parent should complete a personal inventory individually. Then, take time together to compare and discuss your individual values, goals, and expectations for both parenting and career building. It is a good idea to repeat the inventory periodically as your family, personal, and work priorities change.

Personal Inventory Worksheet

1. What is my life purpose?
2. Where do I see myself 5 years from now?
3. What are my parenting goals?
4. What qualities and amount of time do I feel it takes to be a good parent?
5. How do I see myself interacting with my child?
6. What do I want to provide for my child?
7. What does my child need (examples: food, home, clothes, toys, education, etc.)?
8. What values do I want to instill in my child and teach by example?
9. What work am I passionate about?
10. What work do I do well?
11. What do I enjoy about my work?
12. What do I dislike about my work?
13. What material things do I want in the next 5 years?
14. What are my financial and work goals?
15. How do my financial and career goals relate to my parenting goals?
16. What is my ideal parenting-working situation?

A Financial Comparison

After assessing your personal goals and values, review your financial needs. When evaluating financial needs, you can estimate the impact of job options on your financial situation by calculating your projected take home pay and expenditures.

Parents often find there are options to both parents working full time that are also financially feasible. Though the take-home paycheck may be less, expenses such as day care and automobile costs are often lower. This makes overall cash flow equal (and sometimes greater) than with both parents working full time.

By completing both a personal and financial inventory you can make an informed decision about what's best for you and your baby. Single parents benefit from these exercises, also. For example, if staying home with your baby full time is your goal, you may find that the inventories help you identify creative, financially feasible ways to develop a home business or work out of your home.

Ditching the Guilt

Before having a child, parents often envision themselves as patient, kind, organized, and nurturing. When your child arrives, reality sets in. The milk spills, the house is forever a mess, and you lose your patience. As the stress builds, it is easy for the "guilts" to take over. Instead of having the talents of June Cleaver, you may feel more like Oscar, the Sesame Street Grouch. High super-parent expectations can lead to development of enormous guilt between the perfect parent you want to be and the human parent you often are.

Regardless of the work option you choose—full-time mom or dad or full-time or part-time employee—the burden of guilt can lurk behind many corners. Even a stay-at-home parent can get the guilts. Guilt can descend on any parent at any time for not so apparent reasons.

This unwanted baggage takes energy away from your relationship with your child, spouse, friends, and coworkers. Most guilt is unwarranted and unnecessary, and it probably won't make you a better parent anyway.

Steps to Squelching Guilt Attacks

Be confident and comfortable with your decision to work in or out of the home. If you work outside the home, make efforts to participate in work you enjoy. Since you are investing as much as 50 percent of your time away from your family in a job or career, it should be one that makes you eager to get up every day. A healthy attitude about working builds a strong work ethic in children. They learn work has value and purpose, not just a paycheck at the end of a week. Some suggestions:

Find quality child care. Your child's health, well-being, and safety are top concerns. If you feel confident about your day care option, going to work will be much easier (see Chapter 12 on Finding the Best Child Care).

Each parent should live up to his or her responsibilities and expectations. Parents should put forth equal effort and responsibility into raising a child. This means each parent must have and show respect for the work the other parent does. Both parents can pitch in when dividing up household chores. Abandon traditional ideas about stereotypical roles, such as women clean and cook and men take out the garbage. Develop a plan that ensures both parents share household chores, balanced with equal parenting and relaxation time.

Work in a supportive environment. Whether you choose to stay at home or be employed outside the home, strive for a setting that is family-friendly. If you stay at home, your work will be more gratifying if your spouse is supportive. If you work outside the home, look for employers who have strong family policies and practices. Knowing you can stay home to tend to a sick child while being allowed sick time or flex hours or to work at home is more conducive to a positive working relationship than having to dip into vacation time or call in sick yourself to avoid an unexcused absence.

Don't expect perfection. Recognize impatience is part of parenting. Children don't need baths every night. Set realistic goals.

Set aside "guilt-free" time. Identify your personal guilt triggers and explore ways to avoid them. If you feel guilty about not spending enough time with your child, you might try setting a timer for 10 to 20 minutes and giving her undivided attention. When the timer rings, resume your previous tasks. Your child will be content and you will have progressed toward your goal.

Ask yourself if the cause of your guilt is within your control. If the answer is yes, take action. If the answer is no, the guilt feelings are self-deflating—let them go. For example, if you work outside the home, let go of guilty beliefs that good mothers stay home all day. Look for the positive aspects of working, and devote lots of quality time to your child when you are home. Remember you are in good company—more than 50 percent of all mothers work outside the home.

Relish the time that you have with your child. Don't waste precious time feeling bad for moments you missed. Make the most of the here and now.

Trust that you are a good parent. Don't compare yourself to other parents. Listen to your child. Love her unconditionally. Learn from your mistakes, but don't dwell on them. There are numerous parenting books available that can help you build your confidence. Share ideas and concerns with other parents, and use their advice if you feel it fits your parenting philosophy.

Fix simple meals. Mealtime can be fun and delicious without gourmet entrées requiring involved preparations. Keep meals simple and share tasks if possible. If fancy meals are a must, cook large amounts and freeze some or set aside one or two meals a week as "special meals." Mealtime should be fun, not exhausting.

Set a goal of at least four meals a week when the entire family dines together.

Say no. Parenting takes lots of time. Sometimes this means you have to temporarily say no to community or professional organizations. People usually understand you need to spend time with your family. If the work interests you, volunteer to help out in a few years or drop something else before taking on a new responsibility.

Shut out distractions. Turn off the television and the telephone and enjoy quiet time with your family. As a parent you send your child the important message, "I want to spend time with only you for awhile." The outside world can wait. Special family time is important.

Wake up a half hour earlier. An extra half hour in the morning allows you time for yourself or time to get a few household tasks done before the day with baby begins. This extra 30 minutes can leave you feeling more organized and less harried throughout the day.

Create your own family traditions. Holidays can become stressful if you try to carry on a multitude of traditions. Slow down and enjoy the family time. *The Quality Time Family Cookbook* and *Year Round Low-Fat and No-Fat Holiday Meals in Minutes* (see Resource section) are excellent books packed with ideas for creating your own special days.

Delegate, delegate, delegate. At home or work, stop trying to do everything yourself. Do tasks that require your special skills and divide up responsibility for other work with your partner and coworkers as appropriate.

> ## Real Parents Say...
>
> Take advantage of your guaranteed 12 weeks off for maternity or paternity leave if you possibly can. The break from the workplace provides a new parent time to bond with baby, adjust to new responsibility and recuperate.
>
> —*Evie, mother of two*

Take care of your body. Eat well, exercise, and get adequate rest. When you take care of yourself you have more energy for others. Taking care of yourself helps keep your attitude more positive and the guilts are less likely to creep in.

Talk about stressful feelings with your spouse or a friend. It is important to acknowledge, especially to yourself, that it takes a lot of time and energy to raise a child.

Working Parents—The Options

Finding the balance between sufficient child-parent time and an enriching career is no easy task. What works for one parent may not work for another. Take time to listen to your inner voice and you will find an option that works best for you. There are as many parenting-work options available as there are parents.

Option 1—One Parent Stays Home

This option combines the traditions of the '50s and the potential solution to finding quality day care in the '90s. Advocates claim this option is best for child and parent, providing time for consistent parenting and bonding.

How it Works: This option is self-explanatory. One parent works outside the home and one stays at home. Traditionally it has been the woman who undertook the role as primary care giver and dad fulfilled the role of sole breadwinner. Tradition, however, is beginning to give way to some very dedicated, happy, value-centered stay-at-home dads.

Potential Advantages: There is more time available for bonding between parent and child. Your child has the benefit of mom or dad as her primary care giver. She is raised exclusively with your standards, beliefs, and values during the early years. You are there for the "firsts," such as rolling over, crawling, walking, and talking. You have time to make nutritious, economical meals from scratch. You have more time to clip coupons and take advantage of rebates and sales, as well as to make heirlooms for your child.

Your child is exposed to fewer germs and infections by not attending day care. There are fewer child care hassles. And life seems a little more sane when you are not passing baby off at the door.

Potential Disadvantages: Your child may have limited social interaction with other children. There is potential social isolation for the at-home care giver, as well.

Some stay-at-home parents have unrealistic expectations of themselves, such as "I should use this time to prepare gourmet meals every night" or "I should be able to keep the house spotless." There may be increased financial pressure or burden on the sole wage earner or even income loss if the spouse's income was significant in comparison to related expenses. Delayed career opportunities and lesser retirement savings for the parent who stays home may also be factors to consider.

> **Real Parents Say...**
>
> For us, the stay-at-home option was best. There are many hidden costs to working outside the home and you miss your child's growing up.
>
> —*Carol and Jim, parents of one*

Other Things to Consider: Do you like to be with people all day or can you enjoy the company of a baby from 9 to 5? Consider joining or forming a play club which can provide great socialization and support for you and your child. Many stay-at-home parents find maintaining a positive self-esteem can be as challenging as giving up an income because too often in society our worth is tied to earning a salary. Recognize parenting as a worthy profession and follow your gut feeling that staying home is best for you and your family right now. Make sure the stay-at-home parent has some personal time during the day. Be prepared to answer annoying questions like "What do you do?" and "It must be nice not to have to work?"

Dads at Home

It's new and it works—dads at home. Though the majority of stay-at-home parents are moms, dads are successfully breaking tradition. When one parent chooses to stay home, it is usually an economically driven decision. In today's workforce, women continue to typically earn one-third to two-thirds less than their male counterparts, often making it financially logical for moms to stay at home. However, recent studies indicate this trend is beginning to change. As women secure better paying jobs, dads have more opportunities to contemplate the stay-at-home option. Most stay-at-home dads feel fortunate to have the time to develop a close bond with their child.

The lack of support, isolation, and initial out-of-place feelings at their child's play group are often their main frustrations. If you are considering the stay-at-home dad option, focus on the wonderful experiences you will be able to share with your child. Corporate culture can sometimes add to the challenge by sending covert messages to dads encouraging the job commitment priority before family needs.

Be ready to roll with the punches when people ask you what you do. Don't be surprised to receive sidelong looks as they learn you are not the main financial provider. Consider starting a support network with other stay-at-home dads. Look for other parents who are supportive of your new role. Focus on your family's happy lifestyle and the important role you are fulfilling in your child's development.

Option 2—Both Parents Return to Work Full Time

This is a common situation for many families in America.

How it Works: Both parents return to work full time weeks to months following baby's birth (or adoption) or after paternity or maternity leave ends. Time becomes your most precious commodity and you become a master at coordinating work, social, and child care schedules.

Potential Advantages: Financial security. People-contact at work helps you stay up-to-date on business and community activities and provides a mentor or friendship circle. Both parents can continue to pursue career goals. Parents find the work they do outside the home both enjoyable and enriching. Your child develops social and play skills by interacting with other children at day care.

Potential Disadvantages: Finding and retaining quality, affordable child care isn't easy. The need to take your child out of your home in bad weather or at inconvenient times is often stressful. Someone else is raising your child 8 to 10 hours each day. Don't be surprised if you collapse into bed by 9:05 almost every night. The days off go by very fast.

Your child is frequently exposed to colds, flu, and other illnesses at day care.

Other Things to Consider: Some parents arrange to work opposite schedules from their partner to keep child care time and cost to a minimum. This option provides increased parent-child time, but can be stressful on a marriage when spouses find their quality time is almost nonexistent and intimacy dwindles to a mere peck on the cheek as they swap baby at the door.

You may require additional services such as housecleaning, laundry service, and frequent takeout meals to keep up with the day-to-day chores and still allow for family time.

Option 3—One Parent Works Part Time While the Other Parent Works Full Time

This option often appears as the ideal solution to the sometimes insane and hectic lifestyle of both parents working full time.

How it Works: One parent continues to maintain full time employment while the other parent decreases his or her work hours to spend more time at home with baby.

Potential Advantages: Your child is at day care less often. Parents have more time to spend with baby and each other. Reduced child care expenses and work-related savings along with a decrease in taxable income may make this option financially equivalent to both parents working full-time. In some cases, the family actually comes out financially ahead because overall expenses are less. There are fewer time-stresses on the family than when both parents are working full time. Grocery shopping, cleaning, and doctors appointments can be completed during the week so days off can actually be spent doing things together instead of playing catch up.

Potential Disadvantages: You may experience a decrease in income. Career advancement opportunities may be slowed for the parent who switches to part time. Depending on your company's culture and flexibility, you may not be able to pursue certain job duties or responsibilities due to your part-time status. Some child care programs require you pay for full-time care regardless of the number of hours your child is actually there.

Other Things to Consider: When negotiating a part-time position, make sure both you and your employer are clear on your duties and responsibilities. This is an important point if you are going from full-time to part-time status within the same job. Part-time work may allow you to

Real Parents Say...

I love the part-time option. I am home some days so I don't have to wake my children up early. They also love the sitter and I feel it's good for them to be around other children. We seem to have the best of both worlds.

—Sandy and Rick, parents of three

If it's financially possible, I feel part time is the best. This work option gives your child a chance to intermix with other children and allows you a chance to be with other adults. Working full time is a challenge. Sometimes you feel like you miss out on a lot of your child's life.

—Patty, mother of two

I opted to work part time after my children were born and opposite hours of my husband to save money and ensure they had the best care.

—Lisa and Roger, parents of two

explore other options and interest areas you may not have been aware of in your full-time position.

Option 4—Taking Baby to Work

What could be nicer than to take baby with you to work? The child care hassle is solved and you never have to express milk if you are breastfeeding. It is a great solution—if baby never cries!

How it Works: One parent, typically the mother, takes the child with her to work. The child stays in the office with mom during the day. Mom resumes her work duties with baby present.

Potential Advantages: Parent and baby are not separated during the day.

This option is a great convenience for breastfeeding moms. There are minimal child care hassles and costs. This work option is convenient for occasional meetings and educational programs when baby is sleeping or playing contently.

Potential Disadvantages: It may be difficult to concentrate on your work if baby is fussy. It may actually take longer to get work completed if you are continually interrupted or your baby needs attention. Baby's crying may be aggravating to fellow employees. Work group activities may be difficult with baby present. Your baby may feel neglected if you can not attend to her immediately.

Real Parents Say...

We need to put more pressure on employers for options to separating mom and baby. Work flexibility and family-friendly employers are a must. You can't build effective companies on a foundation of broken homes and stressed employees.

—*Linda, mother of three*

Other Things to Consider: This option is great until baby can motor all by herself; child-proofing your office is a must if you plan to have baby present after she is 4 months of age. Share and discuss the idea with your peers. Receptive coworkers can ensure success, while resentful ones can facilitate failure. Develop a plan with your employer to handle work situations that may be disrupted with baby present; make a special effort to reassure your employer that having your child there will not impair your work performance.

Option 5—Job Sharing

Job sharing is a fairly new concept in many workplaces. Though it sounds great on paper, many employers are reluctant to pursue this option. Employers' fears of the lack of dedication to the job and communication challenges are the major areas of concern. However, for those who have successfully accomplished this working option, the reward of balance between career and family is great. While pursuing this new role, the added stress and responsibility of being a precedent-setter is heightened. All eyes are upon you as you strive for success.

How it Works: In a job share, two employees voluntarily share the duties, responsibilities, salary, and benefits of one job. Employees often work opposite days, overlapping once a week to share information, work on joint projects, and complete strategic planning.

Potential Advantages: This option allows both employees to keep their current job while working part time. The employer retains valuable employees, and employee job satisfaction is usually high.

Child care and work-related expenses, such as travel, clothing, and lunch costs are usually lower. This option allows for more time with your child and family.

Potential Disadvantages: Jobsharing may slow or limit career advancement. Some jobs may be difficult to job share, such as management positions. Jobs that entail one type of work, such as journalism or easily divided up caseloads, are easiest to share.

Not all people are compatible to job sharing. Financially, there is a decrease in salary and benefits. Additionally, employers' and fellow employees' misconceptions that part-time employees are not as dedicated to the job or that job sharing can not be successful may add stress to the new situation.

Other Things to Consider: Top qualities that job sharing candidates should possess include: being easy to get along with; being able to work collaboratively as a team player; having a similar work ethic as your job-share partner; having personal and work-related confidence and flexibility; and having good written and oral communication skills. Before proposing a job-share to your employer, investigate and research other successful job share situations in your line of work and develop a detailed plan of how the job share will work (if you know of a potential partner, include that also). Once your job share proposal is accepted and implemented, evaluate and improve it regularly to ensure your success.

Option 6—Flex Time or Compressed Work Weeks

In some situations, job sharing or part-time hours are not viable options. In these situations, flex time or a compressed work week may work well for you.

How it Works: The employer and employee mutually decide on a work schedule that allows the duties of the job to be fulfilled with a nontraditional schedule. A compressed work week by definition is full-time work scheduled in fewer than 5 days in a week. For example, some employees work three or four 10-hour days instead of traditional 8-hour days. Actual hours worked are the same, but there are more full days off.

Potential Advantages: Your care expenses may be lower because of additional full days off work. Employers report there is typically less absenteeism related to sick-child care and doctors appointments. Employers retain valuable employees and save costs incurred to hire, train, and orient a new employee. Employee job satisfaction is usually high.

Many employees find they are actually more productive because they are committed to the work option, feel valued by their employer, and relish their time off with their family.

Potential Disadvantages: This option does not work for all types of jobs. Long days can get tiring and work pressure can be higher as you try to schedule the same amount of work into fewer days. Attending and scheduling company meetings may be more difficult as the employee is at the work site fewer working periods. And it may be difficult to find child care for more than 8 or 9 hours at a time.

Other Things to Consider: Some employers find offering flexible scheduling to all employees actually decreases turnover and improves flexibility.

Develop a written plan with your supervisor that identifies expectations and potential advantages (such as decreased absenteeism and turnover) but also covers potential solutions. Remember to evaluate the plan periodically and communicate regularly with your supervisor to ensure the plan's success.

Option 7—Telecommuting

Some employers allow employees to do the majority of their work at home while communicating via the telephone, computer, and fax machine.

How it Works: As an employee, you typically retain your job duties and responsibilities. Employees who telecommute typically spend 1 to 2 days per week in the office picking up assignments, attending meetings, and presenting completed projects.

Potential Advantages: You maintain your current job, benefits, salary, and seniority. You are doing the majority of work out of your home so child care costs may be less. Your work schedule is up to you as long as your work is done on time. This situation can be great if you can work while baby sleeps or naps. Employer retains the experience and talents of a trained and valued employee; turnover is reduced and employee job satisfaction is high. There is less time spent commuting to and from work, so unused travel time can be spent with baby.

Potential Disadvantages: Child care is still necessary for times when you are at the worksite or have to finish projects without baby underfoot. Not all jobs can be performed via telecommuting. Working at home can get mundane if you miss the activity and social interaction of the office.

It may be tempting to clean the house, pay bills, and fold laundry when office work needs to be done, so time management and self-discipline skills are a must for success. There may be days when you feel you can't get away from the stress of the "office" or "home," which have become one and the same. It helps to keep your office in an area where you can shut the door and keep your work and family life separate.

Other Things to Consider: With your employer, establish who is responsible for the costs of a computer, modem, and fax machine, as well as telephone, electric, and office supply expenses. Present and discuss the idea with your peers. Receptive coworkers can make this option more likely to succeed. Clearly identify job duties, expectations, and deadlines with your supervisor, including how assignments will be handled and if you will be paid by the project, hourly, or salary.

Option 8—Start an At-Home Business

Occasionally, due to personal choice or a less than family-friendly workplace, flexible job options do not work out. Your goal may be to stay home more, yet you find your family financial situation is in need of a second paycheck. Don't despair. Fortunately, there is an exciting and challenging opportunity of home businesses as endless as your creativity.

Before you pursue a home business, ask yourself if you possess these characteristics for success: initiative, determination, perseverance, self-confidence, flexibility, decision-making abilities, leadership and organizational skills, and a genuine interest in people.

How it Works: You decide on a business you would like to pursue. Check out your personal inventory at the beginning of this chapter for work ideas you are passionate about. Explore the current need for your service in your community, and share your idea with friends who will give you both honest feedback and encouragement.

Depending on the nature of your business, set up an office and begin providing the service. Make sure to check with your local zoning agency before opening your doors for business. You may be required to obtain a special permit.

Potential Advantages: Earn a second income while being home with your child. There are often tax breaks, write-offs, and advantages for people who operate a home-based business. Consider talking with an accountant early in the planning stage. Flexible work hours and schedules are determined by you. You can often determine how busy you want to be, making your income potential unlimited.

Potential Disadvantages: Some businesses may be hard to conduct professionally at home with baby. You may still need part-time child care for times when business and baby don't mix. There may be increased wear and tear on your house if your office or study and living room are one and the same. It can be hard to separate work and home life, so many successful at-home entrepreneurs suggest keeping the business in a separate part of the house and maintaining set hours.

Small businesses can take a lot of time and energy to get off the ground. Income can be sporadic and unpredictable. Also, in most situations there are no paid benefits such as insurance and sick or vacation or holiday time.

Other Things to Consider: You may want to rent an office for those times it's not possible to work at home. Develop a plan—formal or informal—of your goals and how to attain them. Read books and literature on starting a home business and consider taking classes at a local technical school, college, or university. Discuss the financial aspects with an accountant who can help you set up proper record keeping from the beginning. Check with your local bank, lending institution, or small business agency; some states offer grants or incentives for businesses owned by women.

Organizations and Brochures

**R
e
s
o
u
r
c
e
s**

These organizations offer ideas on new ways to work. To request information on any of the following publications, send a business size self-addressed, stamped envelope to:

"New Ways to Work," Publications, 149 Ninth St., San Francisco, CA 94103; 415-995-9860

Catalyst, 250 Park Avenue South, New York, NY 10003-1459; 212-777-8900

"A Working Woman's Guide to Her Job Rights," Women's Bureau, United States Department of Labor, PO Box PM, Washington, DC 20210

9 to 5, National Association of Working Women, 614 Superior Avenue, Cleveland, OH 44113-9990; 216-566-9308, or call the National Job Problem Hotline at 800-522-0925

Full-time Dads magazine, PO Box 577, Cumberland, ME 04021; 207-829-5260

At Home Dad newsletter, 61 Brightwood Avenue, North Andover, MA 01845-1702

The Fatherhood Project, 303 Seventh Avenue, 14th Floor, New York, NY 10001

Single Mother Newsletter, The National Organization of Single Mothers, Inc., PO Box 68, Midland, NC 28107-0068

Mothers' Network, 70 West 36th Street, Suite 900, New York, NY 10018; 800-775-MOMS

Working Mother magazine (each October issue lists the 100 most family-friendly companies in America) 230 Park Avenue, New York, NY 10169

Mothers' Home Business Network, PO Box 423, East Meadow, NY 11554

Financial Support

If you require assistance for food, shelter, and basic living costs, you may qualify for certain state and government programs. Check your local telephone book for the following agencies:

Women, Infants and Children
(WIC) program—a supplemental food program

Aid to Families With Dependent Children

Maternal Child Health

Department of Health and Human Services

Books

Staying Home: From Full-Time Professional to Full-Time Parent by Darcie Sanders and Martha M. Bullen, Little, Brown and Company, New York

The Job Sharing Handbook, Ten Speed Press, PO Box 273, Berkeley, CA 94707

Maternity Leave: The Working Woman's Practical Guide to Combining Pregnancy, Motherhood and Career by Eileen L. Casey, Green Mountain Publishing; 802-985-8228

The Quality Time Family Cookbook by Julie M. Cull, RD, Chronimed Publishing, Minneapolis, MN

Year-Round Low-Fat and No-Fat Holiday Meals in Minutes! by M.J. Smith, RD, Chronimed Publishing, Minneapolis, MN

Seven Habits of Highly Effective People and **First Things First** by Stephen Covey, Simon and Schuster, New York

Business References

Growing a Business by Paul Hawken, Simon and Schuster, New York

The Consultant's Calling: Bringing Who You Are to What You Do by Geoffrey M. Bellman, Jossey-Bass, Inc., San Francisco

Writers Digest Books, F&W Publications, Cincinnati

Making Telecommuting Happen by Jack M. Niles, Van Nostrand, Reinhold, NY

The Telecommuter's Handbook by Brad Schepp, McGraw Hill

Telecommuting Review Newsletter, Gil Gordon Associates, 10 Donner Court, Monmouth Junction, NJ 08852; 908-329-2266

The One Minute Commuter: How to Keep Your Job and Stay at Home Telecommuting, Lis Fleming, Ltd., PO Box 1738, Davis, CA 95617-1738; 916-756-6430

Work at Home Days: The Overlooked Solution to Sick Child Care, Lis Fleming, Ltd., PO Box 1738, Davis, CA 95617-1738; 916-756-6430

Small-Time Operator: How to Start Your Own Small Business, Keep Your Books, Pay Your Taxes, and Stay Out of Trouble by Bernard Kamoroff, Nolo Press, Berkeley, CA

Home Sweet Office by Jeff Meade, Peterson's, PO Box 2123, Princeton, NJ 08543-2123; 800-338-3282

Connexions (a newsletter for home-based professionals and mothers), C.J. Hull, PO Box 1461, Manassus, VA 22110; 703-791-6264

Chapter Fourteen

Investing in the Future and Other Financial Matters

"A penny saved is a penny earned."
—*Benjamin Franklin*

As you babyproof your house, purchase a safe car seat, and attend to other baby matters, there are a number of financial concerns you will need to consider during baby's first years. These will include obtaining a social security number for baby, as well as planning for his future education needs. Planning for baby's college or higher education needs may hardly seem a pressing matter in the wake of frequent midnight feedings and diaper changes. However, with college costs rising a hefty 7 percent per year, there is no better time to start saving. First things first, though...

Getting Baby's Social Security Number

When baby arrives, you must notify Uncle Sam of your latest family member. As of January 1995, you need to obtain a social security number for your child at birth in order to claim him as an exemption on your income tax return.

Many hospitals simplify this process by having you complete the necessary paperwork along with the

Necessity Checklist

✿ Obtain baby's social security number

✿ Save for college and retirement

birth registration before you are discharged. If you do not complete this paperwork as part of your hospitalization you can either go to your local social security office or call the Social Security Administration at 800-772-1213 and request an application for a social security number.

You will need to show your baby's birth certificate, hospital, or doctor's bill as documentation of identity. There is no fee for this service. Beware of companies offering to obtain baby's social security number for you for a fee.

If tax time rolls around and baby's social security number has not arrived, write "applied for" on your tax return. If you have not received a social security number within 6 to 8 weeks of application, contact your local social security office to check on the progress of your application.

Real Parents Say...

Savings—what a great idea! Grandparents love to have a part in this! Savings bonds, mutual funds, and stock portfolios all make great baby and special occasion gifts.

—Fran and Lee, parents of three, grandparents of four

We have put $25 a month in a special savings account for each child since birth. We add any cash gifts they receive to this. We estimate each child will have $10,000 by college age—it's a start!

—Ann and Ed, parents of five

Saving even a little is beneficial. Practice putting one dollar a day into a savings bank. When you're up to $100 to $250 put it into a mutual fund or investment.

—Katherine and Martin, parents of one

Starting a College Fund

Are you sitting down? Consider this: If current trends continue, by the time Junior is done with high school, you could be seeing tuition and associated costs of $26,700 per year at a public university and $68,220 per year at a private college.

Once you recover from the sticker shock, you need to devise a plan to prepare for the future. Many financial experts suggest parents do not need to foot the entire college bill. Many families pay for college from a variety of sources, including grants, loans, and scholarships. Some parents want to share the burden with their children by having them chip in money from part-time or summer jobs, or work-study programs.

Even if you don't plan to pay the expenses all by yourself, it is wise to have some type of education savings plan. Early investing allows you the advantage of compounding interest and time for money growth. College financial aid departments, investment companies, and financial planners are good resources for helping you calculate the amount of money you need to save each year to meet these financial educational needs.

When selecting an investment, make sure it meets your needs for growth and accessibility at a level of risk you are comfortable with. Consider seeing a financial planner to establish a savings system that will work best for you. Computer programs such as Quicken and Microsoft Money can also help you identify monthly savings goals.

Be aware that your child may occasionally be eligible to pay taxes. This situation can occur if he earns a certain amount of money or interest in a year. Even if your child is not earning income from a job, he may accumulate unearned income in the form of interest, capital gains, and dividends.

Plan for Your Retirement, Too!

In addition to planning for baby's college education, you need to plan for your own future and retirement. Just as with baby's college fund, saving each month for retirement will really add up.

Sources of retirement income vary. However, one question of today's parenting generation is, "Will social security retire before I do?" In 1945, there were 50 active workers to support each person on social security; by 1985 that number had fallen to only 33 workers. It is projected that by the year 2030 there will be only two active workers to support each social security recipient.[2] With this current trend, investing in other retirement avenues will be important.

When establishing a retirement portfolio, include investments that provide tax deferred growth. These programs allow you to save without paying taxes on your earnings until you withdraw the money. Individual Retirement Accounts (IRAs), Keogh plans, annuities, employee pension plans, 401(K) plans, and profit sharing are some examples of qualifying retirement plans.

In a pinch, you may be able to borrow from your retirement fund to pay for your child's college. Under current tax laws, you can borrow from some tax-deferred savings plans to pay for college. However, before you borrow, be prepared to repay the loan in approximately five years. In most cases, a 10 percent penalty applies if the loan is not repaid in the set time frame.[3]

Though your golden years seem decades away, start saving now so you can spend time watching sunrises and sunsets or traveling foreign lands instead of punching a time clock at age 70.

Budget Helpers

Earning additional income is one avenue for increasing savings. Savvy penny-pinching is another. Unplanned spending can make saving and investing difficult. One way to avoid impulse spending is to put your purchases to the test by asking yourself, "Does my child really need this?" "How long will we use it?"

Some baby products and toys are only suited to meet baby's developmental stages for a few short months. As soon as baby outgrows this toy, he is on to other things and the hardly-used item finds its way to the bottom of the toy box. Tips to minimize impulse spending include:

Make a list before you shop and stick to it. Estimate costs, and decide which items you can afford and need most. Avoid spending outside your list or budget.

If you happen across a great sale, ask to put the item on layaway. This allows you some quiet time outside the store to decide if you really need the item.

Ask yourself, "Is this item a need or a want?" Many things we think are needs are really wants or short-term conveniences.

Ask yourself, "How much will I really use this item?" Wait some time before making the purchase—like a week or two.

Buy in a store with a good return policy and save your receipts. Some stores even allow you to take items home on approval. Leave your new purchase in its packaging for a few days. If you don't have a true need to use it within 3 to 5 days, return it. You're doing great without it.

Be wary of too-good-to-be-true mail order promotions. Today, multitudes of companies have access to your name, telephone number, address, and personal information such as the due date of your baby. Don't be surprised if you are inundated with "new parent" mail before you even arrive home from the hospital.

Smart Parents Do

Record your spending. This helps you monitor where your money goes and helps you keep from making impulsive purchases.

Pay yourself out of every paycheck. Even if it's only a dollar or two, start saving. Ideally, you want to be able to save 5 to 10 percent of your income.

Reduce your expenses. Cutting a little in every area can be easier than trying to completely eliminate areas of spending like dining out or entertainment.

Set a budget for gift-giving times of the year. Love can be expressed in a variety of ways besides the number of toys under the Christmas tree or around the birthday cake.

Avoid shopping as a leisure activity. Recreational shopping can be a costly hobby. Often you buy things you do not need.

Dine in with other family members or friends instead of eating out. The cost is one-fourth to one-half of dining out, and there is no babysitting expense.

Evaluate the products you use. Select products based on both price and quality. An inexpensive brand of baby wipes can end up costing more than a slightly higher priced brand if you find yourself using two wipes instead of one at each diaper change.

When shopping by mail, always remember to add in the shipping and handling costs when comparing prices.

Pay with cash or checks whenever possible and keep a minimal number of credit cards. This helps reduce the urge to overspend.

Make a practice of paying your credit card bills in full. If you can't pay for a purchase in full, postpone buying if possible.

Pay off any debt as quickly as you can. In some situations, it may be beneficial to use your savings to pay down debt. If you are paying 9 percent on a loan and earning 5 percent on money in a savings account, you will be further ahead by paying off the debt and then focusing on building up your savings.

Make extra payments on debts whenever possible. Extra money paid on the principal of a loan adds up quickly. Making 26 biweekly mortgage payments instead of 12 monthly payments can speed up a home mortgage by 5 years or more, saving you thousands of dollars in interest payments.

Never spend change. This is one of the easiest ways to save additional dollars each year. Start a change jar at home. If lunch comes to $5.07, give the clerk $6, don't break out the 7 cents. Put the $.93 in your change jar at home. When the jar is full, deposit the money into an investment account.

Use coupons every time you shop and get in the habit of transferring the amount saved into a savings or investment program.

Take advantage of manufacturer rebate offers. Instead of cashing the rebates for spending money, put them in your child's savings account.

Save all reimbursement from out-of-pocket travel, mileage, and business expenses. Also, save all flexible spending health and child care reimbursements. These dollars add up quickly in a savings program. If you put the money back into your checking account it quickly gets spent on daily living expenses.

Invest any inheritances, windfalls, bonuses, gifts, or lottery winnings. Because this is money you probably were not counting on, it is easier to save it before you cash it.

Regularly increase payroll savings or retirement deductions. An ideal time to do this is when your receive a salary increase. Because you never see the money you often do not miss it.

Evaluate insurance policies and deductibles annually. Having a slightly higher deductible can save you lots on premiums. Put the premium in an emergency savings account in case you need to pay your portion of a deductible on a claim.

Check out a local credit union. Many credit unions waive fees associated with checking accounts and also help you set up automatic savings programs.

Get a credit card with a low interest rate and no annual fee.

Look for a banking institution that offers free monthly checking. Some banks may require that you keep a minimum balance. Think of this balance as part of your emergency fund. A fee-free checking account can easily save you $10 to $20 each month.

Give to a worthy cause. This may seem impossible amid a mountain of debt

Real Parents Say...

Using coupons saves us 20 to 30 percent on grocery bills and up to 10 percent on personal items. We've used one year's rebates to buy $600 worth of savings bonds.

—*Jen and Jack, parents of one*

and new baby expenses, but this act can be very rewarding. Start with a small amount and give for the pure joy of giving.

Seek solvency. This simply means learning to live comfortably and peacefully with the money you have.

When working with a financial planner consider how she or he is paid. Planners often work for a fee, a commission, fee plus commission, or a salary paid by banks or other institutions.

Pamper yourself occasionally. There is not much point to scrimping and saving unless you can occasionally enjoy spending when the occasion and your bank balance is right.

Books

Securing Your Child's Future: A Financial and Legal Planner for Parents, Facade Columbine Books, New York

The College Costs and Financial Aid Handbook, College Board Publications, Box 886, New York, NY 10101

The Bankers Secret, Good Advice Press, Elizaville, NY 12523; 914-758-1400

A Penny Saved: Teaching Your Children the Values and Life Skills They Will Need to Live in the Real World by Neales Godfrey, Fireside Books, 1230 Avenue of the Americas, New York, NY 10020

Magazines

Kiplinger's Personal Finance (mutual fund investing, tax and retirement planning, and other consumer issues); 800-544-0155

Money (mutual funds and money management issues); 800-633-9970

Computer Programs

Quicken, Intuit, PO Box 3014, Menlo Park, CA 94026-9959; 415-322-0573

Money Microsoft Corporation, 1 Microsoft Way, Redmond, WA 98052-6399

Parents Guide to Money (an interactive CD-ROM), Intuit, PO Box 7850, Mountain View, CA 94039-7850; 415-944-6000

Organizations and Other Information

Social Security Administration; 800-772-1213

American Association of Retired Persons (AARP), 601 E Street NW, Washington, DC 20049; 202-434-2277

Office of Public Affairs, U.S. Savings Bond Division, Washington, DC 20226; 1-800-4US-BOND

CHAPTER FIFTEEN

Baby Yourself: Making Time for You

"Keeping house is like threading beads
on a string with no knot at the end."
—Anonymous

As a new parent you may find yourself often wondering if you will ever sleep for 8 uninterrupted hours again. Six hours, at this point, may sound like a vacation! You will adjust, and believe it or not, you will someday be able to make it out of the house, baby in tow, in under an hour.

Though time may seem like a precious commodity these days, time is what you must allow yourself. It is easy to feel the time crunch with the demands of a new baby. There will be days when you feel you accomplish nothing but feeding and changing dirty diapers. This can be especially true for new parents who are used to checking 20 items off their daily "to-do" lists in the "days before baby."

Allowing yourself time to enjoy and adapt to parenthood is the greatest gift you can give yourself, especially during baby's first weeks of life. Take time to get to know your infant and rediscover you. Becoming a parent is a life-changing experience. You have new responsibilities and expectations of yourself. Take time to reflect on these changes and give yourself a break. Pat yourself on the back for doing a terrific job during the past 9 months. Enjoy the moment. The pressures and hectic pace of the outside world will be part of your reality soon enough.

Taking, or more appropriately, "making" time for one's self often seems harder to do for new moms than dads. Maybe there's some mysterious guilt hormone that passes through the placenta right before baby's birth that makes moms feel like motherhood and self-sacrificing are inseparable terms. Maybe men are more "in tune" with their bodies and minds and instinctively know when they need time for themselves. Maybe there is a societal myth that "good moms" always put their children and family before themselves. Maybe it is all three.

Whatever the reason, it is important for both parents to take care of themselves. Saying "yes" to yourself does not mean you are saying "no" to mothering or fathering. In fact, giving to yourself, having a healthy self-esteem, and taking care of your body are all gifts to your child and partner, too. When you pursue mental and physical health, vitality, and balance you tend to be less exhausted and have more energy, patience, and enthusiasm for your new family.

Taking Care of #1

Here are some practical ways to keep yourself mentally and physically healthy rather than exhausted during those first few weeks with baby.

Remember this transition is temporary. In a few weeks you will start to develop a routine that is comfortable for you and your family. Life will seem more organized and your energy level will resume.

Have fewer expectations of yourself. Taking care of a newborn baby is hard work. Assume you will get very little accomplished besides baby care. Remember, caring for a baby is very important work. There may not be a paycheck to reimburse you for your efforts at the end of the week, but instead there is a wonderful feeling that you are nurturing and bonding with baby.

Take a shower and get dressed in the morning. A shower can help energize you and start your day off or end your night—depending on baby's schedule—on the right track. Getting out of your pajamas and into fresh day clothes helps set a positive mood for the day.

Sleep when baby sleeps. Taking care of baby is demanding work. Reject the urge to get 10 things accomplished while baby sleeps. Remember, your body needs to recuperate, too.

Limit visitors. Some visitors are great; too many can be exhausting, leaving you and baby cranky. It is also a good idea to minimize baby's exposure to cold and flu bugs so easily passed to baby via well-meaning hugs and kisses. Politely ask people to call before dropping by. Offer them times when it is convenient for you to have them stop by. They will understand you need to rest.

Take a walk. Get some sunshine and fresh air. Nothing lifts the spirits quite as easily as a brisk walk.

Accept generosity. When people offer to help out, tell them what you need. Precooked meals, a couple hours of babysitting, grocery store pickups, or diaper runs are all things others can do, allowing you some precious moments to yourself.

Forget about the dust bunnies. There will always be time in the future for cleaning. Concentrate on spending lots of quality time with your baby. If the dirt and clutter bother you, hire someone to clean for a few hours a week.

Indulge in those loving feelings—cuddling, singing, and playing with your baby. Babies are only small for a short time. Treasure your special moments together. Focus on bonding, which is so important at this time.

Socialize and get a sitter for a couple of hours. Even nursing moms need an escape from what some days seems like the feeding and changing factory. A chat with friends can help you stay in touch with the world outside your home. Even though you love your baby immensely, a little adult conversation breaks the monotony of singing lullabies and saying "goo-goo-ga-ga." Give yourself some credit. Caring for a baby is some of the most important work you'll ever do. It is a huge responsibility. Take pride in everything from feeding to burping to diapering, realizing you are the most important person baby needs right now. Don't expect to be a child care expert. Avoid criticizing yourself and trust your judgment on how to handle baby.

> **Real Parents Say...**
>
> Cooking and cleaning can wait until tomorrow for babies grow up too fast.
> —*Lois, mother of three*

Reach out to other moms and dads. Other parents' stories can be helpful during this adjustment period. It's nice to know others understand how you feel.

Don't forget about dad. With so much emphasis on mom and baby, it's not surprising that new dads often feel left out. It is important to recognize that the majority of these changes affect dad, too. He, like mom, needs personal time, also. Focus on you two as a couple—as well as being new parents.

Emotions With New Baby on Board

Sometimes new moms feel more than overwhelmed after childbirth. It is not uncommon to feel a wide range of fluctuating emotions. Often there are the anticipated feelings of joy, excitement, and relief that it is over. Some mothers experience feelings of uncertainty, anxiety, and frustration. These feelings may even seesaw back and forth making you feel like you are on an emotional rollercoaster of highs and lows.

The postpartum period, as well as the entire first year of baby's life, involves ongoing social, psychological, and emotional adjustment. Remember that these fluctuating feelings are normal. There are many demands placed on a new mother and her family. These symptoms are not signs of weakness or inadequacy. Time, patience, and the support of friends are all important during this adjustment period.

Sometimes, despite lots of support, women experience more confusing emotions. Health professionals classify these emotions in three ways: the blues, postpartum depression, and postpartum psychosis.

The Blues

More than 80 percent of all new mothers experience the so-called baby blues.[1] This is the most common, most well-known, and least severe of the postpartum reactions. A sudden drop in pregnancy hormones, feelings of letdown after the emotional experience of childbirth, and exhaustion are all thought to contribute to "the blues."

The baby blues typically appear suddenly, usually a few days after birth, but can also occur several weeks after delivery. Signs of the blues include crying for no apparent reason, impatience, anxiety, restlessness, irritability, and episodes of mood swings. Although this common condition usually passes within days to a few weeks, its symptoms can be eased when a new mom takes steps to combat fatigue and isolation. Extra rest, good nutrition, medical care, and some assistance caring for baby can help you recover more quickly.

Postpartum Depression

For 10 to 20 percent of mothers, the blues spiral into various degrees of postpartum depression.[2] For some women there is a feeling that a heavy, gray cloud constantly looms overhead. Postpartum depression is a chronic syndrome that can occur within days of delivery or gradually up to a year later.

Not every new mom with postpartum depression experiences the same signs and symptoms. Symptoms that may indicate you're experiencing more than the blues may include:

✿ unending anxiety attacks;

- ✿ sleep disturbances;
- ✿ appetite disturbances or loss of appetite;
- ✿ overconcern for the baby;
- ✿ lack of concern for the baby;
- ✿ loss of sexual desire (beyond the normal, "I'm too exhausted to make love");
- ✿ fatigue and exhaustion; and
- ✿ in some cases, mothers have obsessive thoughts about hurting themselves or the baby.

Despite the term depression, some mothers feel more nervous or anxious rather than sad. Postpartum depression is not just a bad day, it's a collection of symptoms that are overwhelming and engulfing.

If you find yourself experiencing these symptoms, it's important to contact your physician. Postpartum depression is a physical illness that affects the brain. Finding a support group, talking with a therapist, and in some cases, taking an antidepressant medication are all potential avenues of treatment. If you are breastfeeding, talk to your physician before taking any medication.

Left untreated, postpartum depression can damage a woman's well being and self-esteem, as well as put her baby at risk. The sooner help is sought and treatment is started, the sooner recovery can occur and you can feel well again.

Postpartum Psychosis

Postpartum psychosis is the least common but more severe type of the postpartum reactions.[3] Many of the symptoms are similar to postpartum depression, but more extreme. Other symptoms of this illness may include hallucinations, bizarre feelings or behavior, and insomnia.

The onset of symptoms is usually within the first 2 weeks after baby's birth. Postpartum psychosis is a serious emergency and can be life threatening. If you experience any of the above symptoms, seek immediate medical help.

As Time Goes On—Time Just for Mom

As your life takes on a new sense of normalcy, it is important to build continued time for yourself into your regular routine. Too often, moms and dads alike find they manage to take care of both baby and themselves during the first few months, only to find that when the newness wears off, or the maternity leave is over, the self-care plan collapses.

Moms that are employed outside the home often find returning to the job site similar to cramming one more thing into a diaper bag that is already jammed full. Stay-at-home moms or dads often find the social isolation and lack of adult contact more than taxes them. Both situations can leave parents feeling stressed out, exhausted, and stretched to the limits.

Everyone needs time for him or herself during the day. Time alone nourishes you and gives you a sense of self. This is especially true for women who have been socialized to constantly think of others first. Women sometimes feel that asking for time alone is selfish and self-indulgent. Contrary to this belief, time alone is necessary to maintain both physical and mental health.

Real Parents Say...

You must make time for yourself and don't feel guilty about it. Everyone will benefit from it!

—*Marlene, mother of three*

How Much Time Do You Need?

All this "self-time" sounds great, right? But the big questions are, "How much do I need?" and "Where can I find any more time in a day that's already too full?" The amount of personal time each person requires is very individual. For many people about 30 minutes a day for leisure seems to work well. If daily free time isn't possible, three or four short breaks during the week seem to be more refreshing for people than one 5-hour block on Sunday.

If you are overstressed and low on personal time, you may be experiencing some or all of these typical signs of stress.

Stress Signals
- ❀ Trouble sleeping
- ❀ Headaches
- ❀ Irritability
- ❀ Unable to relax even when you have time to

You may really be stressed if:
- ❀ You have run out of empathy or sympathy for other people
- ❀ You find you can not talk nicely to strangers
- ❀ You feel people close to you take more than they give

A certain amount of stress is good. Stress can help us meet deadlines, take action in emergency situations, and encourage us to maximize our potential. Too much stress, however, can cause health problems, mental anguish, and relationship difficulties.

Developing a Healthy Attitude

An important step to taking care of yourself is to develop a healthy attitude. One way to do this is to see yourself as a bank. Your child, partner, job, home duties, etc., are constantly making withdrawals from the bank. Withdrawals are made when you work, and when you give and do things for others. It is up to you to replenish the funds. One way to revitalize yourself is to take time regularly during the week to do something just for you. If you do not make deposits on a routine basis, your emotional and physical bank will be empty and you will feel like you have little left of yourself to give your child, your partner, yourself, or others.

With a young child, making deposits can be overwhelming. Maintaining the belief that your personal time is important, too, makes it easier to make deposits.

Hints for Making Healthy Deposits

Identify where your time goes. For one week track how your time is spent each day. At the end of the week review the time log. Identify the most and least important things you did. Find ways to postpone, delegate, or eliminate unimportant tasks and use the time for yourself.

Set realistic goals for making healthy deposits. Start slowly. If 30 minutes seems impossible, aim for 15 minutes, three times per week.

Make a list of all the things you enjoy or find relaxing. These should be activities you do only for you that leave you feeling refreshed and energized. For example, take a relaxing bubble bath, shop alone, or read a novel. Try to set aside the time to do at least one relaxing thing each week.

Put yourself at the top of your daily "to do" list. When you are at the end of the priority list you are more apt to be exhausted and skip your personal time.

Don't hinge your self-care success on the cooperation of your family. It's unfortunate, but some spouses, in-laws, or children can be disapproving when you take time for yourself. Remember, you are setting a good example for them and staying healthy.

Evaluate your TV stance. Turn off the TV if necessary. Television may depress rather than revitalize you, especially at the end of a busy day.

Avoid negative people who leave you feeling drained and in a bad mood. Choose instead to spend time with

> ## Real Parents Say...
>
> I tape my favorite TV show and take time to watch it when the kids go to sleep. It gives me 30 to 45 minutes of "think about nothing time."
> —*Anne, mother of two*
>
> Making a date to do something with a friend once or twice a month helps me get out of the house, keep in touch with friends, and socialize. I find that actually setting a golf outing or shopping date keeps me committed to taking care of myself.
> —*Carol, mother of two*

people who leave you feeling positive and good about yourself.

Eat plenty of fruits, vegetables, and other low-fat foods. Avoid high-fat foods, excess caffeine, alcohol, and nicotine. A healthy diet helps keep your stress level in check and provides energy to help you get through your busy days (and nights).

Budget Helpers

Listed below are personal pampering ideas that are free or inexpensive.

- Go for a walk or run with a friend.
- Go to a movie. Matinees are often half price.
- Get a free makeover.
- Attend a lecture.
- Visit a museum.
- Buy some perfumed bath gel and enjoy a relaxing bubble bath.
- Visit the library.
- Play tourist. Visit your local attractions.
- Exercise outdoors.
- Treat yourself to a cup of gourmet coffee in a quiet, relaxing shop.
- Listen to a meditation tape.

Will I Ever Be Productive Again?

With baby under foot, you may often wonder if you will ever be productive again. New parents often look at veteran parents in awe, exclaiming, "How do they get it all done?" Experienced parents know the secret lies in *making* rather than *waiting for* spare time to appear and in keeping organized.

Here are some steps you can take to find more time when baby makes three.

Work with baby close by you. Babies are often content to play as long as mom or dad is within sight. Keep plastic dish buckets full of toys near your work area, but out of baby's reach. Recycle toys, putting new ones out for baby as he becomes bored with the first bucket of toys.

Some babies enjoy being in a front carrier, sling, or backpack. This allows baby to be close to you while you have your hands free to work.

Stop work periodically and spend 5 to 10 uninterrupted minutes with baby. Sometimes all baby wants is reassurance that you are there and a little of your uninterrupted time. Often when baby gets into things or wants to permanently fixate to your leg, he is only asking for attention. Take time out for love and hugs and it will prevent a half hour of tears and frustration later.

Make and use lists. Keep the list short. If you do additional tasks, add them to your list and then cross them off.

Establish some sort of daily routine. This does not need to be a rigid schedule, but baby will nap better and you will tend to be more organized if you follow some sort of routine.

Consider the possibility of hiring help. Often having someone help with routine cleaning can free up time for baby and you. This may be especially necessary if you and your spouse both work outside the home or you are a single parent.

Drop unrealistic standards for house cleaning. Put visions of sparkling windows and shiny woodwork on hold.

Delegate tasks. Divide and conquer everything from the laundry to shopping. Decide what each partner will be responsible for doing. This way things are more manageable and less overwhelming.

Try to do one or two routine chores each evening. This will help prevent Saturdays or days off from becoming total "catch-up" days.

Make a list of all the things that routinely need to be done each month. Write down everything from paying bills to changing oil in the car. Decide how often items really need to be completed. You may need to choose to do something less often to keep your sanity.

While baby sleeps, do tasks you can't do while baby is awake. For example, folding wash can be done with baby in hand while making an important phone call may not be practical when baby is awake. Prioritizing your daily tasks can help you enjoy your time with baby while getting routine chores completed.

Allow an extra 10 minutes to get everywhere. This will keep you from feeling harried and rushed when baby dirties his outfit as you head out the door.

Prepare the night before. Set out clothes, breakfast items, morning mail, and other things before going to bed.

> ## Real Parents Say...
>
> Don't plan on undertaking any major projects (remodeling, building, etc.) while baby is small. You'll just be frustrated and disappointed. Just enjoy.
>
> —*Fran, mother of three*
>
> Waking up 30 to 45 minutes before baby is great. It's tempting to stay in bed, but I find on days I rise early, I have the time to sip on juice or coffee, read, drop notes to friends, write in my journal, or just relax and think. I usually use 5 to 10 minutes of that time to organize the day or start a load of laundry. It's amazing how great the day goes when I take time for myself first.
>
> —*Laurie, mother of one*

Expect bad days. There will be days when all your organization skills fly out the window. Expect it and listen to what your baby needs. Tomorrow you can start again.

Keeping Relationships Alive and Well

When a baby arrives on the scene, life at home changes drastically. Emotions fluctuate, fatigue sets in, and often the focus of the family quickly shifts to a baby who is totally dependent on you. This situation can place considerable stress on any relationship.

Nuturing your relationships is as important as taking care of yourself and your baby. Maintaining your relationship refuels your energy for parenting. Your baby benefits when both his parents are happy.

Real Parents Say...

One night every two weeks, we eat late, after the kids are asleep so we can have a quiet, unhurried, uninterrupted meal.   — *Lisa and Roger, parents of two*

Smart Parents Do

- ✿ Set aside a "date" night each week. Take time to keep the romance in your relationship.
- ✿ Take a class together. Maybe you have always wanted to learn how to dance. Who knows, baby may even enjoy dozing off on your shoulder to a slow waltz.
- ✿ Listen to each other. Open, healthy communication means sharpening your listening skills.
- ✿ Talk, talk, talk. Keep those lines of communication open. A healthy relationship benefits from at least a half hour of communication each day.
- ✿ Plan a weekend getaway. Extended uninterrupted time together can refresh you physically as well as keep the romantic spirit alive in your relationship.
- ✿ Attend a marriage encounter weekend. This is a great chance to rediscover your dreams for the future and enrich the spirituality in your relationship.
- ✿ If the relationship seems really stressed, look for help. Often talking with a therapist can be beneficial.
- ✿ Don't be afraid to say, "I'm sorry."
- ✿ Don't go to bed angry. You probably won't sleep well anyway. By resolving disagreements as they arise, you prevent little molehills from developing into impossible mountains.
- ✿ Send flowers for no reason at all. Keep the romance alive.
- ✿ Have a quiet, romantic meal together.

✿ Kiss and hug on a daily basis. Touch is very important. Without it, we become isolated. So go ahead and hug—share the gift of love.

✿ Leave love notes around the house. Everyone needs to know they are loved and appreciated. Finding an "I love you" note taped to the toothpaste can get your day off to a loving start.

The following national organizations can direct you to resources in your community. Your local hospital or physician's office may also know of local support groups.

Parents Anonymous; 800-421-0353 or 213-410-9732

The American Psychological Association; 202-336-5700

Depression After Delivery; 800-944-4773 or 215-295-3994

Marriage Encounter; 800-795-LOVE (5683)

Postpartum Support International; 805-967-7636

Sources

CHAPTER 1

1. U.S. Department of Agriculture, Center for Nutrition Policy and Promotion, 1120 20th St. NW, Suite 200, Washington, DC, 20036; May 1996.

2, 3. Johnson, Robert V., *Mayo Clinic Complete Book of Pregnancy and Baby's First Year*, New York: William Morrow and Company, 1994, 51, 192.

4, 5. Health Insurance Association of America, *Source Book of Health Insurance Data*, 1025 Connecticut Avenue NW, Washington, DC, 20036–3998, 1991.

CHAPTER 2

1. Rabin, Katherine, "Ten Things You Must Do For Your Kids," *Kiplinger's Personal Finance Magazine*, 2/95, 69-70.

2. Conkling, Winifred, *Securing Your Child's Future: A Financial and Legal Planner for Parents*, Fawcett/Columbine: New York, 1994, pg 3.

3. "Life Insurance Buyer's Guide," National Association of Insurance Commissioners.

CHAPTER 4

1, 2, 3, 4. U.S. Consumer Product Safety Commission, Washington, DC, 20207; July, 1996.

5. Shelov, Steven P., Editor-in-Chief, The American Academy of Pediatrics *Caring for Your Baby and Young Child: Birth to Age Five*, New York: Bantam Books, 1993, pg. 222.

6. U.S. Consumer Product Safety Commission, Washington, DC, 20207; July, 1996.

7. Jones, S., and Freitag, W., *Guide to Baby Products,* New York: Consumer Reports Books, 1991, pg. 178.

8. U.S. Consumer Product Safety Commission, Washington, DC, 20207; July, 1996.

9. Shelov, Steven P., Editor-in-Chief, The American Academy of Pediatrics *Caring for Your Baby and Young Child: Birth to Age Five,* New York: Bantam Books, 1993, pg. 222.

10. Doherty, Shawn, "The Walker Controversy," *Parenting,* 10/93, pg. 164.

CHAPTER 5

1. National Highway Traffic Safety Administration, "Traffic Safety Facts 1994 — Children" 400 7th St. SW, Washington, DC 20590.

2. Iowa Governor's Traffic Safety Bureau, 307 E. 7th St., Des Moines, IA 50319.

3, 4. National Highway Traffic Safety Administration, "Traffic Safety Facts 1994 — Children" 400 7th St. SW, Washington, DC 20590.

5. Iowa Governor's Traffic Safety Bureau, 307 E. 7th St., Des Moines, IA 50319.

6. Jones, Sandy and Werner Freitag, *Guide to Baby Products, 3rd Edition,* Consumer Reports Books: Yonkers, New York, 1991.

7. "What Every Premature or Small Baby Needs to Know... Before Riding in the Car," American Academy of Pediatrics, PO Box 927, Elk Grove Village, IL 60009-0927.

CHAPTER 6

1. "Expenditures on Children by Families," *1995 Annual Report,* U.S. Department of Agriculture, Center for Nutrition Policy and Promotion, 1120 20th Street NW, Suite 200 North Lobby, Washington, DC 20036; April 1996.

CHAPTER 7

1. Jones, Sandy and Werner Freiteg, *Guide to Baby Products, 3rd Edition,* Consumer Reports Books, 1991.

2. "Landfill Excavations," conducted by William Rathje, PhD, professor, University of Arizona, 1990; and Robert V. Johnson, M.D., Editor-in-Chief, *Mayo Clinic Complete Book of Pregnancy and Baby's First Year,* New York: William Morrow and Company, 1994, pg. 208.

3. Benson, Jessica and Maija Johnson, "What a Baby Really Costs," *Parents,* 4/94, pg. 92-93, and estimated costs using current product price averages and number of items needed.

4. Shelov, Steven, The American Academy of Pediatrics *Caring for Your Baby and Young Child: Birth to Age Five,* New York: Bantam Books, 1993, pg. 164.

CHAPTER 8

1. Consumer Product Safety Commission, Washington, DC 20207.

2. "The Toy Manufacturer of America Guide to Toys and Play" The American Toy Institute, Inc., New York, NY, 11/94.

3. Jones, S., and Freitag, W., *Guide to Baby Products,* Consumer Report Books, 3rd Edition, Yonkers, New York, pg. 290.

4. Shelov, Stephen, *Caring For Your Baby and Young Child: Birth to Age 5,* The American Academy of Pediatrics, Bantam Books, New York, 1991, pg. 395.

5. Fulghum, Robert, *All I Really Need to Know I Learned in Kindergarten,* Villard Books, New York, 1986, pg. 7.

CHAPTER 10

1, 2, 3, 4, 5. Shelov, S., *Caring for Your Baby and Young Child: Birth to Age Five,* New York: Bantam Books, 1993, pg. 59, 64, 478, 584.

6, 7. "Back to Sleep," P.O. Box 2911, Washington, DC 20040.

8. Johnson, Robert V., *Mayo Clinic Complete Book of Pregnancy and Baby's First Year,* New York: William Morrow and Company, 1994, 104.

9. Sudden Infant Death Syndrome Institute, 11/95.

10. Shelov, S., *Caring for Your Baby and Young Child: Birth to Age Five,* New York: Bantam Books, 1993, pg. 583-584.

CHAPTER 11

1, 2, 3. National Safe Kids Campaign, 1301 Pennsylvania Avenue, NW, Suite 1000, Washington, DC, 20004-1707; August 1996.

4. Consumer Product Safety Commission, Washington, DC 20207.

5. National Safe Kids Campaign, 1301 Pennsylvania Avenue, NW, Suite 1000, Washington, DC, 20004-1707; August 1996.

6, 7. Thoman, Mike, "Bicycle Safety," Iowa Chapter of the American Academy of Pediatrics Accident Prevention Committee.

8. "Prevention, Pesticides, and Toxic Substances (7404)," U.S. Environmental Protection Agency, Washington, DC 20036, March 1996.

9. "Vinyl Miniblinds Are a Hazard for Young Children," *ISU Extension Newsletter Bulletin*, ISU Extension, Ames, IA 50011.

10. Shelov, Steven, *Caring for Your Baby and Young Child, Birth to Age Five*, The American Academy of Pediatrics, Bantam, 1991, pg. 463.

11. American Association of Poison Control Centers, 3201 New Mexico Avenue NW, Suite 310, Washington, DC 20016.

12. National Safe Kids Campaign, 1301 Pennsylvania Avenue NW, Suite 1000, Washington, DC, 20004-1707; August 1996

CHAPTER 12

1. "Expenditures on Children by Families: 1995 Annual Report," Center for Nutrition Policy and Promotion, U.S. Department of Agriculture, 1120 20th Street NW, Suite 200 North Lobby, Washington, DC 20036; April 1996.

2. Casper, Lynne M., "Who's Minding Our Preschoolers," *Current Population Reports*, U.S. Department of Commerce, Bureau of the Census, Washington, DC 20233-0001, March 1996.

3. "It Is Time to Join the Campaign for Quality, Affordable Child Care in America," Child Care Action Campaign, 330 7th Avenue, 17th Floor, New York, NY.

4, 5, 6. Conkling, Winifred, *Securing Your Child's Future: A Financial and Legal Planner for Parents*, New York: Fawcett Columbine, 1994, pg. 141.

7. Shelov, et al, *Caring for Your Baby and Young Child: Birth to Age Five*, Bantam Books: New York, 1991, pg. 434-435.

CHAPTER 13

1. Casper, Lynne M., "Who's Minding Our Preschoolers?", *Current Population Reports*, U.S. Department of Commerce, Bureau of the Census, Washington, DC, 20233-0001, March 1996.

CHAPTER 14

1. The College Board, 45 Columbus Avenue, New York, NY 10023-6992.

2. *Personal Financial Management*, Emerald Publications, 11555 Rancho Bernardo Road, San Diego, CA 92127, pg. 13-14, 101.

3. Conkling, Winifred, *Securing Your Child's Future: A Financial and Legal Planner for Parents*, New York: Columbine, 1994, pg. 189.

CHAPTER 15

1, 2, 3. Johnson, Robert V., *Mayo Clinic Complete Book of Pregnancy and Baby's First Year*, New York: William Morrow and Company, 1994, pg. 426-427.

Index

abuse, child care and, 232
accidents, home, 193
air travel, 87
alcohol,
    breastfeeding and, 146
    pregnancy and, 12-13
    safety and, 186, 196
allergic reactions, 158, 178
alpha-fetoprotein screening (AFP), 5
amniocentesis, 4
antibiotics, 187
appliance safety, 196, 197, 198, 210
at-home businesses, 253-255

baby blues, 273
baby bottles, 153, 165
baby clothes, 91-106
    basic, 92-96
    resources, 105-106
    safety issues, 100-101
    sizes of, 97-98
    sleepwear, 98-99
baby food, homemade, 164
baby powder, 111
baby toys, 86, 116, 121-138
baby wipes, 72, 87, 111
    homemade, 119
babyproofing your home, 191-214
    resources, 213-214
babysitters, selecting, 229-230
babysitting co-ops, 219-220
backpack baby carriers, 60
bags, diaper, 115-117
balloons, safety of, 132
bassinets, 61-62, 185

bath sets, hooded, 96
bathing, 56-58, 199
    safety and, 199
    washcloths and, 95
bathroom safety, 198-199
bedding, 185
    cribs, 45-51
    youth, 49
bedroom safety, 200
beds,
    water, 46
    youth, 49
bibs, 95
bicycle safety, 201-202
blankets,
    electric, 51
    receiving, 51
blood tests, prenatal care, 3
bonnets, 94
books, reading to baby, 122, 126-129
booties, 94
bottlefeeding, safety, 161
bottles, baby, 153, 165
bras, maternity, 36-37, 39, 166
breast pumps, 144
breastfeeding clothes, 36-37, 39, 166
breastfeeding problems, 148-152
breastfeeding resources, 169-171
breastfeeding, 140-152, 188
    bras for, 36-37, 39
    involving fathers in, 146-148
    pumps for, 144
    SIDS and, 185
    vitamin D and, 143
    work and, 155-156

breastmilk, storing of, 144, 148
budget, working with, 22-24, 262-263
bunting, 95

caffeine,
    breastfeeding and, 145
    illness and, 188
car seat resources, 88-89
car seats, 60, 75-85
    booster, 79
    convertible, 78, 84
    infant, 77
career issues,
    family leave, 26-27
    maternity leave, 26-27
    resources, 256-258
    working options, 237-258
carriers, baby, 60-62
cereal, rice, 158
cesarean section, costs of, 6
chairs,
    high, 51-53
    hook-on, 62-63
changing tables, 60-61
checkups, medical, 176-178
child care centers, 225-227
child care costs, 14, 216-217
child care resources, 234-236
child care,
    away-from-home, 223-227
    family, 223-225
    in-home, 221-223
    selecting, 215-236
    sick, 228-229
    tax issues, 217-218
choking, 161
    bottle feeding and, 154
    toys and, 133
chronic conditions, prenatal care and,
    2
cigarettes, pregnancy and, 12-13
climbing, play and, 122
cloth diapers, 94-95, 108-110, 118
clothes, baby,
    resources, 105-106
    sizes of, 97-98
    sleepwear, 98-99
    winter, 95
clothes, maternity, 33-42
    casual, 35
    exercise and, 39
    fabrics, 34
    formal, 39
    resources, 42
    sizes of, 34
    underwear, 38-39, 41
    work-related, 35
clothes, nursing, 36-37, 39, 166

clothing, baby, 91-106
    basic, 92-96
college funds, 1, 260-261
colostrum, 142
Consumer Product Safety Commis-
    sion, 72
coping, 240-244, 269-283
    resources, 283
cords, window covering, 194-195
cow's milk, 163
cradles, 61-62, 185
crawling, play and, 122
crib gyms, 131
cribs, 45-50, 185
    costs of, 45
    linens for, 50-51
    mobiles and, 64
    selecting of, 45-50
    used, 47-48

day care, see child care
dehydration, 182-184
delivery costs, prenatal and, 6
detergents, laundry, 70, 113
development, child, play and, 122-123
diabetes, gestational, 5
    resources, 15
diabetes, prenatal care and, 2, 3, 6
Diaper Genie, 114
diaper bags, 115-117
diaper pails, 114, 115
diaper pins, 117
diaper rash, 112
diaper services, 109
diapers, 60-61, 107-120
    cloth, 94-95, 108-110
    disposable, 110, 117
    resources, 120
diarrhea, 154, 182
dieting, 168
disability insurance, 25, 29
    resources, 32
disposable diapers, 110, 117
Down's syndrome, 5
drowning hazards, 195
drugs, pregnancy and illicit, 12-13

education funds, 1, 260-261
eggs, 162
electrical outlets, safety, 194
exercise,
    maternity clothes and, 39
    pregnancy and, 12
    strollers and, 54
Exersaucer walker, 62

fabric, synthetic, 96, 98-99, 101
family leave, 26-27
    resources, 32

fathers,
   breastfeeding and, 146-148
   stay at home, 246
feeding problems, 151
feeding, 139-171, 242-243
   encouraging good habits, 166-168
   fluid needs, 183
   high chairs and, 51-53
   hook-on chairs and, 62-63
   introducing solids, 157-161
   involving fathers in, 146-148
   recommended amounts, 156-157,
      158, 160-161
   travel and, 86
fever, 178-182, 186
   child care during, 228
financial planning, 18-19, 21-30, 240,
   259-267
   emergency fund, 21-22
   record keeping, 28
   resources, 15, 31, 267
fire safety, 210-211
fluid needs, 183
fluoride supplements, 143, 154, 163
Food Guide Pyramid, 160-161
food safety, 161-163
food, baby, 157-163
   homemade, 164
formula feeding, 152-156
   costs of, 141
   homemade, 165-166
furniture, nursery, 43-50, 60-62

games, baby, 124-126
gates, safety, 67-68, 194, 212
generic medications, 188
gestational diabetes, 5
   glucose challenge test, 5
   resources, 15
goat's milk, 163
gowns, 92
grasping, play and, 122
guardian, selecting of, 20-21
gyms, crib, 131
gynecologist, 2

hair care, baby, 70
hats, 94
health care resources, 15
health care spending accounts, 14
health coverage, home, 10
health insurance, 7-12, 13-14
   for baby, 11-12
   hospital stay and, 13-14
health records, 175
helmets, bicycle, 201
high blood pressure,
   prenatal care and, 2, 3-4, 6
high chairs, 51-53

home safety measures, 191-214
home safety resources, 213-214
honey, 162
hook-on chairs, 62-63
hosiery, maternity clothes, 38-39
hospital stays, postnatal, insurance
   coverage and, 9-10, 13-14
human chorionic gonadotropin, 3
hypertension, prenatal care and, 2, 3-4,
   6
illness references, 190
illness, 173-190, 228-229
   child care during, 228-229
immunizations, 176-178, 187, 188
infants, low weight, travel and, 82-83,
   84
infection,
   breast, 150
   Group B streptococcus (GBS), 4
insurance, 24-26, 29, 265
   disability, 25, 29
   health, 7-11
   for baby, 11-12, 30
   life, 25-26
intolerance, food, 158
iron, breastfeeding and, 143

jackets, 95-96
job sharing, 250-251
juice, 154-155, 159
jumpers, baby, 63-64
Juvenile Products Manufacturers
   Association, 43-44

kitchen safety, 196-198, 210

lactation, see breastfeeding or nursing
language skills, play and, 122
laundry tips, 99-100
laundry, diapers and, 113-114, 118
lead poisoning, 163, 202-204
life insurance, 25-26
   for baby, 11-12, 30
linens, baby, 50-51
lotion, baby, 70

maternity clothes, 33-42
   casual, 35
   exercise-related, 39
   fabrics, 34-35
   formal, 39
   resources, 42
   sizes of, 34
   underwear, 38-39, 41
   work-related, 35
maternity leave, 26-27
Medicaid, 7-8
medical supplies, basic, 187

medical tests,
  postnatal, 7
  prenatal, 2-6
medications,
  child care and, 228
  generic, 14, 188
  safety and, 186, 198, 204-206
midwife, 2
milk, 140
  cow's, 163
  goat's, 163
minerals, 154
mittens, 95
mobiles, 64, 131
monitors, baby, 65
multiple births, breastfeeding and, 145

National Highway Traffic Safety
  Administration, 85
neglect, child care and, 232
newborn clothing, 96, 97
night lights, 65-66
nonstress test, prenatal care and, 6
nurse-midwife, 2
nursery furniture, 43-50, 60-62
  safety and, 43
nursery rhymes, 122, 128
nursing bras, 36-37, 39, 166
nursing resources, 169-171
nursing, 140-152
  breast pumps and, 144
  involving fathers in, 146-148
  iron and, 143
  SIDS and, 185
  vitamin D and, 143
  work and, 155-156
nutrition, 139-171
  fluid needs, 183
  prenatal, 12

obstetrician, 2
Onesie-style shirts, 92
outdoor safety, 200-201, 210

pacifiers, 66-67, 131, 153
pads, nursing, 166
pail, diaper, 114, 115
Pap smear, prenatal care and, 4
perinatalogist, 2
pets, safety and, 195
physical skills, play and, 122
pins, diaper, 117
plane travel, 87
planning, financial, 21-30, 259-267
  resources, 267
plant safety, 207-209

play,
  child development and, 122-123
  parent's role, 123-124
  simple games, 124-126
playpens, 67
poisoning, 204-209
portions, 167
postnatal checkups, 7, 176-178
postpartum depression, 273-274
postpartum psychosis, 274
powder, baby, 70, 111
preeclampsia, 4
pregnancy clothes, 33-42
pregnancy resources, 15
pregnancy,
  exercise and, 12
  medical tests during, 2-6
  planning of, 185
  shoes and, 40
  smoking and, 12-13
premature babies, travel and, 82-83, 84
prenatal care, 2-6, 17-32
  nutrition, 12
  resources, 15
prenatal costs, delivery and, 6
priorities, 239
problem-solving skills, play and, 123
product safety, baby, 72
productivity tips, 278-280
products, baby, 43-74
  resources, 74
pumps, breast, 144

rash, diaper, 112
rattles, 131
reactions, allergic, 158, 178
record keeping,
  financial, 28
  health, 175
retirement planning, 261-262
running, play and, 122

sacque sets, 96
safety gates, 67-68, 194, 212
safety resources, 213-214
safety, 191-214
  bathroom, 198-199
  bedroom, 200
  bicycle, 201-202
  fire, 210-211
  high chairs and, 51-52
  kitchen, 196-198, 210
  medications and, 186, 204-206
  nursery furniture and, 43
  outdoor, 200-201, 210
  plants, 207-209
  resources, 213-214
  strollers and, 53, 54
  toys, 131-134

seats, car, 60, 75-85
  booster car, 79
  convertible car, 78, 84
  resources, 88-89
shoes, 94, 96-97
  pregnancy and, 40
shots, baby, 176-178, 187
sickle cell anemia, 3
SIDS, resources, 190
skin care, 70, 72, 100, 112, 116, 152
sleep positions, 185
sleepers, 92-93
  blanket, b94
sleepwear, 98-99, 116
  SIDS and, 185
slings, baby, 60
smoking, 18
  insurance and, 29
  pregnancy and, 12-13
  safety and, 195
snacks, 116
snowsuits, 95
Snugli baby carriers, 60
soap, baby, 70
social security number, baby's, 259-260
social skills, play and, 122-123
socks, 94
solid foods, introducing, 157-161
songs, language skills and, 122
spending habits, financial planning
  and, 22-23
stress test, prenatal care and, 6
stress, parental, 240-244, 269-273, 275-282
strollers, 53-56
stuffed toys, 132
Sudden Infant Death Syndrome
  (SIDS),. 184-186
sugar, baby food and, 159
sun protectors, 86
supplements,
  breastfeeding and, 143
  formula feeding and, 154
suppositories, acetaminophen, 187
sweaters, 95-96
swings, baby, 69
synthetic fabric, 96, 98-99, 101

T-shirts, baby, 92
table, changing, 117
Tay-Sachs disease, 3
teeth, bottle feeding and, 154-155
teethers, 131
telecommuting, 252-253
television viewing, 130
temperature, measuring of, 178-182
thermometers, selecting of, 180-182
toiletries, baby, 70
toxemia, 4

toxoplasmosis, 3
toy lending library, 134, 135
  resources, 137
toys, 86, 116, 121-138
  basic, 129-130
  battery-powered, 132
  crib, 47
  resources, 137-138
  safety of, 131-134
  selecting of, 133-134
  stuffed, 132
  washing of, 135
  wooden, 132
travel precautions, 75-89, 186
  resources, 88-89
triplets, breastfeeding and, 145
twins, breastfeeding and, 145

ultrasound, prenatal care and, 5-6
undershirts, baby, 92
underwear, maternity clothes, 38-39, 41
urinalysis, 3

videos, 130
vitamin D, breastfeeding and, 143
vitamins, 154
vomiting, 182

walkers, baby, 62, 70-71
walking, 71
warmers, diaper wipe, 119
washcloths, 95
water beds, 46
water supplementation, 143, 163
water,
  lead and, 203
  safety and, 199
weaning, 152
weight gain,
  infant, 156
  sudden, pregnancy and, 3
wills, writing of, 18-19
  resources, 31, 32
windows, safety and, 195
winter clothes, 95
wipes, baby, 72, 87, 111
  homemade, 119
  warmers, 72, 119
work options, 237-258
work resources, 256-258
work,
  breastfeeding and, 155-156
  child care options, 217-219